Skills and Musicianship Workbook to Accompany
The Complete Musician

An Integrated Approach to Tonal
Theory, Analysis, and Listening

Third Edition

Steven G. Laitz

Eastman School of Music

New York   Oxford
OXFORD UNIVERSITY PRESS

Oxford University Press, Inc., publishes works that further Oxford University's
objective of excellence in research, scholarship, and education.

Oxford   New York
Auckland   Cape Town   Dar es Salaam   Hong Kong   Karachi
Kuala Lumpur   Madrid   Melbourne   Mexico City   Nairobi
New Delhi   Shanghai   Taipei   Toronto

With offices in
Argentina   Austria   Brazil   Chile   Czech Republic   France   Greece
Guatemala   Hungary   Italy   Japan   Poland   Portugal   Singapore
South Korea   Switzerland   Thailand   Turkey   Ukraine   Vietnam

For titles covered by Section 112 of the US Higher Education Opportunity
Act, please visit www.oup.com/us/he for the latest information about
pricing and alternate formats.

Published by Oxford University Press, Inc.
198 Madison Avenue, New York, New York 10016
www.oup.com

Library of Congress Cataloging–in–Publication Data
Laitz, Steven G. (Steven Geoffrey)
  Skills and musicianship workbook to accompany The complete musician : an
  integrated approach to tonal theory, analysis, and listening / Steven G. Laitz.
  —3rd ed.
    p. cm.
  ISBN 978–0–19–974280–6
  1. Music theory—Textbooks.   2. Tonality.   3. Musical analysis.   I. Title.
MT6.L136C66 2011b
781.2—dc23

                                                                    2011023575

Printing number: 16 15 14 13 12 11

Printed in the United States of America
on acid-free paper

CONTENTS

PREFACE

New to the Third Edition

The workbooks accompanying the third edition of *The Complete Musician* feature a new organization designed specifically for greater flexibility.

- Whereas Workbook 1: *Writing and Analysis* is devoted to written skills, this workbook is devoted to musicianship skills with an emphasis on crucial skill-development exercises, such as singing model progressions (through arpeggiation), extensive and varied keyboard studies, improvisation, and many types of harmonic dictation (with an emphasis on the music literature, and all are performed on the instruments designated by the composers).

- Each workbook chapter aligns with the corresponding chapter in the text. Within each chapter of the workbook, activities are organized by type, beginning with singing (one- and two-voice), listening (dictation, correction, analysis and notation, etc.), and keyboard (including sing-and-play activities). There are more introductory-level musicianship exercises and, for the dictation activities, considerably more notational information and specific guidelines.

- Several new skills components are included in this edition, the most extensive of which is one- and two-voice singing excerpts. There are more than 300 new melodies, 200 of which are taken from the literature. These are organized by harmonic device (for example, in the augmented-sixths chapter, 12 examples contain that chord). The emphasis is on hearing these tunes within the context of their underlying harmonic implications. To that end, left-hand pitches (including figured-bass symbols in some cases) or chords are occasionally included to guide the student in sing-and-play activities.

- There are new aural exercises, such as correcting a notated melody, series of chords, or bass line based on what is heard; and there are new keyboard exercises, including easy (five-finger) harmonically oriented examples, outer-voice harmonic paradigms, and creative sing-and-play activities.

- The recordings on the included CD—from solo piano to full orchestra—range from excerpts to complete pieces and are played by students and faculty from the Eastman School of Music. Between the two workbooks, there are over 3,900 recorded analytical and dictation examples and over 15 hours of recorded music, all of which are in high-quality mp3 format.

- Additional supplementary material is available on the new companion website (www.oup.com/us/laitz).

CHAPTER 1

Musical Space and Time

SINGING AND PERFORMING

EXERCISE 1.1 Singing Scale Degrees

A. Play $\hat{1}$ in any major or minor key. Sing this pitch, and then be able to sing any other scale degree(s) in that key above or below it. In the beginning, you may find it easier to sing to the required scale degree if you sing the scalar pitches between it and $\hat{1}$. For example, given the scale of E (natural) minor and $\hat{1}$, and the instruction to sing $\hat{5}$, you would sing $\hat{1}$–$\hat{2}$–$\hat{3}$–$\hat{4}$ and then $\hat{5}$.

B. Given $\hat{3}$ or $\hat{5}$ of any major or minor key, be able to sing to any other scale degrees.

EXERCISE 1.2 Scales: Pattern Continuation

Study the following scale degree patterns, and continue them until you return to the tonic. Sing in both the major mode and the three forms of the minor mode. Feel free to make up some patterns of your own.

SCALE DEGREE NUMBERS:	MOVEABLE DO SOLFÈGE:
A. $\hat{1}$–$\hat{2}$–$\hat{3}$, $\hat{2}$–$\hat{3}$–$\hat{4}$, $\hat{3}$–$\hat{4}$–$\hat{5}$, . . .	do-re-mi, re-mi-fa, mi-fa-sol, . . .
B. $\hat{1}$–$\hat{7}$–$\hat{1}$, $\hat{2}$–$\hat{1}$–$\hat{2}$, $\hat{3}$–$\hat{2}$–$\hat{3}$, . . .	do-ti-do, re-do-ti, mi-re-mi, . . .
C. $\hat{1}$–$\hat{7}$–$\hat{1}$–$\hat{2}$–$\hat{3}$, $\hat{2}$–$\hat{1}$–$\hat{2}$–$\hat{3}$–$\hat{4}$, . . .	do-ti-do-re-mi, re-do-re-mi-fa, . . .
D. $\hat{1}$–$\hat{3}$–$\hat{2}$–$\hat{1}$, $\hat{2}$–$\hat{4}$–$\hat{3}$–$\hat{2}$, $\hat{3}$–$\hat{5}$, . . .	do-mi-re-do, re-fa-mi-re, mi-sol, . . .

EXERCISE 1.3 Scale Degree Patterns

Sing the following scale degree fragments from any given pitch in both major and minor modes. Arrows represent raised and lowered forms of the scale degree number they precede.

A. $\hat{1}$–$\hat{2}$–$\hat{3}$
B. $\hat{1}$–↑$\hat{7}$–$\hat{1}$
C. $\hat{1}$–$\hat{3}$–$\hat{5}$–$\hat{1}$
D. $\hat{1}$–$\hat{2}$–$\hat{3}$–↑$\hat{7}$–$\hat{1}$
E. $\hat{5}$–$\hat{4}$–$\hat{3}$–$\hat{1}$–↓$\hat{6}$–$\hat{5}$
F. $\hat{3}$–$\hat{2}$–$\hat{1}$–$\hat{5}$
G. $\hat{3}$–$\hat{1}$–$\hat{4}$–$\hat{5}$–$\hat{1}$

EXERCISE 1.4 Singing Melodies

Sing the following short melodies using scale degree numbers. The key and mode are given for exercises A–F. You must determine the key and mode for exercises G–S.

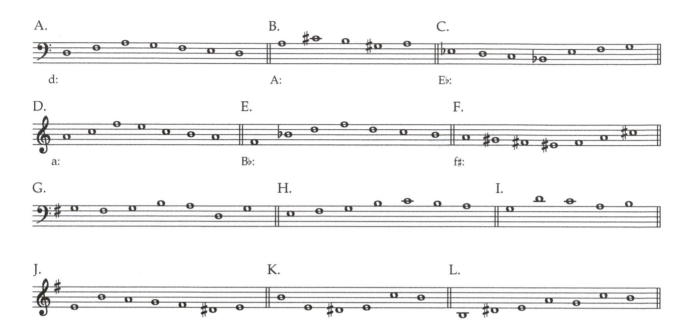

M. Brahms, Intermezzo, op. 117, no. 1, *Andante moderato*

N. Beethoven, "Freudvoll und leidvoll," op. 84, no. 4

Freud - voll und leid - voll, ge - dan - ken - voll sein,
Joy - ful and woe - ful, and wist - ful in fine,

O. Dvořák, Symphony no. 9 in E minor, "New World Symphony," op. 95, *Largo*

P. Tchaikovsky, *Capriccio Italien*, op. 45, *Andante un poco rubato*

Q. Schubert, "Wonne der Wehmut," op. posth. 115, no. 2, D. 260

Etwas geschwind (Allegretto)

Trock - net__ nicht, trock - net__ nicht, Trä - nen der e - wi-gen Lie - be,

Ach, nur dem halb - ge - trock - ne-ten Au - ge, wie ö - de, wie tot die Welt_ ihm er-scheint!

R. Mozart, "Mädchen, so treibt ihr's mit allen," from *Cosi fan tutte*, act 2

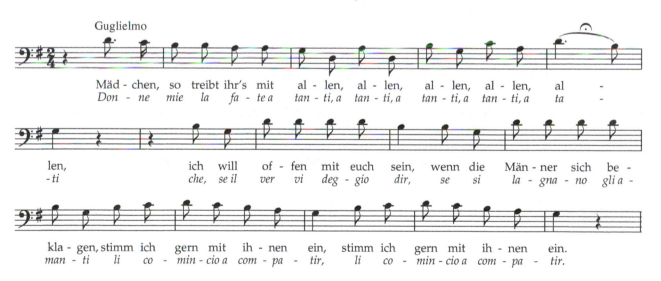

Guglielmo

Mäd - chen, so treibt ihr's mit al - len, al - len, al - len, al - len, al -
Don - ne mie la fa - te a tan - ti, a tan - ti, a tan - ti, a tan - ti, a ta -

len, ich will of - fen mit euch sein, wenn die Män - ner sich be -
-ti che, se il ver vi deg - gio dir, se si la - gna - no gli a -

kla - gen, stimm ich gern mit ih - nen ein, stimm ich gern mit ih - nen ein.
man - ti li co - min - cio a com - pa - tir, li co - min - cio a com - pa - tir.

S. Schubert, "Wiegenlied," op. 105, no. 2, D. 867

Wie sich der Äu-glein kind - li-cher Him mel, schlum-mer-be - las tet, läs - sig ver-schliesst!

EXERCISE 1.5 Singing Rhythmic–Metric Disruptions

Melodic fragments are given that illustrate syncopation and hemiola. Label and bracket examples of these disruptions. Then sing each pattern, continuing it until you return to the tonic. Finally, be able to conduct yourself while singing. Exercise A has been labeled for you.

A.

B.

C.

D.

EXERCISE 1.6 Transforming Melodic Fragments

Sing each fragment as written and in other major or minor keys. Continue the pattern until you return to the tonic. Then transform the tunes by adding syncopations. The easiest way to disrupt the rhythms is to move strong-beat accents to a weak beat by making the strong-beat duration shorter than that of the weak beat.

EXERCISE 1.7 Melodies with Triplets and Syncopations

A. Brahms, Piano Concerto no. 2 in B♭ major, op. 83

Allegro ma non troppo

B. Mozart, Violin Sonata in F major, K. 377

VAR. III.

C. Mozart, Symphony no. 40 in G minor, K. 550, III

D. Morley, "Sweet Nymph, Come to Thy Lover"

Sweet Nymph come to_____ thy lov - er, to_____

__ thy lov - er, sweet Nymph come to_____ thy lov - er,

E. Pergolesi, "Se tu ma' mi"

Andantino

Se tu,_ m'a - mi, se tu so - spi - ri Sol_ per me,_ gen - til_ pa - stor,
If thou_ lov'st me, and sigh - est ev - er But_ for me,_ O gen - tle_ swain,

F. R. Strauss, "Mit deinen blauen Augen," op. 56, no. 4

Andante

Mit dei - nen blau - en Au - gen siehst du mich lieb - lich an, da
Your eyes so blue_____ and ten - der, They gaze in - to mine own; As

ward mir so träu - mend zu Sin - ne, dass ich nicht spre - chen kann.
if in a dream world_ I wan - der, And speech from me has flown.

EXERCISE 1.8 Integrating Rhythm, Meter, Singing, and Keyboard

Complete the following tasks while sitting at the keyboard.

A. Tap quarter notes on any pitch. From this pitch, sing ascending and descending scales in quarter notes, then in eighth notes, and again in dotted-quarter-plus-eighth rhythms.

B. Tap quarter notes with one foot and eighth notes with one hand on any pitch on the keyboard. Sing ascending and descending scales in quarter notes, and then in eighth notes, and then in dotted-quarter-plus-eighth rhythms.

C. Tap the following rhythms on any pitch on the keyboard while singing scales in even quarter notes and then eighth notes:

1.    etc.

2.    etc.

3. ♩ 𝄿𝄿𝄿♩ 𝄿𝄿𝄿♩   etc.

4. 𝄿𝄿𝄿 𝄿𝄿𝄿   etc.

5. ♪ ♩   ♪ 𝄿𝄿 ♪ ♩   ♪ 𝄿𝄿

D. Tap a series of pulses at a tempo of one pulse per second (for example, the same as a metronome set to 60). The quarter note receives the pulse.

   1. Sing ascending and descending scales in eighth notes and then in triplet eighth notes.
   2. Sing ascending and descending scales in eighth notes. Start with an accent, and then accent every fourth note after the accent to create a $\frac{2}{4}$ meter; then accent every sixth note after the accent to create a $\frac{3}{4}$ meter.

E. Tap a series of quarter-note pulses on any note of the keyboard at a tempo of two pulses per second (for example, the same as a metronome set to 120). Sing ascending and descending scales in quarter notes. Create meters of $\frac{3}{4}$, $\frac{4}{4}$, and $\frac{6}{8}$ by accenting the appropriate members of the scale.

LISTENING

EXERCISE 1.9 Mode Identification

Identify the mode (major or minor) for each of the musical excerpts drawn from well-known theme-and-variation movements. What is unusual about letter F?

A. _____   B. _____   C. _____   D. _____   E. _____   F. _____

EXERCISE 1.10 Correction

Renotate Examples A–H to reflect what is played.

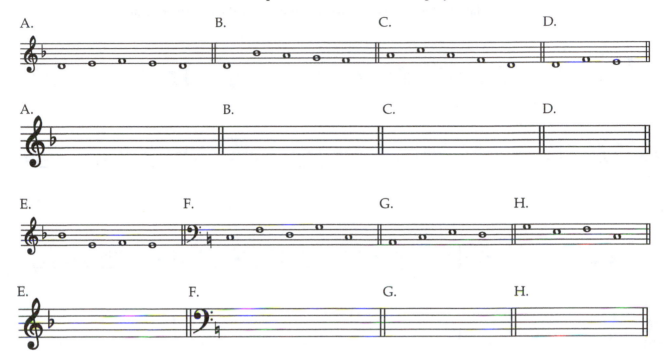

EXERCISE 1.11 Melodic Dictation

Notate scale degrees of the major- and minor-mode melodies that are played in different keys. Scale degrees 1–3–5 are played before you hear each example.

A. ___ ___ ___ ___ ___ ___ ___   D. ___ ___ ___ ___ ___

B. ___ ___ ___ ___ ___ ___ ___   E. ___ ___ ___ ___ ___ ___ ___

C. ___ ___ ___ ___ ___ ___ ___   F. ___ ___ ___ ___ ___ ___ ___

EXERCISE 1.12 Melodic Dictation

You will hear five-pitch major-mode melodies. Listen to the entire melody and be able to sing (1) the tonic pitch and (2) the entire fragment. Then, notate the scale degree numbers. $\hat{1}$ is played before you hear each example.

A. ___ ___ ___ ___ ___   F. ___ ___ ___ ___ ___

B. ___ ___ ___ ___ ___   G. ___ ___ ___ ___ ___

C. ___ ___ ___ ___ ___   H. ___ ___ ___ ___ ___

D. ___ ___ ___ ___ ___   I. ___ ___ ___ ___ ___

E. ___ ___ ___ ___ ___

EXERCISE 1.13 Melody Correction

Several of the pitches notated in the following exercises do not correspond to what is played. Rewrite a corrected version below the incorrect version.

A.

B.

C.

EXERCISE 1.14 Meter and Mode Identification: Simple Meters

Identify the meter and mode (major or minor) of each of the following excerpts as follows:
- Identify the basic pulse.
- Locate the regularly recurring accented beat that is followed by one or more weak beats.
- Determine the generic meter, which will be duple or triple.
- Refine your decision by assigning $\frac{2}{4}$ or $\frac{3}{4}$.

A. Schubert, "An mein Klavier"   meter: _____   mode: _____

B. Tchaikovsky, "Old French Song"   meter: _____   mode: _____

C. Schubert, "Dance"   meter: _____   mode: _____

D. Bach, "Dance"   meter: _____   mode: _____

E. Purcell, "Hornpipe"   meter: _____   mode: _____

EXERCISE 1.15 Meter and Mode Identification: Simple and Compound Meters

This exercise requires you to identify both simple and compound meters. Your choices are: $\frac{2}{4}$, $\frac{3}{4}$, $\frac{4}{4}$, $\frac{6}{8}$, and $\frac{9}{8}$. Each exercise contains a recurring rhythmic pattern; based on the meter you choose, notate the rhythmic pattern.

A. Schubert, "Frühlingstraum," from *Winterreise*   meter: _____ mode: _____ rhythmic pattern: _____

B. Schubert, "Des Müllers Blumen," from *Die schöen Müllerin*

meter: _____ mode: _____ rhythmic pattern: _____

EXERCISE 1.16 Meter and Mode Identification: Simple and Compound Meters

Identify the meter and the mode (major or minor) in the following examples. Your choices are $\frac{2}{4}$, $\frac{3}{4}$, $\frac{4}{4}$, and $\frac{6}{8}$.

A. Brahms, "Wie Melodien zieht es mir" ("As if Melodies Were Moving"), op. 105, no. 1:   meter: _____ mode: _____

B. Chopin, Nocturne in F minor, op. 55, no. 1, BI 152:   meter: _____ mode: _____

C. Schumann, "Reiterstück," *Album für die Jugend*, op. 85:   meter: _____ mode: _____

D. Bach, Prelude in B♭ major, BWV 866, *Well-Tempered Clavier*, Book 1:   meter: _____ mode: _____

E. Mozart, Trio in E♭ for Clarinet, Viola, and Piano, K. 498, *Allegretto*:   meter: _____ mode: _____

EXERCISE 1.17 Rhythmic Correction

Several of the rhythms notated in the following exercises do not correspond to what is played. Rewrite a corrected version below the incorrect version.

A.

B.

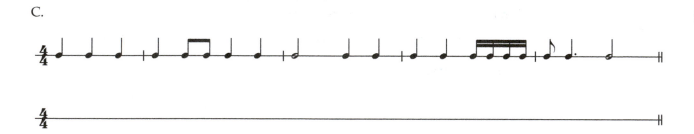

C.

EXERCISE 1.18 Error Detection

The following examples include intervals of M2 (M9), m2 (m9), M3 (M10), m3 (m10), P4, A4, P5, d5, and P8. Listen to each interval as it is played. If what you hear is correctly notated, write "Y" (yes). If what you hear is not notated, write "N" (no) and correctly notate what you hear by changing the upper pitch and maintaining the lower pitch.

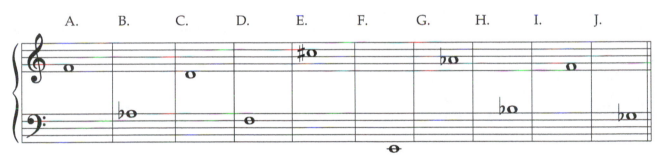

EXERCISE 1.19 Intervals: Seconds, Thirds, Fourths, Fifths, Octaves, and Tritones

Notate and label the ascending or descending intervals that you hear. The first note is given in A–E, the second in F–J.

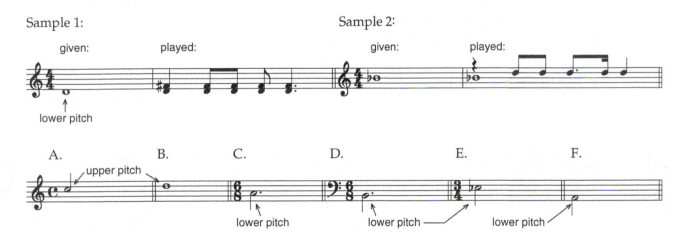

EXERCISE 1.20 Rhythm and Intervals

You will hear a single interval played in a one-measure rhythmic pattern. Notate the rhythmic pattern that will fill one measure of the given meter and identify the interval.

EXERCISE 1.21 Three-Pitch Intervals

You will hear three pitches as follows:
- two pitches will sound together (forming a harmonic interval);
- the following third pitch creates both a second harmonic interval and another melodic interval.

Notate the missing pitch and label all three intervals. An arrow indicates which of the three pitches is missing.

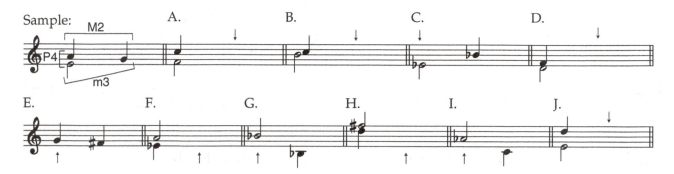

EXERCISE 1.22 Three-Pitch Intervals

This is the same as Exercise 1.21, but this time you are given only one of the three pitches. Notate the missing pitches and label all three intervals. Arrows indicate which two pitches are missing.

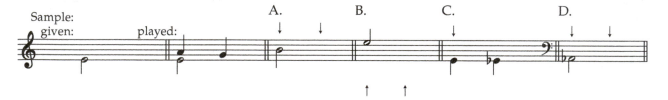

PLAYING AND SINGING

EXERCISE 1.23 Reading in Bass and Treble Clefs, Ledger Lines

1. Say the names of the following pitches, including their octave designations (e.g., the D above middle C is D^4).
2. Play the pitch in the notated octave.
3. Sing each of the pitches in a comfortable octave after you play it.
4. Play half steps (diatonic and chromatic) and whole steps above and below each pitch, saying aloud the pitch name.
5. Viewing each given pitch as scale degree 1, play one-octave ascending and descending major and three forms of minor scales (in a comfortable octave).

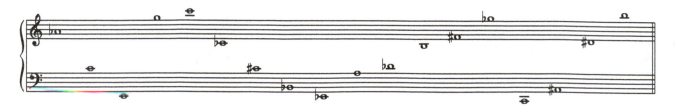

EXERCISE 1.24 Sing and Play (I)

Continue the given scale degree patterns until you return to the tonic. Alternate playing and singing such that you begin a pattern by playing it, then sing the first repetition, then play again, and so on until the end. Use scale degrees or solfège when you sing. Be able to transpose the patterns to major and minor keys up to two flats or two sharps.

A. $\hat{1}$–$\hat{2}$–$\hat{3}$, $\hat{2}$–$\hat{3}$–$\hat{4}$, $\hat{3}$–$\hat{4}$–$\hat{5}$, etc.
B. $\hat{1}$–$\hat{7}$–$\hat{1}$–$\hat{2}$–$\hat{3}$, $\hat{2}$–$\hat{1}$–$\hat{2}$–$\hat{3}$–$\hat{4}$, $\hat{3}$–$\hat{2}$–$\hat{3}$–$\hat{4}$–$\hat{5}$, etc.
C. $\hat{1}$–$\hat{3}$–$\hat{2}$–$\hat{1}$, $\hat{2}$–$\hat{4}$–$\hat{3}$–$\hat{2}$, $\hat{3}$–$\hat{5}$–$\hat{4}$–$\hat{3}$, etc.
D. $\hat{3}$–$\hat{4}$–$\hat{3}$–$\hat{2}$–$\hat{1}$, $\hat{4}$–$\hat{5}$–$\hat{4}$–$\hat{3}$–$\hat{2}$, $\hat{5}$–$\hat{6}$–$\hat{5}$–$\hat{4}$–$\hat{3}$, etc.
E. $\hat{1}$–$\hat{3}$–$\hat{5}$–$\hat{2}$–$\hat{1}$, $\hat{2}$–$\hat{4}$–$\hat{6}$–$\hat{3}$–$\hat{2}$, $\hat{3}$–$\hat{5}$–$\hat{7}$–$\hat{4}$–$\hat{3}$, etc.

EXERCISE 1.25 Sing and Play (II)

Perform the exercises as required. Use the right hand to play in the treble clef and the left hand to play in the bass clef. Since the piano part guides what you will then sing, listen carefully as you play.

EXERCISE 1.26 Scales

Play major and minor scales with key signatures up to and including four sharps and four flats. Use the tetrachord fingering as follows:

scale degrees: 1̂ 2̂ 3̂ 4̂ ——————→ 5̂ 6̂ 7̂ 1̂

left hand: 5 4 3 2   right hand: 2 3 4 5

EXERCISE 1.27 Harmonies in Texture

Using the fingerings given, play the following pitch and rhythmic patterns. Determine the key(s) implied in each exercise. Then be able to sing (and sustain) the bass by playing the first right-hand pitch.

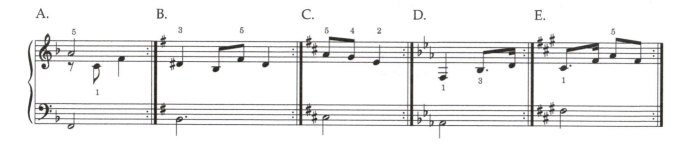

EXERCISE 1.28 Sign and Play

1. Sing one voice and play the other using the indicated fingerings; reverse.
2. With a partner, sing both voices in a comfortable octave.
3. Play both voices as written. Thinking in scale degrees, transpose to D minor.

A.

B.

EXERCISE 1.29 Meter Determination

Play the following examples and determine a suitable meter signature.

EXERCISE 1.30 Intervals Within the Scale

Be able to play all intervals of the same generic size that occur between any scale degrees of major and minor scales. For example, all of the thirds in a D-major scale would be: D–F♯, E–G, F♯–A and so on.

EXERCISE 1.31 Intervals Within the Scale

Be able to play all instances of intervals with the same specific size that occur between any pitches of the major and minor scales. For example, all of the minor thirds in a D-major scale would include: E–G, F♯–A, B–D, C♯–E. What intervals occur most often? Least often? Not at all?

EXERCISE 1.32 Singing and Playing

- Play any pitch in the middle of the piano.
- Sing the pitch. Then consider the pitch to function as Î ("do" in moveable do solfège) and sing a M2 (2̂, or "re") and then a P5 (5̂, or "sol") above the given pitch. Transpose to at least five different major keys.
- Then repeat the process, this time singing a M3 (3̂, or "mi"), a M2 (2̂, or "re"), and then a M6 (6̂, or "la"), and transpose to five different major keys.
- Finally, repeat the process, this time singing a P5 (5̂, or "sol"), a m3 (3̂, or "me") a m6 (6̂, or "le"), and a M2 (2̂, or "re"), and transpose to five different minor keys.

EXERCISE 1.33 Analysis, Playing, and Singing

- Label each given interval using its specific name. [The specific name includes the generic (numerical) size and the specific quality (perfect, major, or minor)].
- Then play the lower pitch and sing the upper pitch.
- Finally, play the upper pitch and sing the lower pitch.

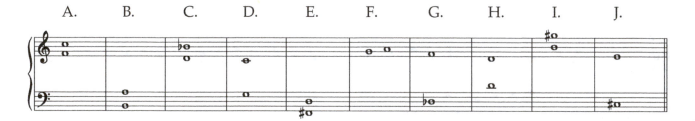

EXERCISE 1.34 Interval Play

Sing the following pitches, and say the letter names. Then play major and minor thirds, sixths, and sevenths above and below the given pitches. Finally, be able to sing the pitch and the interval above and below before you play it.

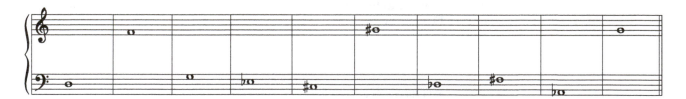

EXERCISE 1.35 More Interval Play

Play each pitch given in any register, then play the required intervals above and below that pitch. Finally, find a comfortable register in which you can sing the required intervals above and below the given pitch.

1. given F: Play major and minor sixths and thirds.
2. given D: Play major and minor sevenths and sixths.
3. given F♯: Play major and minor sevenths and thirds and perfect fifths.
4. given B: Play major and minor thirds, sixths, and sevenths.
5. given A: Play any of the intervals.
6. given E♭: Play and sing all perfect intervals and major and minor seconds and sixths.

INSTRUMENTAL APPLICATION

EXERCISE 1.36 Transposition and Performance

- For each of the following melodic fragments (A–I), label scale degree numbers and perform the fragment on your instrument.
- Then, perform the fragment again, transposing it to the key implied by the given pitch. *Note:* The given pitch will be the first pitch of the fragment, but, like the fragment, may not necessarily be the tonic.

   For example, given the fragment D–G–A–B–F♯–G and the first pitch of the transposed version (B♭), you would:

1. Study the melody to determine the key. The sample solution is in G major (1a).
2. Label the scale degrees of the melody ($\hat{5}$–$\hat{1}$–$\hat{2}$–$\hat{3}$–$\hat{7}$–$\hat{1}$) (1b).
3. Transfer the scale degree number of the first pitch of the original melody to the given new pitch, since this will be the first pitch of the transposed version (2a). Given that the first pitch of the original melody is D, which functions as $\hat{5}$ in G, then the given B♭ will also function as $\hat{5}$, but now in the key of E♭ major.
4. Play the transposed version: B♭–E♭–F♮–G–D–E♭ (2b). (Notice that F♮ is necessary to cancel the retained F♯ from G major.)

Sample solution:

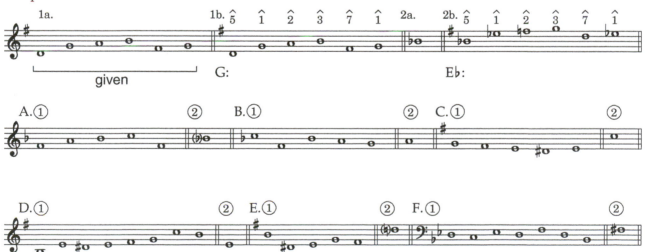

G.① ② H.① ② I.① ②

EXERCISE 1.37 Melodic Fragments

Play on the piano or your instrument, or sing each melodic fragment and:

1. determine its key;
2. memorize its scale degrees; and
3. perform the fragment in keys up to and including two sharps and two flats.

CHAPTER 2

Harnessing Space and Time: Introduction to Melody and Two-Voice Counterpoint

SINGING

EXERCISE 2.1

Sing the following melodies, many of which are in the minor mode and feature the various forms of $\hat{6}$ and $\hat{7}$.

A. Schubert, "Ländler," no. 4, D. 366

B. Haydn, Trio in G major, no. 25, Hob XV

C.

D. Schubert, Piano Sonata in A minor, D. 845, *Moderato*

E. Schubert, Impromptu, op. 90, no. 1, *Allegro molto Moderato*

F. Brahms, "Des Abends Kann ich nicht schlafen gehn"

G.

EXERCISE 2.11 Two-Voice Dictation

Listen to the recording and notate the counterpoint voice.

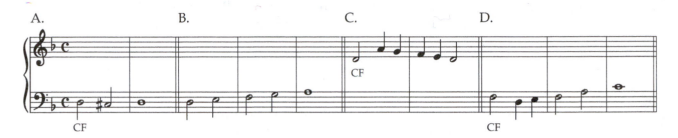

EXERCISE 2.12 Two-Voice Dictation

This exercise is the same as Exercise 2.11, but now only the starting pitches are given in each voice.

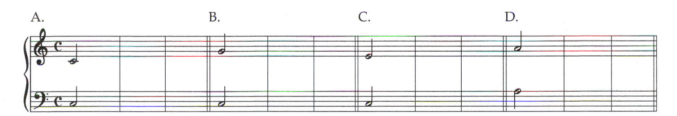

EXERCISE 2.13 Dictation: Notation of One Voice in Two-Voice Counterpoint

You will hear examples of two-voice counterpoint. The cantus firmus is given. Using your ear and knowledge of permissible pitches, notate the counterpoint voice. Check your work by labeling the interval making sure that each is consonant.

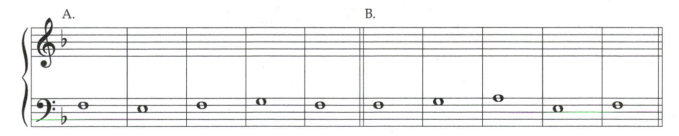

EXERCISE 2.14 Dictation of 1:1 Counterpoint Fragments

Notate the 1:1 counterpoint voice against the given cantus firmus. Exercises A–E are in G major (the CF is in the bass). Exercises F–J are in E minor (the CF is in the treble). Use both your ear as well as your knowledge of permissible intervals.

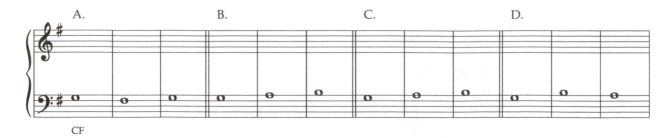

EXERCISE 2.15 Dictation of 2:1 Counterpoint Fragments

Notate the 2:1 counterpoint voice against the given cantus. Exercises A–E, in major, place the CF in the bass, and Exercises F–J, in D minor, place it above.

EXERCISE 2.16   Dictation: Notation of One Voice in Second-Species Counterpoint

Notate the second-species counterpoint above the cantus firmus and label each interval.

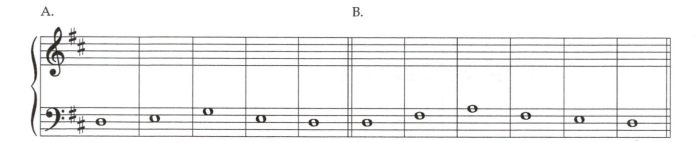

EXERCISE 2.17   Dictation: Notation of One Voice in Second-Species Counterpoint

Notate the second-species counterpoint below the cantus firmus and label each interval.

PLAYING AND SINGING

EXERCISE 2.18

Perform the following two-voice examples as follows:

1. Play one of the voices while playing the other; reverse.
2. Sing one voice while listening to the recording of the other; reverse.

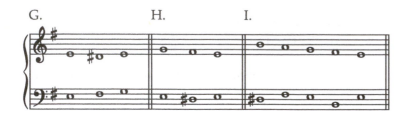

EXERCISE 2.19 Singing Against Another Voice

Sing either the upper or lower voice of the 1:1 examples written in varied rhythms. Then listen to either the upper or lower voice and while that plays, sing the other voice against it. Reverse the process, singing the opposite voice and playing the recording for the other voice.

EXERCISE 2.20 First Species

Play the following exercises in the major mode (as written) and in the minor mode with a steady tempo. Begin by playing each hand separately; add the second hand only when you are comfortable with each hand alone. Play the lowest notes with the thumb of your right hand and the fifth finger of the left hand. Transpose each to the keys of G, E, and B♭ major and minor. Be able to sing one part while playing the other. Finally, analyze each exercise, marking the intervals and the types of contrapuntal motions.

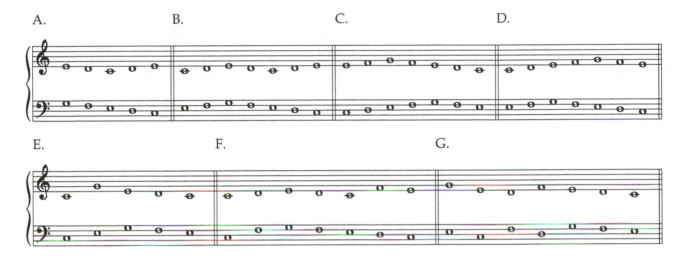

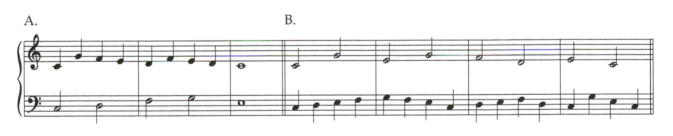

EXERCISE 2.21 Sing and Play

Sing one voice while playing the other; switch. Play as written and in the minor mode with a steady tempo. Begin by playing each hand separately; add the second hand only when you are comfortable with each hand alone. Play the lowest notes with the thumb of your right hand and the fifth finger of the left hand. Transpose each to the keys of D and B♭ major and minor.

D.

E.

CHAPTER 3

Musical Density: Triads, Seventh Chords, and Texture

SINGING

EXERCISE 3.1 Arpeggiation of Inverted Triads

Given any pitch, sing root-position major, minor, or diminished triads. Next, arpeggiating from the root-position triad, sing first-inversion then second-inversion triads, ending with root position. For example, to arpeggiate a minor triad from the pitch D, you would sing D–F–A, F–A–D, A–D–F, and end by ascending to root position (D–F–A).

EXERCISE 3.2 Reinterpreting Pitches to Create Triads

Given a pitch, treat it as the root, the third, or the fifth of a major, minor, or diminished triad. For example, given the pitch G, consider it to be the root of major, minor, and diminished triads. Then treat it as the third of an E♭-major triad and the third of E-minor and E-diminished triads. Finally, treat G as the fifth of C-major and C-minor triads and as the fifth of a C♯-diminished triad.

EXERCISE 3.3 Seventh Chords

From any pitch, be able to sing root-position major-minor, major-major, minor-minor, diminished-minor, and diminished-diminished seventh chords.

EXERCISE 3.4 Seventh Chords in Inversion

Given that Mm seventh chords occur more often than other seventh chords do, you must be familiar not only with their root-position sound but also with the sound of their inverted forms. Be able to arpeggiate from root position through each inversion until you return to root position. For example, given a B♭ Mm chord, you would sing:

EXERCISE 3.5 Singing Major-Minor and Minor-Minor Seventh Chords from Given Pitches

Given any pitch, treat it as the root, third, fifth, or seventh of a Mm or mm seventh chord. For example, given the pitch C, consider it the root of Mm and mm seventh chords. Then, consider C as the third of a Mm seventh chord (built on A♭) and then as a mm seventh chord (built on A).

EXERCISE 3.6 Singing Seventh Chords from Given Scale Degrees

Choose a major key, play its tonic pitch, and arpeggiate an ascending and descending MM seventh chord constructed above $\hat{1}$. Continue singing seventh chords built on the other diatonic scale degrees, making sure that you arpeggiate the correct seventh-chord type (e.g., a ii^7 chord is a mm seventh, a IV^7 chord a MM seventh, etc.). Do the same for a minor-mode key (use only the lowered form of $\hat{6}$ [Mm], but use both the lowered [Mm] and raised [dd] forms of $\hat{7}$).

EXERCISE 3.7 Melodic Singing

Study the following longer tunes, noting repetitions of material and basic contours (stepwise, arpeggiating, etc.). Then sing the tunes using scale degree numbers while you conduct.

A.

B. Brahms, "Da unten im Tale"

C. Brahms, "Ach, englische Schäferin"

D. Brahms, "Wo gehst du hin, du stolze?"

E.

F. Mozart, "Wer ein Liebchen hat gefunden," from *The Abduction from the Seraglio*, act 1, scene 2

Doch sie   treu   sich zu   er - hal - ten,   schließ er   Lieb - chen sorg - lich   ein;

EXERCISE 3.8 Two-Part Singing

Be able to sing each part in a comfortable octave. Then with a partner, sing the exercises as duets, pausing briefly at each *fermata* in order to make sure the intervals are in tune. Finally, switch parts. You should also practice this exercise as a sing and play (i.e., play one part while singing the other)

A.

B.

C.

D.

E.

EXERCISE 3.16 Dictation: Notation of One Voice in Two-Voice Counterpoint

You will hear examples of two-voice counterpoint. The cantus firmus is given. Using your ear and knowledge of permissible pitches, notate the counterpoint voice. Check your work by labeling the interval making sure that each is consonant.

A.   B.

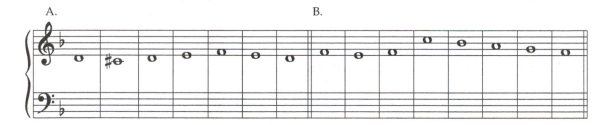

PLAYING

EXERCISE 3.17 Improvising Counterpoint

On the piano, play the given bass pitches with the left hand and create two-voice counterpoint by playing a note taken from the triad that is indicated by the fig- ured bass with the right hand. Move from one upper-voice pitch to the next by the shortest possible distance; however, make sure the counterpoint is correct (e.g., avoid parallel perfect intervals). Then sing one of the voices while playing the other. Play each exercise in the parallel minor, and transpose each to one other key of your choice. Exercises A–E are entirely diatonic and permit few choices.

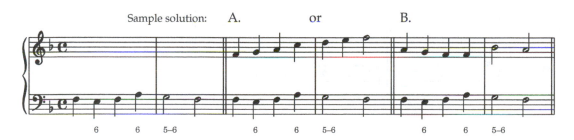

Exercises F–J contain some chromaticism and allow for more melodic choices for the upper voice.

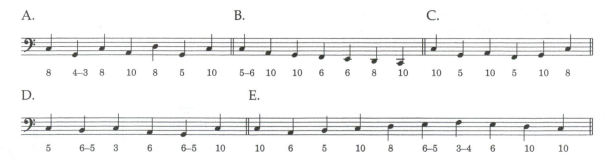

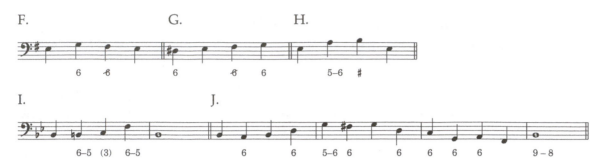

F.   G.   H.

6   6   6   6   6   5–6   #

I.   J.

6–5 (3) 6–5   6   6   5–6 6   6   6   6   6   9 – 8

EXERCISE 3.18 Two-Part Counterpoint and Figured Bass

On the piano play the given bass pitches with the left hand and create two-voice counterpoint by playing the interval indicated by the figured bass with the right hand. The result will be a mix of 1:1 and 2:1 counterpoint. Move from one upper-voice pitch to the next by the shortest possible distance. Then sing one of the voices while playing the other. Be able to play each exercise in the parallel major or minor and transpose each to one other key of your choice.

A.

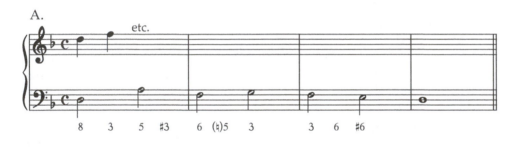

8   3   5   #3   6   (♮)5   3   3   6   #6

B.

5   3   2   6   3   3   4   6   5   6   5   3

C.

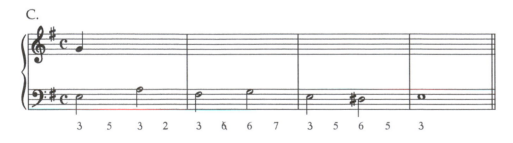

3   5   3   2   3   ♭   6   7   3   5   6   5   3

D.

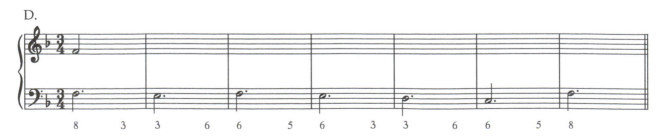

8   3   3   6   6   5   6   3   3   6   6   5   8

EXERCISE 3.19 Outer Voices and Keyboard Style

In the following examples, the bass is always the root of the triad. Determine the chordal function of the soprano, then add the missing triad note(s); double the root. Play three voices in the right hand and the root in the left. Analyze with roman numerals.

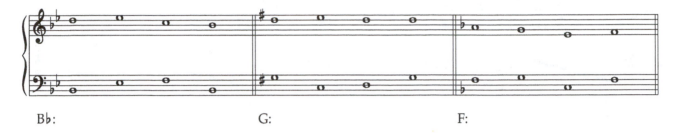

Bb: G: F:

EXERCISE 3.20 Soprano Voice and Building Chords

You are given a soprano line, the chordal function of each note (1 = root, 3 = third, 5 = fifth), and the key. Play the resulting triads below the soprano, using keyboard style to create a four-voice texture. The root will be in the bass. Name the quality of each triad. *Note*: Triads built on $\hat{5}$ will be major in both major and minor keys; that is, raise $\hat{7}$.

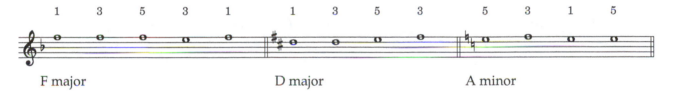

F major   D major   A minor

EXERCISE 3.21 Soprano Voice and Building Chords

You are given the soprano and the letter name of the triad. Add necessary notes to create complete right-hand triads; then double the root in the bass to create a four-voice, keyboard-style texture. Notice how little each voice moves to the next chordal pitch. Often, in fact, there is no motion, given the common tones between the chords.

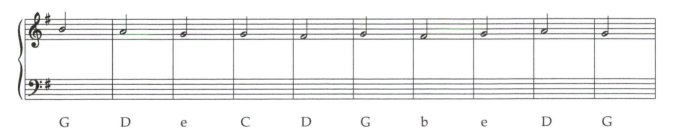

G   D   e   C   D   G   b   e   D   G

EXERCISE 3.22 Playing and Singing Seventh Chords

Play the arpeggiated three-pitch pattern and sing the missing pitch to complete the required root-position seventh chord.

Note: LH = left hand, RH = right hand

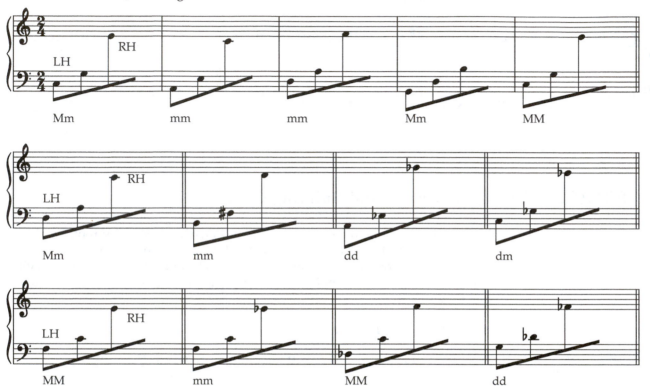

CHAPTER 4

When Harmony, Melody, and Rhythm Converge

SINGING

EXERCISE 4.1 Singing Longer Melodies

Using scale degree numbers, sing the following melodies and conduct. Begin by scanning each tune: determine the key, look for patterns of large-scale repetition and melodic fluency.

A.

B.

C. Brahms, "Des Markgrafen Töchterlein"

D. Handel, Overture from *Music for the Royal Fireworks*

E. Purcell, "Nymphs and Shepherds"

Nymphs and shep - herds,   come a - way,   come a - way,   Nymphs and shep - herds

come a - way,   come a - way, come, come, come,   come a - way!   In ye

grove,   in ye grove let's sport and play, let's sport and play, let's sport and play!

F. Mozart, Piano Concerto in E♭ major, K. 482

Allegro

G. Bach, *Mass in B minor,* Gloria

Vivace

EXERCISE 4.9 Two-Chord Progressions

Each example presents three different seventh chords, each of which leads to the same major or minor triad. Label each seventh-chord type, then listen to the recording and circle the notated pair of chords that is played.

PLAYING

EXERCISE 4.10 More Triads and Doublings

Inversions are included in this exercise. Add missing pitches in the right hand below the soprano to create full triads, and play the bass note as required by the figured bass and given root. Double the root of the chord.

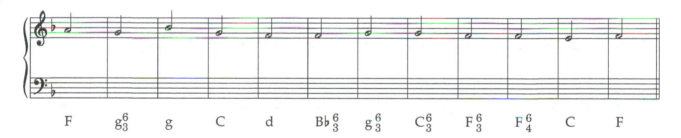

EXERCISE 4.11 Figured Bass and Doublings

In keyboard style, realize the following figured basses. Double the root in each example. When shifting to the next chord, move the right hand the shortest possible distance—by step preferably, or, not at all if there is a common tone.

EXERCISE 4.12 Figured Bass and Seventh Chords

Construct seventh chords in keyboard style according to the figured bass. Watch accidentals. Identify the quality of each seventh chord. Since there is no underlying key in this example, thus no key signature, you must add necessary accidentals.

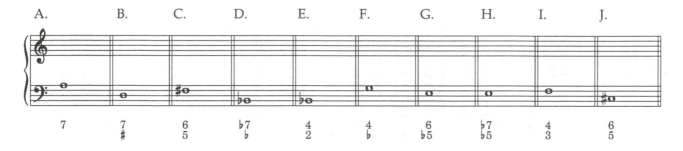

EXERCISE 4.13 Playing Figurated Triads

Play the following short pieces. You will use right-hand fingerings of 1–3–5 or 1–2–5, with your thumb (1) always playing the lowest pitch in the chord.

- Determine the roman numerals for each chord.
- Play the excerpt in the parallel major.
- Transpose to any other minor key and its parallel-major form.
- For letter B, play the right hand while singing the bass voice.

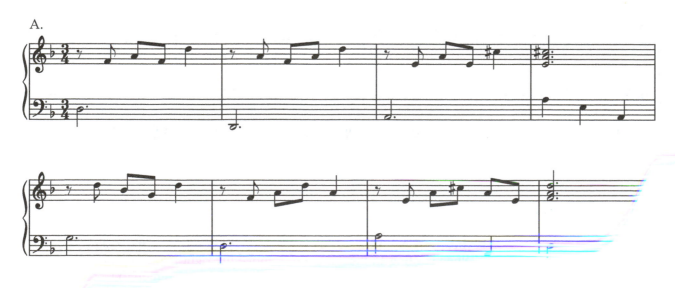

B.

Tonic and Dominant as Tonal Pillars and Introduction to Voice Leading

SINGING

EXERCISE 5.1 Melodies Implying Tonic and Dominant

Given are many tunes whose melodic structure is based primarily on the tonic and dominant harmonies. Sing these using scale degree numbers. You might also wish to play these tunes on your instrument, thinking in terms of scale degree numbers, and then transpose each tune to a different key.

- Examples A–D are pure arpeggiations of I and V (a harmonic analysis is included).
- Examples E–Q also rely on tonic and dominant, but these tunes (from the literature) also include various embellishing tones, most of which are passing tones. As you sing these melodies, add roman numerals (I and V) to measures or groups of measures that unfold these harmonies.
- As always, scan each melody before singing it, looking for formal repetitions (including repeated phrases), melodic fluency, and local pitch patterns (e.g., repeating rhythmic gestures).

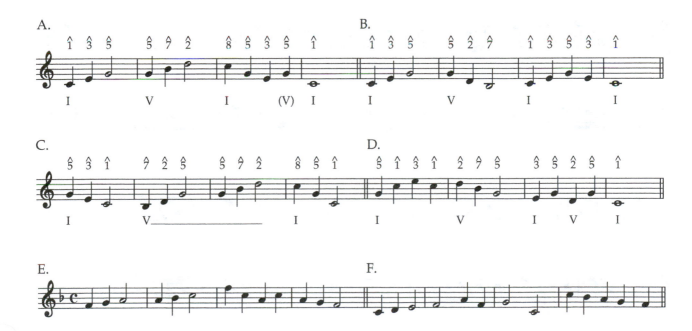

G.

H.

I.

J.

K.

L.

M.

Tonic and Dominant as Tonal Pillars and Introduction to Voice Leading

SINGING

EXERCISE 5.1 Melodies Implying Tonic and Dominant

Given are many tunes whose melodic structure is based primarily on the tonic and dominant harmonies. Sing these using scale degree numbers. You might also wish to play these tunes on your instrument, thinking in terms of scale degree numbers, and then transpose each tune to a different key.

- Examples A–D are pure arpeggiations of I and V (a harmonic analysis is included).
- Examples E–Q also rely on tonic and dominant, but these tunes (from the literature) also include various embellishing tones, most of which are passing tones. As you sing these melodies, add roman numerals (I and V) to measures or groups of measures that unfold these harmonies.
- As always, scan each melody before singing it, looking for formal repetitions (including repeated phrases), melodic fluency, and local pitch patterns (e.g., repeating rhythmic gestures).

G.

N.

O.

P. Handel, *Semele*

Leave_____ me,   leave   me,   loath - some

light!   Re - ceive   me,   re - ceive   me, si – lent night

Q. Durante, "Vergin, tutto amor"

Ver - gin,   tut - to a - mor,   o   ma - dre di bon -
Vir - gin,   fount   of   love,   Dear Moth - er, thou   of

ta - de,   o   ma - dre   pi - a,   ma - dre   pi – a,
mer - cy, whose heart was   riv - en,   whose heart   was   riv – – en,

LISTENING

EXERCISE 5.2 Warm-Up for Metrical Hearing

We now review metrical patterns, since the upcoming harmonic dictations will nearly always be cast in a meter. We focus on three meters for our dictations: $\frac{3}{4}$, $\frac{4}{4}$, and $\frac{6}{8}$. (We will also encounter $\frac{2}{4}$, $\frac{2}{2}$, $\frac{9}{8}$, and $\frac{12}{8}$ in analysis and writing.) $\frac{3}{4}$ and $\frac{4}{4}$ are easily distinguished. $\frac{6}{8}$ is a compound meter: it subdivides the beat into threes, rather than into the twos of $\frac{3}{4}$ and $\frac{4}{4}$. Listen to the following excerpts from the literature and identify a probable meter and an appropriate tempo indication that would correspond to that meter. If you hear the following patterns, for example,

two possible meters arise, one a fast $\frac{4}{4}$ (or $\frac{2}{4}$) (as notated above), and the other a slow $\frac{4}{4}$ notated as follows:

Your tempo indications are *andante* (slowish, walking), *allegro* (fast), and *molto allegro* (very fast).

	meter	tempo		meter	tempo		meter	tempo
A.	_____	_____	B.	_____	_____	C.	_____	_____
D.	_____	_____	E.	_____	_____	F.	_____	_____
G.	_____	_____						

EXERCISE 5.3 Cadence and Meter Identification

Examples A–D are in homophonic texture. Examples E–G are from Haydn's "Sun" Quartets. Determine a possible meter, and label the final cadence of each excerpt. Remember that you must listen to the outer-voice counterpoint to determine the type of cadence. Your choices are perfect authentic cadence (PAC), imperfect authentic cadence (IAC), contrapuntal cadence (CC), and half cadence (HC).

A. _____   _____

B. _____   _____

C. _____   _____

D. _____   _____

E. _____   _____

F. _____   _____

G. _____   _____

EXERCISE 5.4 Progressions from the Literature

The following excerpts employ tonic and dominant harmonies. The harmonic rhythm is one chord per measure. Write the correct roman numeral for each measure. Label cadences.

A. Quantz, Trio Sonata in G major for Oboe and Bassoon, *Adagio*

Note: Consider only the downbeat harmonies of each measure, which are in root position; ignore the bass line's chordal leaps on beat 2, which seem to create inversions.

m.   1   2   3   4
$\frac{3}{4}$:   ____   ____   ____   ____

B. Corelli, Concerto Grosso in D major, op. 6, no. 1, *Allegro*

m.   1   2   3   4
$\frac{3}{4}$:   ____   ____   ____   ____

C. Handel, Concerto Grosso in G minor, op. 6, no. 6, *Largo*

m.   1   2   3
$\frac{3}{4}$:   ____   ____   ____

D. Corelli, Sonata, op. 1, no. 9, *Allegro*

m.   1   2   3   4   5   6   7   8
$\frac{3}{4}$:   ____   ____   ____   ____   ____   ____   ____   ____

E. Schubert, "Waltz," from *38 Waltzes, Ländler, and Ecossaises*, D. 145

m.   1   2   3   4
$\frac{3}{4}$:   ____   ____   ____   ____

F. Vivaldi, Violin Sonata in C major, "Manchester," RV 754, *Corrente*

m.   1   2   3   4   5   6
$\frac{3}{8}$:   ____   ____   ____   ____   ____   ____

EXERCISE 5.5 Identification of Tonic

You will hear chord progressions that employ numerous diatonic chords. Label only tonic (I or i) harmonies on the appropriate lines; leave remaining lines blank. Each exercise is in a different key; you will hear I–V–I in the appropriate key to orient you. It is best to sing the tonic triad softly before listening to the exercise. The durations of harmonies are shown by the proportional length of lines. Identify cadences in each example, except for letter C.

A. $\frac{4}{4}$: ____ ____ ____ ____ | ____ ____ _____ || cadence type:

B. $\frac{4}{4}$: ____ | ____ ____ ____ ____ | ____ ____ _____ || cadence type:

C. $\frac{4}{4}$: ____ ____ ____ ____ | ____ ____ ____ ____ || cadence type:

D. $\frac{4}{4}$: ___ ___ ___ ___ | _____ _____ || cadence type:

E. $\frac{3}{4}$: _____ ___ | _____ __ | _____ ___ | _____ | _____ ___

| _____ | _____ || cadence type:

EXERCISE 5.6 Identification of Tonic and Dominant

Once again, you will hear progressions that use numerous diatonic chords. Label only the I (or i) and V chords, using roman numerals. Identify cadence types.

A. $\frac{4}{4}$: __ __ __ __ | __ __ | __ __ __ | _____ || cadence type:

B. $\frac{3}{4}$: __ | __ __ __ __ | __ __ __ | __ __ __ | _____ || cadence type:

C. $\frac{4}{4}$: ___ ___ | ___ ___ | ___ ___ | _____ || cadence type:

D. $\frac{4}{4}$: ___ ___ | __ __ ___ | ___ ___ | _____ || cadence type:

E. $\frac{6}{8}$: ___ __ _____ | ___ __ _____ | _____ ___ __ | _____ ||

cadence type:

EXERCISE 5.7 Differentiating Between I and V

Listen to the following progressions that employ only tonic and dominant chords in root position. Vertical slashes represent bar lines, and note values represent durations of harmonies. Write either I or V to indicate the sounding harmony in the blanks provided. Be aware that the same harmony may be repeated in different spacings. The first four are in D major, the second four are in B minor. The first one has been done for you.

Sample solution:

A. $\frac{4}{4}$:   ♩   ♩   ♩   ♩ ||
        I   V   V   I

B. $\frac{3}{4}$: ♩ | ♩ ♩ ♩ | ♩ ♩ ♩ | ♩ ♩ ♩ | ♩ ♩ ♩ | ♩ ♩ ♩ ||
     ___   ___   ___   ___   ___   ___

C. $\frac{4}{4}$: ♩ ♩ ♩ ♩ | ♩ ♩ ♩ ||
     ___ ___ ___ ___ ___ ___ ___

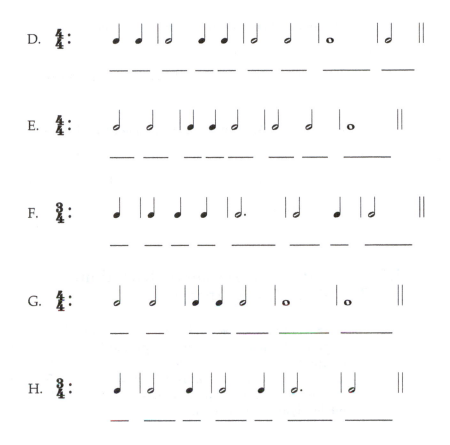

D. 𝄴 :

E. 𝄴 :

F. ¾ :

G. 𝄴 :

H. ¾ :

EXERCISE 5.8 Identification of Tonic and Dominant from the Literature

Label only tonic and dominant harmonies in the appropriate spaces given, ignoring any other diatonic harmonies. Identify the final cadence in each excerpt.

A. Schubert, "Frühlingstraum" ("A Dream of Springtime"), *Winterreise*, D. 911, no. 11

m.:   1   2   3   4

6/8: ____ | ____ | __ __ | ____ || cadence type:

B. Handel, "Air," Concerto Grosso no. 10 in D minor, op. 6, HWV 328

m.:   1   2   3   4

3/4: ____ __ | _____ | __ __ __ | _____ || cadence type:

C. Schubert, Impromptu in A♭ (major), *Six Moments musicaux*, op. 94, D. 780

m.:   1   2   3   4   5   6   7   8

3/4: ____ | ____ | ____ | ____ | ____ | ____ | ____ | ____ ||

cadence type:

D. Chopin, Mazurka in G minor, op. 67, no. 2

m.:   1   2   3   4   5   6

3/4: ___ | ___ | ___ | ___ | ___ | ___ || cadence type:

E. Schubert, Waltz in A major, *17 Ländler*, D. 366

m.:   1   2   3   4   5   6   7   8

3/4: _____ | _____ | _____ | _____ | _____ | _____ | _____ | _____ :||

cadence type:

EXERCISE 5.9 Preparation for Harmonic Dictation: Two-Voice Counterpoint

Notate both the upper and lower voice of the short examples of two-voice counterpoint. Each example moves primarily in note-against-note style. Use the
rhythms provided (a few pitches are given). Check your work by analyzing each
interval: all verticalities must be consonant (6, 3, 5, or 8) and weak-beat moving
lines (oblique motion) may be dissonant (2, 4, and 7) but must pass between two
pitches lying a third apart.

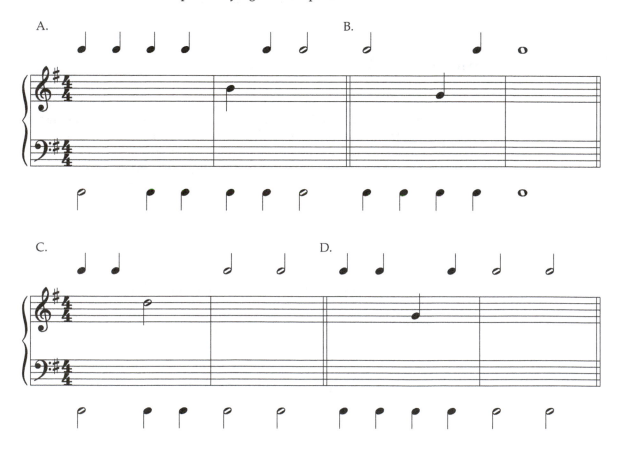

EXERCISE 5.10 Notation of Two-Voice Counterpoint

Notate the following two-voice exercises. In this exercise a few pitches are provided. Analyze your work by labeling each interval. Exercises A and B are in B♭ major and C–E are in G minor.

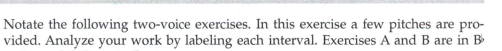

E.

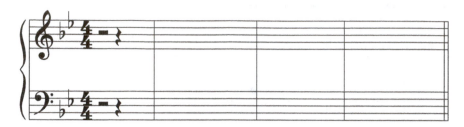

EXERCISE 5.11 Harmonic Dictation

Notate the bass and soprano voices. Next, provide roman numerals for each chord and identify the type of cadence for the following homophonic progressions. Observe the following steps:

1. Listen to the entire exercise, notating the first harmony and final cadence.
2. Listen for individual chords, focusing on soprano steps and leaps.
3. Check your final product.
   a. Are there any missing notes?
   b. Are there any contradictions between harmony and melody? For example, remember that a dominant harmony cannot support $\hat{3}$ in the melody and that it is important to use the leading tone (i.e., raised $\hat{7}$ in minor).

A.

B.

C.

D.

EXERCISE 5.12 Dictation from the Literature

Listen to the following excerpts from the literature that employ only I and V. Notate the single controlling bass pitch for each measure. Provide roman numerals (when you encounter an accompanimental figure, focus on the lowest-sounding pitch, since it determines the harmony).

A.   B.

C.

EXERCISE 5.13 Dictation from the Literature

Listen to the following excerpts from the literature that employ only I and V. Notate the single controlling bass pitch for each measure. Provide roman numerals (when you encounter an accompanimental figure, focus on the lowest sounding pitch, since it determines the harmony).

A. Mozart, Symphony no. 13 in F major, K. 112, *Andante*
B. Mozart, Symphony no. 25 in G minor, K. 183, *Allegro*

A.   B.

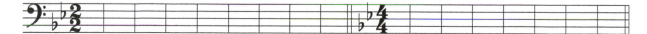

PLAYING

We will apply each harmonic concept to both the keyboard and to your own instrument, since such work greatly helps our hearing and allows us to apply concepts in a musical medium. Adding the keyboard and your instrument completes the third side of what we can consider the learning triangle: hearing, thinking, and feeling. By activating the tactile sense a powerful synthesis of concepts will result.

EXERCISE 5.14 Keyboard: Authentic Cadences

Study the following chord progressions, in which the soprano voice either remains stationary or features a passing tone or neighbor note. The arrows in exercises A, B, and C show how the three upper voices simply circulate through the three positions of soprano, alto, and tenor. Note that $\hat{5}$ is held as a common tone between the tonic and the dominant (and shown by dotted lines), except in exercise D (stepwise motions between chords are shown with solid lines).

At the keyboard:

1. Play the progressions as written, in C major and C minor.
2. Transpose the progressions to major keys up to one sharp and one flat and in the relative minors of these keys.

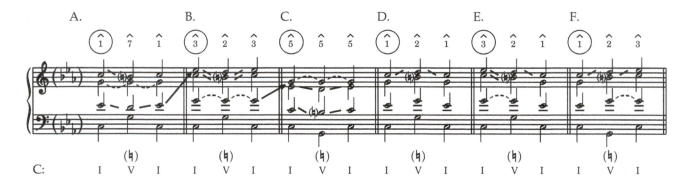

EXERCISE 5.15

Construct triads (no seventh chords) from the figured bass to create a four-voice keyboard spacing. Double the root. Then, follow each dominant harmony with its tonic harmony. Move each right-hand pitch as little as possible to the next pitch. Following the sample solution, revoice the right-hand chords as shown.

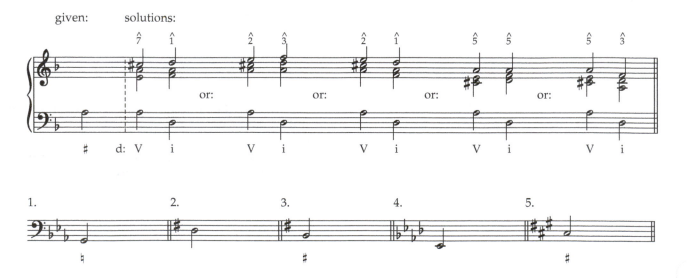

EXERCISE 5.16 Soprano Harmonization

In keyboard style, harmonize each pitch of the following soprano fragments. Use only root-position I and V chords. Except for $\hat{5}$, no other soprano scale degrees provide you with multiple chord choices. Play as written in both major and parallel minor and transpose to F and D major and minor.

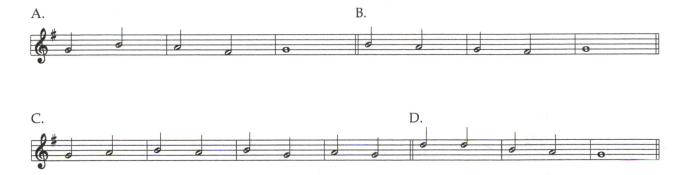

EXERCISE 5.17 Bass-Line Harmonization

Play a soprano in note-against-note style that works with the given bass and harmonize, using only I and V chords in root position. Then add inner voices (played along with the soprano in the right hand). Transpose the bass to D major and add a different soprano melody and inner voices.

EXERCISE 5.18 Longer Soprano Harmonization

Add a bass line to the soprano melody using only I and V harmonies in root position. Then add tenor and alto. Transpose to F major. Be able to sing either outer voice while playing the remaining three voices.

EXERCISE 5.19 Sing and Play: Harmonizing Melodies

- Study (scan) each melody, then sing it using scale degree numbers. Identify all cadences.
- Determine the harmonic rhythm and the underlying harmonic structure (I or V). Embellishing tones include chordal leaps, arpeggiations, passing tones, and neighboring tones.
- Sitting at the piano, add the root of the chord in the bass using your left hand. If you like, you may use your right hand to add the third and fifth of the chord in close position, moving to the next chord using proper voice leading.

A. Brahms, "Ich weiss mir'n Maidlein," *49 Deutsche Volkslieder*, WoO33, no. 40

B. Rossini, *William Tell*, act 2

C. Mozart, Horn Concerto no. 2 in E♭ major, K. 417

D. Mozart, Horn Concerto no. 1 in D major, K. 412

The Impact of Melody, Rhythm, and Meter on Harmony; Introduction to V⁷; and Harmonizing Florid Melodies

SINGING

EXERCISE 6.1

The following arpeggiations create progressions that incorporate V^7. Sing in the parallel minor as well; remember to raise $\hat{7}$ for the leading tone.

A.   B.

EXERCISE 6.2

Following are tunes whose melodic structure is based on I and V^7. Sing these using scale degree numbers. You might also wish to play these tunes on your instrument, thinking in terms of scale degree numbers, and then transpose each tune to a different key.

- Study each melody, observing its harmonic rhythm and whether tonic or dominant control the span (e.g., a measure, two measures, etc.).
- Accompany your singing at the piano by adding a single bass pitch, the root, of either tonic or dominant.

A.

B.

C.

D.

E.

F. Mozart, Symphony no. 39 in E♭ major, K. 543, *Allegretto*

G.

H.

I. Beethoven, Symphony no. 8 in F major

J. Haydn, Sonata in E major, Hob XVI.13, *Presto*

K. Schubert, "Wiegenlied," op. 98, no. 2

L. Mozart, String Quartet in A major, K. 464, *Allegro*

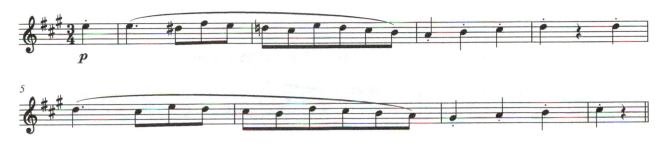

M. Handel, Concerto Grosso, op. 6, no. 3

N. Handel, Concerto Grosso in B♭ major, op. 3, no. 2

O. Mozart, *Le Nozze di Figaro (The Marriage of Figaro)*

P. Mozart, "Der Vogelfänger bin ich ja," from *The Magic Flute*

Andante

Der— Vo - gel - fän - ger— bin ich ja stets— lu - stig hei - ßa hop - sa - sa!

Q. Vivaldi, Violin Sonata in E♭ major, no. 11, Giga

Q.

R. Handel, Sonata no. 3 for Two Violins and Continuo, op. 5, HWV 398, Rondeau

S. Schubert, "Der Schmetterling," op. 57, no. 1, D. 633

S.

Wie soll— ich nicht tan - zen? Es macht— kei - ne

Mü - he, und rei - zen - de Far - ben

T. Handel, Concerto Grosso in B minor, op. 6, no. 12, *Allegro*

Violino I.

U. Haydn, Piano Sonato in E major, Hob XVI.47, III

Tempo di Menuet

V. Haydn, Symphony no. 13, in D major, *Allegro molto*

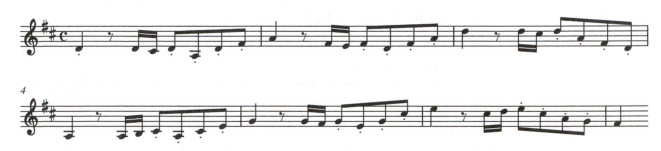

W. Mozart, String Quartet in B♭ major, K. 458

Allegro vivace assai

X. Mozart, Horn Concerto no. 2 in E♭, K. 417, *Allegro*

LISTENING

EXERCISE 6.3 Distinguishing Between V, V⁷, and V⁸⁻⁷

For each short harmonic progression that you hear, identify the following:

1. mode (major or minor)
2. scale degree of first soprano pitch
3. type of cadence (IAC, PAC, HC)
4. whether V, V⁷, or V⁸⁻⁷ is used at the cadence

	mode	scale degree of 1st pitch	cadence type	type of V
A.	_____	_____	_____	_____
B.	_____	_____	_____	_____
C.	_____	_____	_____	_____
D.	_____	_____	_____	_____

EXERCISE 6.4 Dictation and Second-Level Analysis

Notate the bass and the soprano lines and provide roman numerals for the following homophonic examples. Then step back to determine which harmonies in a measure are more important than others by focusing on their metrical placement and on the soprano line. Finally, based on these decisions, bracket entire measures in the bass and provide a second-level analysis in which a single roman numeral represents the underlying harmony that controls each measure. Note that the penultimate measure often contains two harmonies, such as I followed by V, which leads to a final tonic.

A.

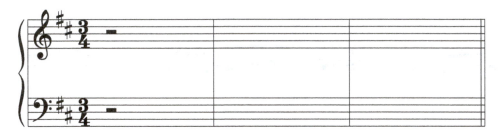

B.

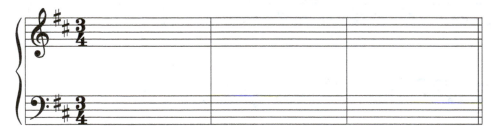

C.

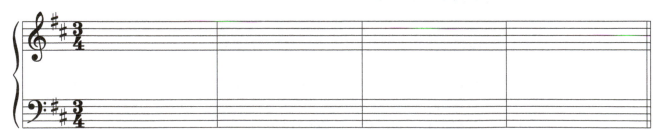

D.

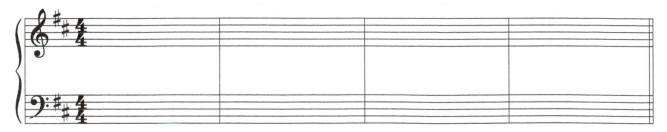

E.

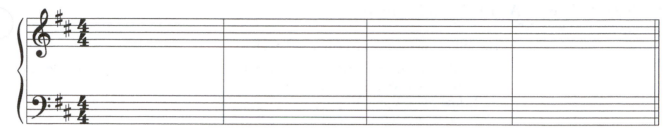

EXERCISE 6.5 Analysis and Dictation

The following excerpts do not have bass lines.

1. After listening to each example, notate the missing bass notes. Consider the given pitches to be helpful hints.
2. Identify I, V, and V^7 using roman numerals.
3. Circle and label any embellishing tones in the melody.

A. Schubert, Minuet in G major, Trio, *20 Minuets*, D. 41, no. 20

B. Haydn, German Dance in D major, *Seven German Dances*, Hob IX.12

EXERCISE 6.6 Analysis and Dictation

The following excerpts do not have bass lines.

1. After listening to each example, notate the missing bass notes. Consider the given pitches to be helpful hints.
2. Identify I, V, and V^7 using roman numerals.
3. Circle and label any embellishing tones in the melody.

A. Schubert, Waltz in B minor, *38 Waltzes, Ländler, and Ecossaises*, op. 18, no. 6, D. 145
   The right-hand G in m. 4 is a dissonant upper neighbor to the harmony's F♯.

B. Haydn, String Quartet in C major, op. 50, no. 2, Hob III.45, *Allegro*

C. Haydn, String Quartet in G major, op. 33, no. 5, *Largo*

D. Bach, Sonata for Flute and Continuo in E minor, BWV 1034, *Allegro*

EXERCISE 6.7 Analysis/Dictation

These incomplete scores from the literature omit the bass lines. You are to:

1. Listen to each example and notate the missing bass notes. *Note:* In addition to I and V, you may encounter other chords. Listen for their appearance and notate their bass notes only, but do not analyze them.
2. Circle and label embellishing tones in the melody.

A. Mozart, Serenade in B♭ major, K. 361, Trio II

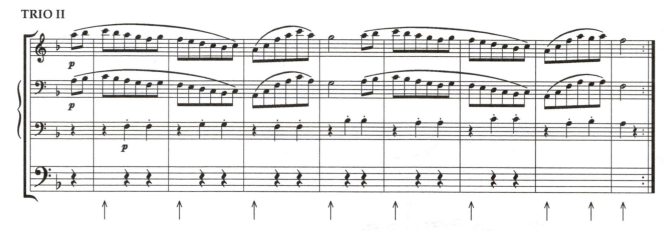

B. Schumann, "Jemand," *Myrten*, op. 25, no. 4

C. Schumann, String Quartet in A major, op. 41, Scherzo

EXERCISE 6.8 Dictation: Melodies with Accompaniments

Provide this information on the following staves:

1. key and mode
2. meter
3. number of measures
4. cadence type at close of example
5. bass line and roman numeral analysis

A.

B. Chopin, Etude in E, op. 10, no. 3, BI 74

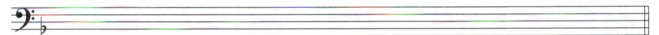

C. Beethoven, Ecossaise in G

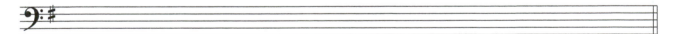

D. Haydn, String Quartet in E♭, op. 64, no. 6, Hob III.64

EXERCISE 6.9 Outer-Voice Dictation

Notate the outer voices of the four-voice homophonic examples. Provide a roman numeral analysis.

A.

B.

C.

D.

E.

F.

EXERCISE 6.10 Outer-Voice Dictation

Notate the outer voices of the four-voice homophonic examples. Provide a roman numeral analysis.

A.   B.

C.   D.

E.

PLAYING

EXERCISE 6.11 Broken Chords

Play the following broken-chord exercise, which features a dominant seventh chord in root position and each inversion. Transpose to major keys up to three sharps and three flats.

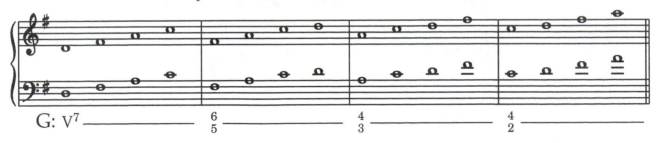

G: V⁷ ———————   6   ———————   4   ———————   4   ———————
                     5   3   2

EXERCISE 6.12

Identify the major key of each example, and play authentic cadences in *three* voices from the given V^7. Focus on resolution of tendency tones. Be able to sing any of the three voices while playing the other two.

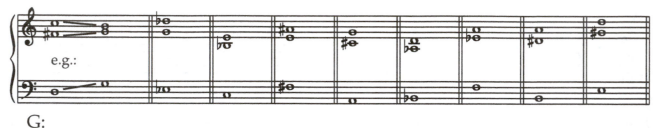

G:

EXERCISE 6.13

The following two-voice models demonstrate common settings of I–V^7–I. Add inner voices, and play in four-voice keyboard style in C and in major and minor keys up to and including three sharps and three flats. Be able to sing either the bass voice or the soprano voice while playing the other three voices.

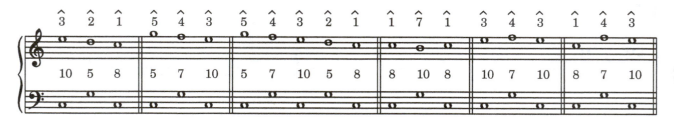

EXERCISE 6.14

Play the progression I–V^7–I in four voices, keyboard style, in any major or minor key up to three sharps and three flats. Be able to demonstrate the various complete and incomplete voicings. Also, be able to sing either the bass voice or the soprano voice while playing the other three voices.

EXERCISE 6.15 Figured Bass

In keyboard style, realize the following figured bass by adding alto and tenor voices. Play in the parallel minor. Then transpose to any two major keys and their parallel minor forms.

EXERCISE 6.16 Unfigured Bass

Realize the following two unfigured basses in four voices. Use only root positions of I, V, and V⁷. Analyze with roman numerals.

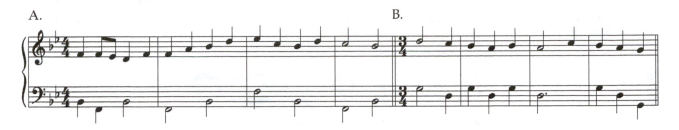

EXERCISE 6.17 Soprano Harmonization

Choose three soprano melodies from the four melodies given and harmonize each pitch by adding the three lower voices in keyboard style. Use only I, V, and V⁷. Circle all sevenths that occur in the soprano melodies and trace their resolutions. Transpose each melody to one other key of your choice.

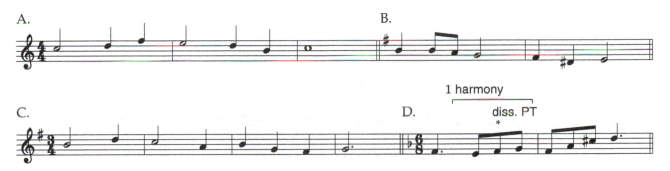

EXERCISE 6.18 Sing and Play: Harmonizing Melodies with Slow Harmonic Rhythm

- Study (scan) each melody, then sing each one using scale degree numbers. Identify cadences.
- Determine the harmonic rhythm and the underlying harmonic structure (I or V). Embellishing tones include chordal leaps, arpeggiations, passing tones and neighboring tones. Notes in parentheses are dissonances that resolve to the following note.
- Sitting at the piano, add the root of the chord in the bass using your left hand. If you like, you may use your right hand to add the third and fifth of the chord in close position, moving to the next chord by using proper voice leading.

A. Mozart, "Voi, che sapete," from *Le Nozze di Figaro (The Marriage of Figaro)*, K. 492, act 2

B. Mozart, "Batti, batti, o bel Masetto," from *Don Giovanni*, K. 527, act 1

Bat - ti, bat - ti, o bel Ma - set - to, la tua po - ve - ra Zer - li - na: sta - rò
Beat me, Beat me, dear Ma - set - to, Pun - ish your Zer - li - na mook - ly: Like a

qui co-me a-gnel - li - na le tue bot - te ad__ a - spet - tar.
lamb - kin, hum - bly, sweet - ly, I re - pent - ant __ shall __ sub - mit.

C. Mozart, "Longing for Spring," K. 596, *Giocoso*

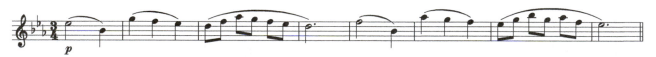

D. Mozart, Symphony no. 39 in E♭ major, K. 543, *Allegretto*

E. Haydn, Symphony in G major, "Surprise," no. 94, *Allegro*

F. Russian folk tune, *Andante grazioso*

G. Mozart, "Tutto e disposto . . . Aprite un po' quegli occhi," from *Le Nozze di Figaro (The Marriage of Figaro)*, K. 492, act 4

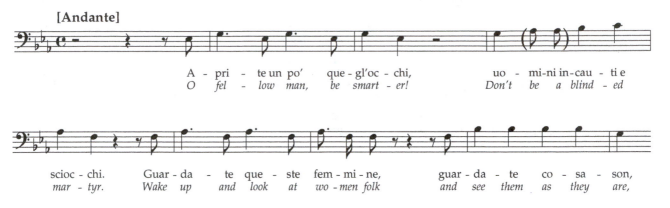

A - pri - te un po'   que - gl'oc - chi,   uo - mi - ni in - cau - ti e
O   fel - low man,   be   smart - er!   Don't   be   a   blind - ed

scioc - chi.   Guar - da - te   que - ste fem - mi - ne,   guar - da - te   co - sa - son,
mar - tyr.   Wake up   and look   at   wo - men folk   and   see   them   as   they   are,

H. Mozart, *Die Zauberflöte (The Magic Flute)*, K. 626, act 1, Finale

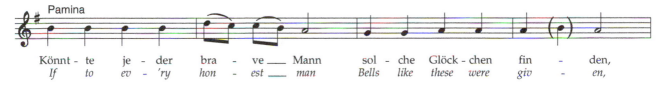

Könnt - te   je - der   bra - ve ___ Mann   sol - che   Glöck - chen   fin - den,
If   to   ev - 'ry   hon - est ___ man   Bells   like   these   were   giv - en,

I. Mozart, *Die Zauberflöte (The Magic Flute)* act 2, Finale

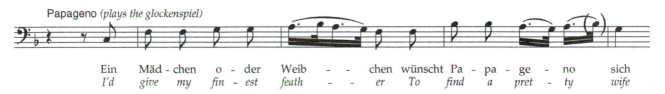

Ein   Mäd - chen   o - der   Weib - - chen wünscht Pa - pa - ge - no   sich
I'd   give   my   fin - est   feath - - er To   find   a   pret - ty   wife

J. Mozart, "Se vuol ballare, Signor Contino," from *Le Nozze di Figaro*, act 1, no. 3

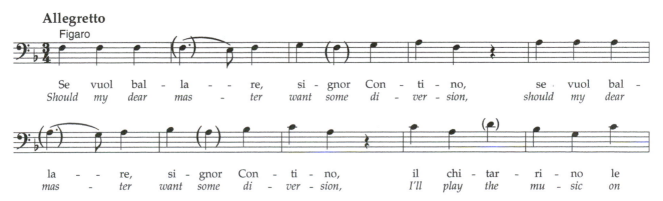

Se   vuol   bal - la - - re,   si - gnor   Con - ti - no,   se   vuol   bal -
Should   my   dear   mas - ter   want   some   di - ver - sion,   should   my   dear

la - - re,   si - gnor   Con - ti - no,   il   chi - tar - ri - no   le
mas - ter   want   some   di - ver - sion,   I'll   play   the   mu - sic   on

suo — ne rò,   il chi - tar - ri - no le suo - ne -
my ____ gui - tar,   I'll play the mu - sic on my gui -

rò, sì,   le suo - ne - rò, sì,   le suo - ne - rò.
tar, yes,   on my gui - tar, yes,   on my gui - tar.

CHAPTER 7

Contrapuntal Expansions of Tonic and Dominant: Six-Three Chords

SINGING

EXERCISE 7.1

The following melodies incorporate common uses of I^6, V^6, vii^{o6}, and IV^6. Sing them using scale degree numbers. Note how often harmonies change. Also, sing each in its parallel major or minor keys. *Remember:* Raise $\hat{7}$ for the leading tone, unless it passes down to $\hat{6}$, in which case use the lowered form.

A.

B.

C.

D.

E.

F.

G. Brahms, "Guten Abend"

H.

I.

J.

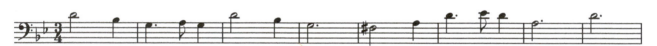

9

K. Mozart, Horn Concerto no. 4 in E♭ major, Rondo

5

L. Bellini, "Mecco all'atar di Venere," *Norma*, act 1, scene 2

Me pro - teg - ge,___ me di - fen - de un___ po -

5

ter mag - gior di___ lo - ro: è il pen - sier___ di___ lei___ che a - do

EXERCISE 7.2 Duet

Be able to sing either voice part, then with your partner sing the duets. Switch parts. It is a good idea to practice these as sing-and-play exercises before meeting with your partner.

LISTENING

EXERCISE 7.3 Root and First-Inversion Progressions

Listen to the following examples that contain tonic and dominant triads, their expanding $\frac{6}{3}$ inversions, and V^7 in root position. The meter signature is given, and the blanks indicate chord changes. Specify roman numerals and figured bass for each chord. Then, supply a second-level analysis that summarizes the harmony underlying each progression.

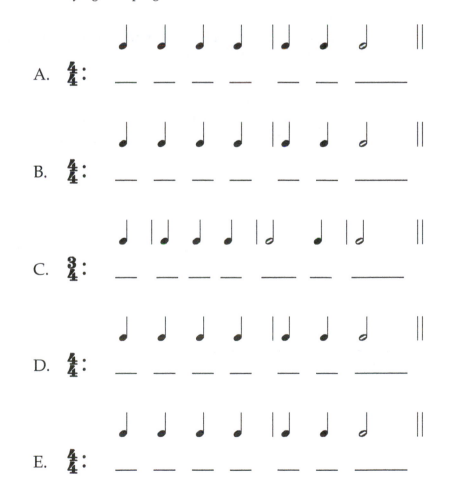

EXERCISE 7.4 Bass-Line Notation

Listen to, memorize, and then notate the bass lines in the following examples, which use I (i), I⁶ (i⁶), V, V⁷, and V⁶. Provide a two-level harmonic analysis.

A.   B.   C.

D.   E.

EXERCISE 7.5 Bass-Line Notation

Notate the bass part for each example. Then place a roman numeral that best fits each bass note, and also provide a second-level analysis. All examples are cast in either $\frac{3}{4}$ or $\frac{4}{4}$; you will need to determine which of the two meters best fits each example. Listen first to an entire example without notating anything. Focus on:

1. Whether the meter is $\frac{3}{4}$ or $\frac{4}{4}$.
2. The location of the tonic harmonies—there should be a sense of return to the pitches of the tonic chord.

A.   B.

C.   D.

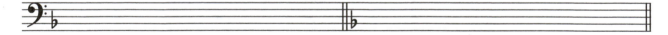

E.

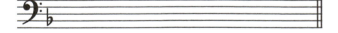

EXERCISE 7.6 Bass-Line Dictation

Listen to, memorize, and notate the bass lines in the following examples, and provide a two-level harmonic analysis.

A.　　　　　　　　　　　B.　　　　　　　　　　　C.

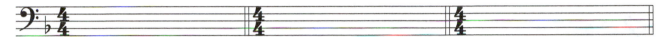

D.　　　　　　　　　　　E.　　　　　　　　　　　F.

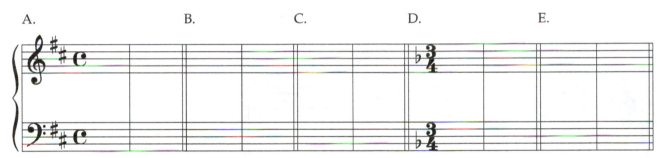

EXERCISE 7.7 Two-Voice Dictation

You will hear short (four- to six-chord) outer-voice counterpoints. Notate the two voices and provide roman numerals based on their harmonic implications.

A.　　　　　B.　　　　　C.　　　　　D.　　　　　E.

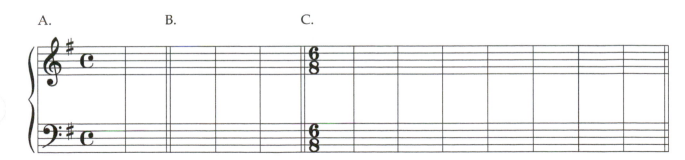

EXERCISE 7.8 Two-Voice Dictation: 2 + 2 = 4

You will hear how the two-voice counterpoint of the bass and soprano provides the skeleton for the added inner voices of alto and tenor. The result is a four-voice texture, the harmonies of which are essentially by-products of the confluence of voices. Outer-voice counterpoint is played for one beat, immediately followed by the added inner voices, their combination resulting in four-voice harmony. Notate the outer voices only, using both their counterpoint and the addition of the inner voices to label the harmonies.

A.　　　　　B.　　　　　C.

EXERCISE 7.9 Outer-Voice Notation and Analysis

1. Listen to the four-voice examples and notate their outer voices. To do this, listen to the entire example and determine the opening and closing harmonies. Then, start filling in the second level by distinguishing between harmonic progressions and contrapuntal expansions. Finally, memorize and notate one melodic line at a time. (Do not notate individual pitches as they are played; this is an inefficient and dangerous means of taking dictation because the pitches are not within a larger musical context.) A few pitches are provided.
2. Based on the harmonic implications of the outer voices, provide a two-level roman numeral analysis.

A.

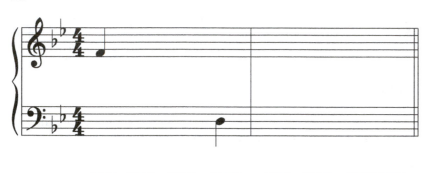

B.

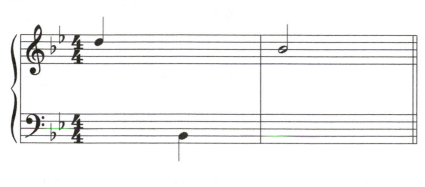

EXERCISE 7.10 Two-Voice Dictation

Notate the two voices and provide roman numerals based on their harmonic implications.

EXERCISE 7.11 Two-Voice Dictation: 2 + 2 = 4

The two-voice counterpoint of the bass and soprano provides the skeleton for the added inner voices of alto and tenor. The result is a four-voice texture. You will hear the outer-voice counterpoint for one beat, immediately followed by the added inner voices, their combination resulting in four-voice harmony. Notate the outer voices only, using both their counterpoint and the addition of the inner voices to label the harmonies.

EXERCISE 7.12 Two-Voice Notation and Analysis

You will hear a mix of two- and four-voice examples. Notate the pitches of the two-voice examples and the outer voices of the four-voice examples. Remember to listen for context and attempt to memorize lines. Analyze with two levels.

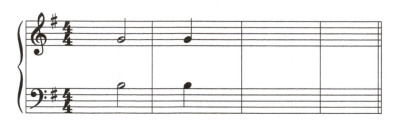

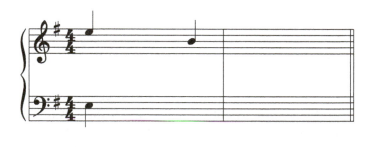

EXERCISE 7.13 Potpourri

A. You will hear short (four- to six-chord) outer-voice counterpoints. Notate the two voices and provide roman numerals based on their harmonic implications.

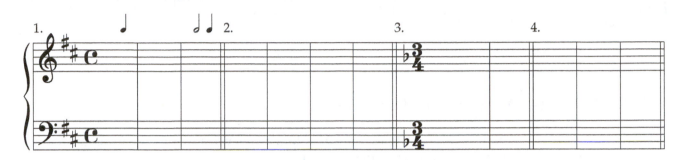

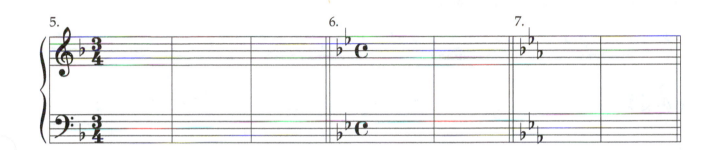

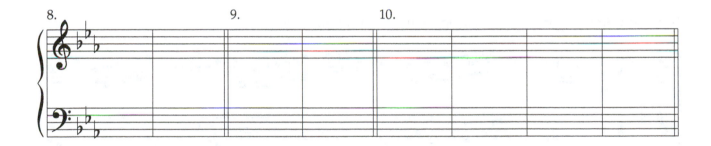

B. Two-Voice Dictation: 2 + 2 = 4. You will hear the outer-voice counterpoint for one beat, immediately followed by the added inner voices, their combination resulting in four-voice harmony. You are to notate the outer voices only, using both their counterpoint and the addition of the inner voices to label the harmonies.

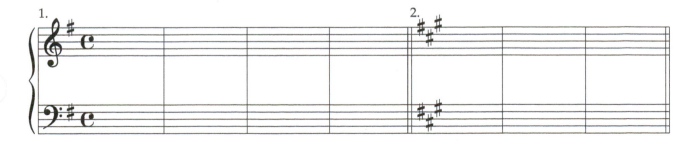

3.

EXERCISE 7.14 Analysis and Dictation

Notate the bass lines and provide a two-level harmonic analysis on the incomplete scores from the literature.

A. Vivaldi, Violin Sonata no. 11 in C major, Corrente

B. Haydn, String Quartet in B minor, op. 64, no. 2, Hob III.68, *Presto*

C. Bach, Flute Sonata in A minor, BWV 1033, *Adagio*

D. Brahms, "Muss es eine Trennung geben?" ("There Must Be a Parting?") ("Romances from Tieck's Magelone"), op. 33, no. 12
   Add eighth-note bass pitches on beats 1 and 4.

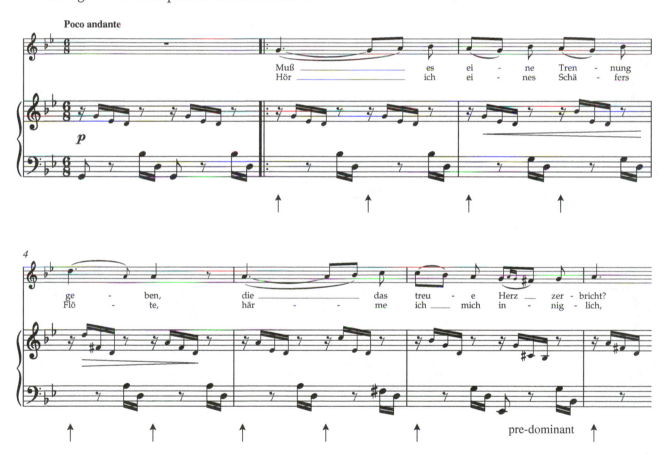

EXERCISE 7.15 Variation and Contrapuntal Expansion
of a Harmonic Model

You will hear contrapuntal expansions of a I–V–I harmonic progression. The model bass line will be fleshed out in six variations that maintain the metric placement of the given harmonies implied by the bass notes. Complete the following tasks:

1. Notate the bass and soprano voices of the contrapuntal chords that embellish the given harmonic structure.
2. Provide a two-level harmonic analysis. Your harmonic vocabulary now includes I, I⁶, IV⁶, V, V⁶, V⁷, and vii°⁶.

Model:

Var. 1   Var. 2

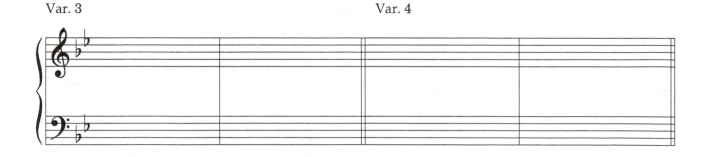

Var. 3   Var. 4

Var. 5   Var. 6

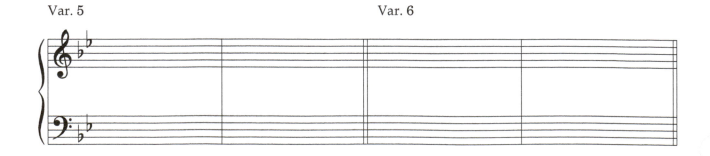

EXERCISE 7.16 Variation and Contrapuntal Expansion of a Harmonic Model

You will hear contrapuntal expansions of a I–V–I harmonic progression. The model bass line will be fleshed out in six variations that maintain the metric placement of the given harmonies implied by the bass notes. Complete the following tasks:

1. Notate the bass and soprano voices of the contrapuntal chords that embellish the given harmonic structure.
2. Provide a two-level harmonic analysis. Your harmonic vocabulary now includes I, I⁶, IV⁶, V, V⁶, V⁷, and vii°⁶.

Model:

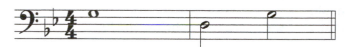

Var. 1   Var. 2

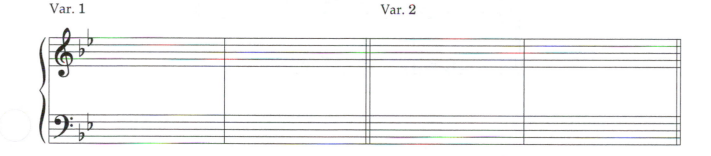

Var. 3   Var. 4

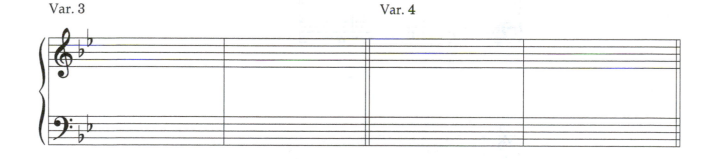

Var. 5   Var. 6

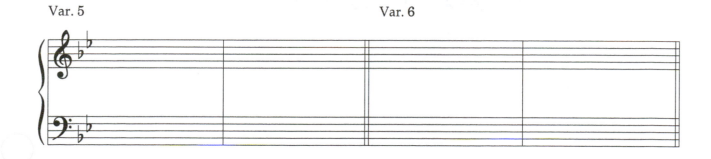

PLAYING

Up to this point, your keyboard chord progressions have been restricted to root-position triads and seventh chords. When the chord's root was in the bass, your right hand played a close-position chord that automatically doubled the root. However, the strategy of doubling the bass won't work for a first-inversion dominant triad (V^6), because doubling its third means doubling the leading tone.

EXERCISE 7.17 Playing Six-Three Chords

The following figured basses incorporate I^6 and V^6 chords. Play each in four-voice keyboard style (bass note in the left hand; upper voices in the right hand). Apply "doubled unisons" and "neutral position" when possible. Next, transpose the progressions to major and minor keys with key signatures up to two sharps or two flats—remember that in minor keys, you raise $\hat{7}$ for the leading tone.

A.

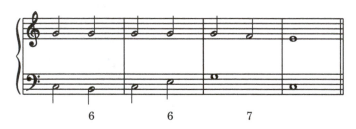

B.

C.

EXERCISE 7.18 Harmonization of Soprano Fragments

Harmonize each soprano melodic fragment in two different ways. Your chord choices are I (i), I⁶ (i⁶), V, V⁶, V⁷, vii°⁶, and IV⁶ (iv⁶). Harmonize all in D minor.

EXERCISE 7.19 Combining Fragments

Create a single melody by arranging the fragments from Exercise 7.18 in a logical order. Harmonize this melody in D minor using only i, i⁶, V, V⁶, V⁷, vii°⁶, and IV⁶. *Optional:* Add embellishing tones to the upper voices of your homophonic setting.

EXERCISE 7.20 Figured and Unfigured Bass

Play the outer voices as given. Determine the implied harmonies, adding roman numerals and second-level analysis. Then add inner voices, playing soprano, alto, and tenor in the right hand and bass in the left hand. In Example B, you will need to determine the implied harmonies without the aid of a given figured bass.

A.

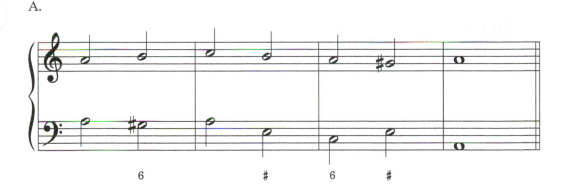

B.

EXERCISE 7.21 Melody Harmonization

The following two melodies offer the chance to incorporate first-inversion tonic and dominant chords in four-voice keyboard style. Harmonize Example B in both a major key and its relative minor. You may write in a few bass notes and roman numerals to aid your playing.

A.

B.

EXERCISE 7.22 Unfigured Bass

Determine a logical chord progression for the harmonic implications of the following unfigured bass; iv^6 and vii^{o6} are important possibilities. Add inner voices and play in keyboard style.

EXERCISE 7.23 Harmonic Implications of Two-Voice Counterpoint

Play the outer-voice counterpoint as written and determine a logical implied harmonic progression. Transpose the counterpoint to at least three different major and minor keys. Sing one voice while playing the other; switch.

EXERCISE 7.24 Singing and Playing

Sing the upper-voice quarter-note melody as you accompany yourself by playing the four-voice progression. Transpose to one other minor key. Be able to analyze.

EXERCISE 7.25 Figured Bass from the Operatic Literature

Sing the following operatic excerpts, then realize their figured basses in keyboard style. Finally, combine the two activities and accompany yourself while singing. Be aware that the key signatures do not represent the keys.

A. Handel, *Samson*, act 1, scene 2

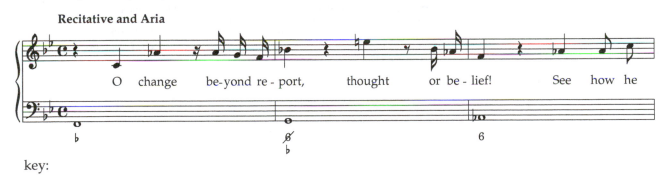

key:

B. Handel, *Susanna*, act 3, scene 2

key:

EXERCISE 7.26 Longer Unfigured Bass

Determine a logical chord progression for the harmonic implications of the following unfigured bass. Two important possibilities are IV⁶ and vii°⁶. Add inner voices and play in keyboard style. Be able to sing either outer voice while playing the remaining three voices.

EXERCISE 7.27 Expansions of Harmonic Pillars

Based on the instructions beneath the staff and the rhythms above, expand the root-position tonic and dominant chords in this four-measure excerpt.

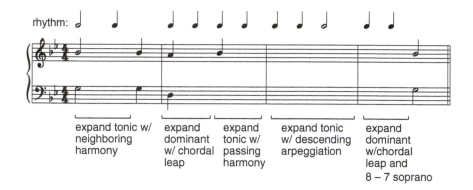

CHAPTER 8

More Contrapuntal Expansions: Inversions of V⁷, Introduction to Leading-Tone Seventh Chords, and Reduction and Elaboration

SINGING

EXERCISE 8.1 Singing and Playing Inversions of V⁷

The following arpeggiations create progressions that incorporate inversions of V⁷. Sing them and determine how often harmonies change; then analyze the progressions with roman numerals. Next, perform the exercises in the parallel minor. Remember that in minor keys you raise $\hat{7}$ to create the leading tone.

A.

B.

EXERCISE 8.2 Singing Leading-Tone Seventh Chords

Using solfège or scale degree numbers, sing the following minor-key patterns that contain vii°⁷ and the major-key pattern that contains viiø⁷.

A.

B.   C.

D.

E. Bach, "Schweigt stille, plaudert nicht," Cantata no. 211, "Coffee Cantata"

Aria

Mäd - chen, die von har - ten Sin - nen, die____

____ von__ har - ten Sin - nen, sind nicht leich - te__ zu ge - win - nen.

EXERCISE 8.3 Longer Singing Examples

The following tunes contain examples of harmonic and melodic techniques that we studied in previous chapters.

A.

B.

C.

EXERCISE 8.4 Duets

The following duets contain examples of V^7 and vii^{o7} and their inversions. Be able to sing either voice part, then, with your partner sing the duets. Switch parts. It is a good idea to practice these as sing-and-play exercises before meeting with your partner.

A.   B.   C.

LISTENING

EXERCISE 8.5 Comparison of Bass Lines

Listen to the recording, then circle the bass line that represents what was played and analyze it using roman numerals.

A.   B.

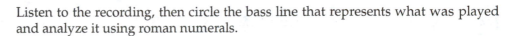

C.   D.

E.

EXERCISE 8.6 Notation of Bass Lines

Listen to each example, studying the given upper voices and then notate the bass line and provide a two-level harmonic analysis.

A. Mendelssohn, *Lieder ohne Wörte (Songs Without Words)*, Book 7, op. 85, no. 5

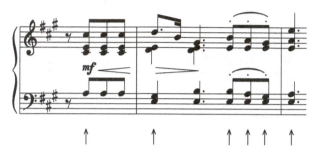

B. Mozart, Symphony no. 15 in G major, K. 124, Trio

C. Mozart, String Quartet in B♭ major, K. 172, Trio

D. Mozart, Symphony in A major, K. 114, Trio

E. Grieg, "Ingrid's Complaint," *Peer Gynt Suite* no. 1.

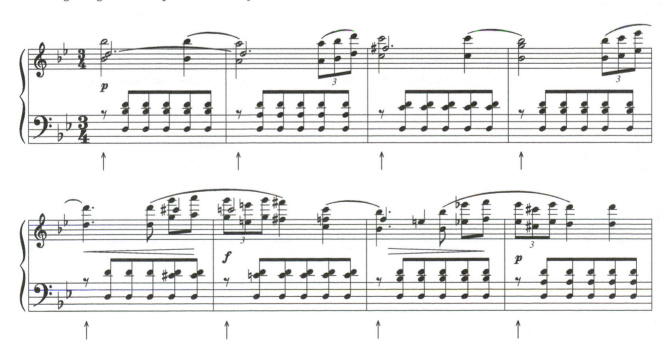

EXERCISE 8.7 Two-Voice Dictation: Paradigms

Notate the pitches of the missing voice (either bass or soprano). Then, based on the harmonic implications of the two voices, provide roman numerals (your choices are I, I^6, V, V^6, and V^7, and its inversions).

A.   B.   C.   D.   E.   F.

F:

G.   H.   I.   J.   K.

e:

EXERCISE 8.8 Two-Voice Dictation: 2 + 2 = 4

You will hear the outer-voice counterpoint for one beat, immediately followed by the added inner voices (alto and tenor), their combination resulting in four-voice harmony. Notate the outer voices only, and label each harmony.

A.   B.   C.

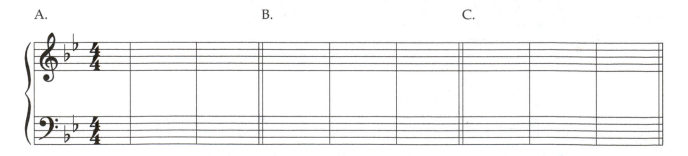

D.

EXERCISE 8.9 Two-Voice Dictation: Unmetered Paradigms

Notate the outer voices; then, based on the harmonic implications of the two voices, provide roman numerals (your choices are I, I⁶, V, V⁶, and V⁷, and its inversions).

A.   B.   C.   D.

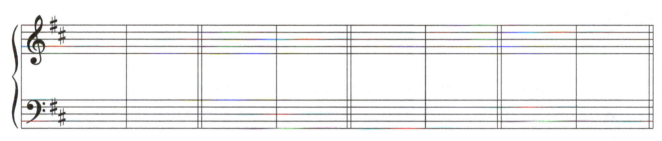

D:

E.   F.   G.

c:

EXERCISE 8.10 Dictation from the Literature

Notate the bass lines of the following contrapuntal progressions and include a single-level harmonic analysis. Some of the exercises provide a few pitches to guide you.

A. Chopin, Waltz in B minor, op. 69, no. 2, op. posth., BI 95, no. 2

B. Sammartini, Recorder Sonata no. 1 in G minor, *Allegro*

C. Beethoven, Piano Sonata no. 6 in F major, op. 10, no. 2, *Allegro*

D. Beethoven, String Quartet in C♯ minor, op. 131, *Andante*

E. Chopin, Nocturne in E minor, op. 72, no. 1, op. posth., BI 11

F. Rossini, "Ehi Fiorello," from *Il Barbiere di Sivigila* (*The Barber of Seville*), act 1, scene 3

EXERCISE 8.11 Dictation of Figurated Examples

The chords in this exercise are presented as horizontal melodies, and you must aurally stack the chordal members to create a vertical harmonic structure. Notate the bass. Focus on the "sonic dimension" in this exercise rather than the outer-voice counterpoint. That is, listen not only for underlying tonic or dominant progressions but exactly how they are expanded in time.

A.

B.

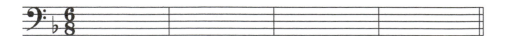

C.

EXERCISE 8.19 Variation and Contrapuntal Expansion of a Harmonic Model

You will next hear contrapuntal expansions of two I–V–I progressions. Each of the following two progressions will be fleshed out with various contrapuntal expansions that maintain the harmonic rhythm of the model progressions. Complete the following tasks:

1. Notate the bass and soprano voices of the contrapuntal chords that embellish the given harmonic structure.
2. Provide a two-level harmonic analysis. Your harmonic vocabulary now includes I, I^6, IV^6, V, V^6, V^7, V^6_5, V^4_3, V^4_2, vii^{o6}, vii^{o7}, vii^{o6}_5, and vii^{o4}_3.

Variation

Variation 4

on 5

Variation 5

Variation 6

Variation 6

Variation 7

Variation 7

PLAYING

EXERCISE 8.20 Completing Dominant Sevenths

Given are three notes of a dominant seventh chord. Determine the missing member, and then add it to the right hand to create four-voice chords. Be aware of inversions. Regard the missing note as either soprano or tenor (top or bottom of right hand), and play each chord in both positions. Say aloud the inversion or figured bass. An example is provided.

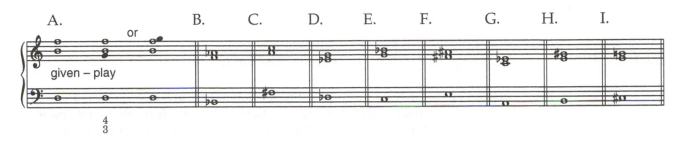

EXERCISE 8.21 Figured Bass

Realize the figured basses shown in four voices. Transpose to the keys of C major and F major. Play each example in parallel and relative minor keys.

EXERCISE 8.22 Keyboard: Warm-Up with vii°⁷ and viiø⁷

Complete the following tasks in four voices. You may use either close position with keyboard or SATB spacing. Play:

A. i–vii°⁷–i in minor keys up to five sharps and five flats (begin with $\hat{}$ soprano)

B. i–vii°⁶₅–i⁶ in C, A, and F♯ minor (begin with $\hat{1}$ in the soprano)

C. i–vii°⁴₃–i⁶ in C♯, E, and G minor (begin with $\hat{3}$ in the soprano)

D. I–viiø⁷–I in B♭, D, and C major (begin with $\hat{5}$ in the soprano)

EXERCISE 8.23 Keyboard: Completion of vii°⁷ and V⁷ Chords

EXERCISE 8.24 Voicing Inverted Dominant Seventh Chords

Given are right-hand voicings for root-position and inverted dominant seventh chords in F major. Note that root position is the only form that contains four (rather than three) possible voicings because root position may omit the fifth (as shown by the asterisk). Inverted seventh chords, however, must be complete; angle brackets illustrate the "gap" that occurs between various voicings because the missing note lies in the bass. Transpose to keys up to and including two sharps and two flats.

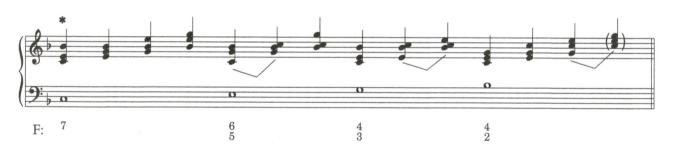

EXERCISE 8.25 Progression Incorporating vii°⁷

Play the two-measure progression that incorporates vii°⁷. Transpose it by ascending perfect fourths until you reach G minor. Part of the first transposition is given; the final chord of m. 2 is a link that transforms the tonic into the dominant of the upcoming key. Sing bass or soprano while playing.

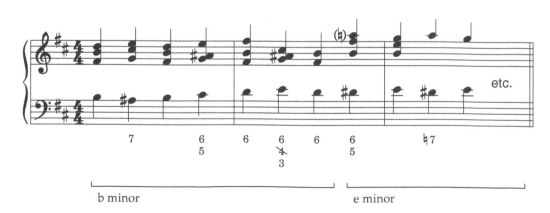

EXERCISE 8.26 Melodic-Fragment Harmonization

Determine a possible key for each of the following unmetered melodic fragments. Choose a meter and rhythmic setting and harmonize each in four voices using inversions of V^7 or $vii^{\circ 7}$ to create contrapuntal expansions of the tonic.

EXERCISE 8.27 Bass Harmonization

Harmonize three of the four bass fragments. Follow the instructions for Exercise 8.26. You may write out the soprano voice.

A.   B.   C.   D.

EXERCISE 8.28 Outer-Voice Progressions

Play the outer-voice counterpoint examples and transpose each to at least two keys. Analyze.

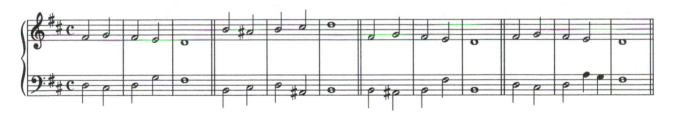

SINGING AND PLAYING

EXERCISE 8.29 Keyboard Reduction

Play the opening of Haydn's song, analyze it, and reduce it to a four-voice homophonic texture. Play your four-voice reduction while singing the melody.

Haydn, "Das strickende Mädchen" ("The Knitting Maiden"), *XII Lieder für das Clavier*, Book 1, Hob XXVIa.1

1. Und   hörst   du,_ klei - - ne
2. In   dei - - nen_ Au - - gen
3. So   man - - chen. Tag,   so

Phyl - - lis, nicht der Vög - lein ___ sü ___ Bes
herrscht ___ der Gott der Lieb ___ und ___ zau - bert ___
man - - ches Jahr schlich ich ___ dir ___ ein - sam ___

EXERCISE 8.30 Figured Bass from the Operatic Literature

Sing the following tunes, then realize the figured bass in keyboard style. Combine the two activities by accompanying yourself as you sing.

Handel, *Semele*, act 1. scene 2

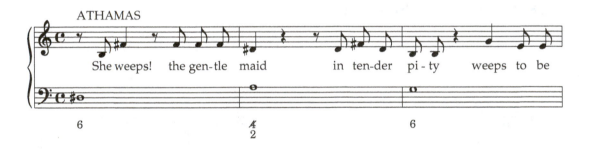

ATHAMAS

She weeps! the gen-tle maid in ten-der pi - ty weeps to be

6   4   6
           2

Handel, *Giulio Cesare*, act 2, scene 2

RECITATIV und ARIE

Ich fühl es wohl zu mei - nem tief - sten Un - glück, dass

6   5

ihr im Her-zen ra-send schon die Flam-me ent - lo-dert;

6   ♭7
5

INSTRUMENTAL APPLICATION

EXERCISE 8.31 Harmonic Reduction

Reduce the florid texture of the following short excerpts. Analyze, verticalize (into a four-voice homophonic texture), and then arpeggiate each example. Play each reduction.

A. Corelli, Concerto Grosso in F major, op. 6, no. 12, Sarabanda

B. Handel, Concerto Grosso in D major, op. 3, no. 6, *Allegro*

C. Handel, Concerto Grosso in A minor, op. 6, no. 4, *Allegro*

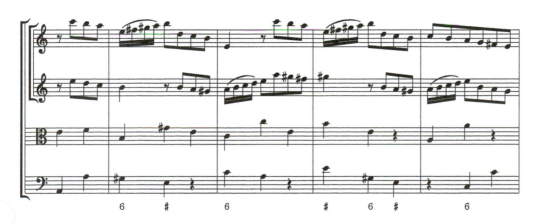

D. Handel, Concerto Grosso in G major, op. 6, no. 1, *Allegro*

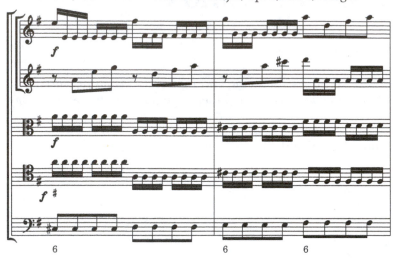

EXERCISE 8.32 Embellishment

Elaborate the following figured basses and scale degree melodies (with roman numerals) by arpeggiating in strict ascending four-voice chords that maintain good voice leading between chords. Then embellish your solution by adding changes in contour and embellishing tones. Refer to the discussion in this chapter for a detailed procedure.

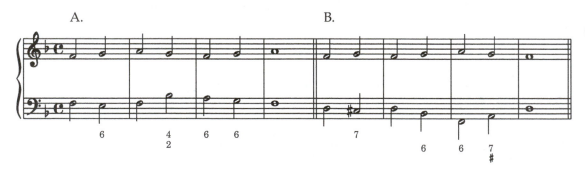

CHAPTER 9

The Pre-Dominant Function and the Phrase Model

SINGING

EXERCISE 9.1 Melodies Incorporating the Pre-Dominant Function

The following arpeggiations create progressions that incorporate the pre-dominant function. Sing them and note how often harmonies change. Then analyze the progressions with roman numerals. Play A and B in the parallel minor. (Exercise C should be performed only in the minor mode.)

A.

B.

C.

minor
only

D.

E.

F.

EXERCISE 9.2 Melodies from the Literature

Sing each tune, each of which contains one or more phrases and implied predominant harmonies. Determine the harmonic rhythm, then, at the keyboard, add a bass pitch that represents each of the underlying harmonies.

A. English

B. American

C. Brahms, "Vergebliches Ständchen"

D. Gluck, "Schweizer Heimweh"

E. Haydn, Sonata in C major, *Allegro con brio*

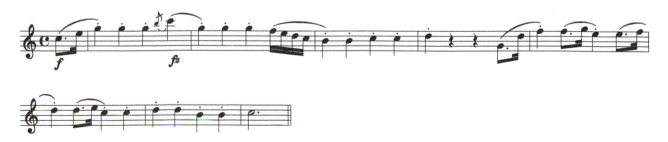

F. Mozart, Piano Trio in G major, K. 564, *Allegretto*

LISTENING

EXERCISE 9.3 Aural Identification of Pre-Dominants

Listen to each of the following short phrases in the major mode, and identify the pre-dominant chord with a roman numeral. Your choices are ii, ii⁶, and IV. The following hints will be helpful.

- If there is a bass leap into the V chord, the pre-dominant must be a root-position ii chord.
- If the pre-dominant harmonizes $\hat{2}$ in an upper voice, it must be a supertonic chord.
- If the pre-dominant harmonizes $\hat{1}$ in an upper voice, it must be a sub-dominant chord.

A. _____   D. _____

B. _____   E. _____

C. _____

EXERCISE 9.4 Aural Identification of Pre-Dominants

Listen to the following phrases in the minor mode, and identify the pre-dominant with a roman numeral. Your choices are ii°⁶, iv, and iv⁶. In addition to the hints for the previous exercise, here are some more tips.

- If the bass steps into the V chord from above, the pre-dominant must be a iv⁶ chord.
- Remember that there will be no root-position ii° chords in minor.

A. _____   E. _____

B. _____   F. _____

C. _____   G. _____

D. _____   H. _____

EXERCISE 9.5 Aural Discrimination

Circle the progression that is played, and analyze it using roman numerals.

EXERCISE 9.6 Aural Identification of Pre-Dominants

Provide the roman numeral (RN) of the pre-dominant that occurs in each short (six-to eight-chord) example. Your choices are ii (root position in major only), ii⁶, and IV (major and minor modes), and iv⁶ (in minor only, as part of half cadence). Then, given the key for each example, write the names of the pitches of the pre-dominant harmony in ascending order from the bass note. To hear the PD, work backward from the dominant of the cadence and listen for the bass motion: $\hat{4}$–$\hat{5}$, $\hat{2}$–$\hat{5}$, and $\hat{6}$–$\hat{5}$ are possible lines, then listen to the melody to discern the exact chord.

Sample solution:

A. RN: __iv__ Key: d minor: G B♭ D   G. RN: ____ Key: f minor: _____

B. RN: ____ Key: D Major: _____   H. RN: ____ Key: F Major: _____

C. RN: ____ Key: d minor: _____   I. RN: ____ Key: G Major: _____

D. RN: ____ Key: D Major: _____   J. RN: ____ Key: g minor: _____

E. RN: ____ Key: F Major: _____   K. RN: ____ Key: G Major: _____

F. RN: ____ Key: f minor: _____   L. RN: ____ Key: g minor: _____

EXERCISE 9.7 Dictation and Analysis

The upper voices are given. Notate the bass and provide roman numerals and second-level analysis. Begin by listening to the examples and by studying the harmonic implications provided by the upper voices.

A.   B.

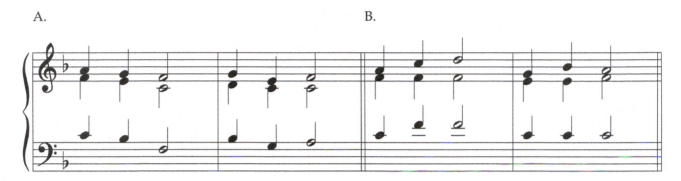

C.   D.

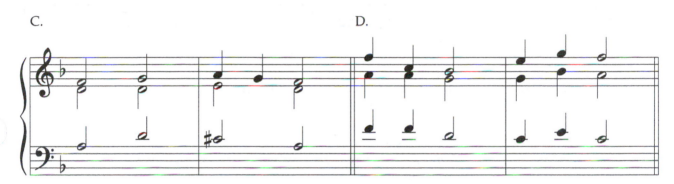

EXERCISE 9.8 Two-Voice Dictation

Notate the bass and soprano voices and provide roman numerals given their harmonic implications.

EXERCISE 9.9 Two-Voice Dictation: 2 + 2 = 4

You will hear how the two-voice counterpoint of the bass and soprano provides the skeleton for the added inner voices of alto and tenor. The result is a four-voice texture, the harmonies of which are essentially by-products of the confluence of voices. You will hear the outer-voice counterpoint for one beat, immediately followed by the added inner voices, their combination resulting in four-voice harmony. You are to notate the outer voices only, using both their counterpoint and the addition of the inner voices to label the harmonies.

A.   B.   C.

EXERCISE 9.10 Dictation and Analysis: The IV–ii Complex and the Phrase Model

The upper voices are given in the following examples from the literature. Notate the bass and provide roman numerals and second-level analysis. Begin by listening to the examples and by studying the harmonic implications of the upper voices.

A. Haydn, String Quartet in G major, op. 76, no. 1, Hob III.75, Menuetto

B. Haydn, String Quartet in D major, op. 76, no. 5, Hob III.79, Menuetto

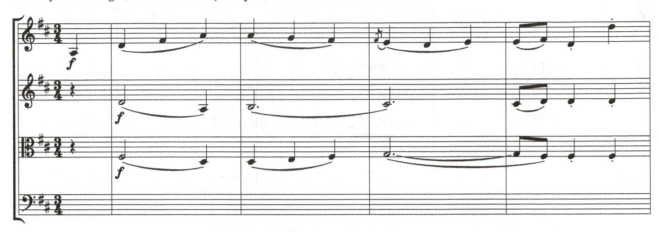

C. Schubert, String Quartet, op. 168, D. 112, *Allegro*

D. Kozeluch, String Quartet in F major, op. 33, no. 3, *Adagio ma non troppo*

E. Beethoven, String Quartet no. 6 in B♭ major, op. 18, no. 6, *Adagio ma non troppo*

EXERCISE 9.11 Notation of Pre-Dominants

Memorize each progression's basic harmonic structure, focusing on the bass. Then notate the bass line and provide roman numerals.

A.   B.

C.   D.

E.   F.

EXERCISE 9.12 Homophonic Dictation

Use roman numerals to label the underlying harmonic progression and the cadence type in the following phrase models. There is usually one chordal function per measure; be aware that the pre-dominant and dominant may occupy the same measure.

A.

B.

C.

D.

E.

EXERCISE 9.13 Figurated Dictation from the Literature

Use roman numerals to label the underlying harmonic progression in the phrase models. Also, label the cadence type. Horizontal lines indicate harmonic placement and vertical lines indicate measures.

A. Vivaldi, Concerto in C major for Violin, Ryom 176, *Largo*

¾: ___ | ___ | ___ | ___ ||

B. Schumann, "Tief im Herzen trag' ich Pein" ("Deep in My Heart I Suffer"), *Spanisches Liebeslieder (Spanish Love Songs)*, op. 138, no. 2

$\frac{3}{4}$: ___ | ___ | ___ ___ | ___ ___ | ___ ||

C. Haydn, String Quartet in B♭ major, "Der Frosch," Menuetto op. 50, no. 6, Hob III.49, *Allegretto*

$\frac{3}{4}$: ___ | ___ | ___ | ___ ||

D. Bach, "Wo soll ich fliehen hin," Cantatas 163 and 148, BWV 163 and 148

$\frac{4}{4}$: _ | _ _ _ _ | ____ _ | _ _ _ _ | ___ ||

E. Schubert, "Litanei auf das Fest aller Seelen" ("Litany for the Feast of All Souls"), D. 343

$\frac{4}{4}$: ___ ___ | _ _ _ _ |

F. Loeillet, Trio Sonata in B♭ major, op. 2, no. 9, *Largo*

$\frac{3}{4}$: ___ _ | ___ _ | ___ _ | ____ |

PLAYING

EXERCISE 9.14 Figured Bass

Each of the following two-voice cadential models moves through tonic, predominant, dominant, and back to tonic. Realize the figured bass, and play in four-voice keyboard style. Then transpose each to major and minor keys (up to two flats or two sharps). You should not play parts B1 and C2 in minor keys. Why not?

EXERCISE 9.15 Melody Harmonization

Determine logical meters and progressions for the given melodic fragments. You may change the rhythms of the fragments. Parts A–D are soprano fragments; Parts E–H are bass fragments. Harmonize in four-voice keyboard style. Be aware that progressions may work in major and/or minor mode.

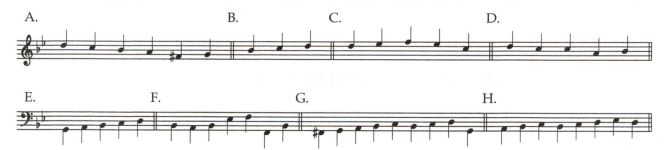

EXERCISE 9.16 Paradigms

Play the following progressions in all major and minor keys that contain one and two sharps and flats.

A. Soprano: $\hat{3}$–$\hat{2}$–$\hat{7}$–$\hat{1}$ B. $\hat{5}$–$\hat{4}$–$\hat{2}$–$\hat{1}$ C. minor only: $\hat{3}$–$\hat{4}$–$\hat{5}$

   Harmony: I–ii^6–V^7–I   I–IV–V–I   i–iv^6–V

EXERCISE 9.17 Reduction

Each of the following examples represents an elaboration of a two-voice counterpoint. Play each example, then reduce the texture to simple four-voice homophony by determining each measure's governing harmony and omitting repeated notes and nonchord tones. Look for a melodically fluent soprano voice. Play your reduction in four voices.

A.

B.

C.

PLAYING AND SINGING

EXERCISE 9.18 Unfigured Bass

Realize the unfigured bass in four-voice keyboard style. Be able to sing one of the outer voices while playing the other three voices. Analyze.

EXERCISE 9.19 Figured Bass from the Operatic Literature

Sing the tunes from the following excerpts, then realize the figured bass in keyboard style. Finally, combine the two activities by accompanying yourself while you sing. Be aware that the key signature may not reflect the key of the excerpt.

A. Handel, "Mein Kelch ist voll" ("My Cup is Full,"), from *Joshua*, act 3, scene 1

Mein Kelch ist voll, welch' se-gen voll-Ge-schenk! wie sag' ich würd gen-Dank dem Herrn und dir!

B. Handel, "Of My Ill-Boding Dream," from *Semele*, act 3, scene 8

Of my ill-bod-ing dream   be-hold   the dire e - vent!

♭5   ♭5 – ♭6   ♭5   (♭5)

EXERCISE 9.20 Instrumental Application: Reduction and Elaboration

Reduce the textures in the following Mozart symphonic excerpts. Analyze, verticalize (into a four-voice homophonic texture), and then perform each example as
follows. If you are a pianist, simply play your four-voice realization. If you are
a melodic instrumentalist, arpeggiate each example. If necessary, refer to the
discussion in Chapter 8 for a detailed procedure. Play each reduction in the key
in which it is written; then transpose to one other key of your choice.

A. Mozart, Symphony in D major, K. 81, *Andante*

B. Mozart, Symphony in D major, K. 95, *Andante*

EXERCISE 9.21 Embellishment

Embellish the following four-voice progressions and figured basses by arpeggiating in strict ascending four-voice chords that maintain proper voice leading
between chords. Then embellish your solution by adding changes in contour and
embellishing tones. Refer to the discussion in Chapter 8 for a detailed procedure.

A.   B.

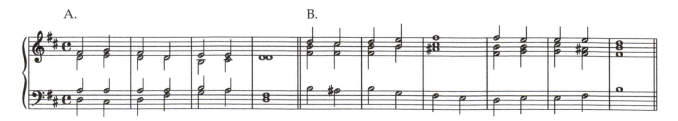

C.   D.

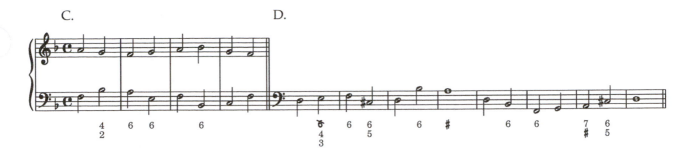

EXERCISE 9.22 Reduction

Reduce the texture in the following Mozart symphonic excerpt. Analyze, verticalize (into a four-voice homophonic texture), and then perform as follows. If you are a pianist, simply play your four-voice realization. If you are a melodic instrumentalist, arpeggiate. If necessary, refer to the discussion in Chapter 8 for a detailed procedure. Play your reduction in the key in which it is written; for extra credit, transpose to one other key of your choice.

Mozart, Symphony in D major, K. 97, *Allegro*

CHAPTER 10

Accented and Chromatic Embellishing Tones

SINGING AND PLAYING

EXERCISE 10.1 Singing Accented and Chromatic Embellishing Tones

Be able to sing either voice while playing the other using scale degrees or solfège in major and minor modes up to and including two sharps and two flats. Label all embellishing tones.

EXERCISE 10.2 Improvising Suspensions in Two Voices

A. Play the lower voice and sing the upper voice as written. Then add suspensions as shown in the figured bass. The result will be a continuous 2:1 counterpoint; the faster note values may occur in either voice.

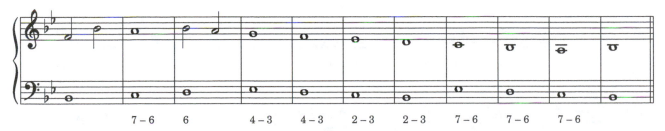

7 – 6   6   4 – 3   4 – 3   2 – 3   2 – 3   7 – 6   7 – 6   7 – 6

B. Proceed as in letter A, but no figured bass is given. Add a minimum of one each of the typical suspension figures (9–8, 7–6, 4–3, and 2–3). Analyze using roman numerals. The result will be a continuous 2:1 counterpoint; the faster note values may occur in either voice.

SINGING

EXERCISE 10.3 Melodies from the Literature

Sing the following melodies that include chromatic and accented embellishing tones. Determined implied harmonies for each example. For Exercise F, play the bass notes while singing the melody.

A. Schubert, Mass in G major, Kyrie

B. Mozart, *Cosi fan tutte*, act 2, scene 1

C. Mozart, *Abduction from the Seraglio*, Belmonte's Aria, act 2, no. 15

D. Haydn, Cello Concerto in D, Hob VIIb.2, *Allegro*

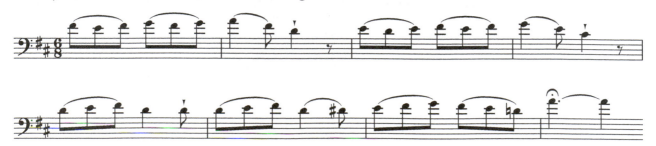

E. Bellini, "Morte io non temo," from *I Capuleti e i Montecchi*, act 2, no. 1

Mor-te io non te - mo il   sa   -   i,   sem-pre la chie - si a___ te_____ sì.

Pur non pro-va - to   ma - i   sor - ge un ter - ro - re in___ me

F. Verdi, "Bella Figlia dell'amore," from *Rigoletto*

(8va bassa)

G. Bellini, "No: non ti son rivale," from *La straniera*, act 1, no. 7

Andante

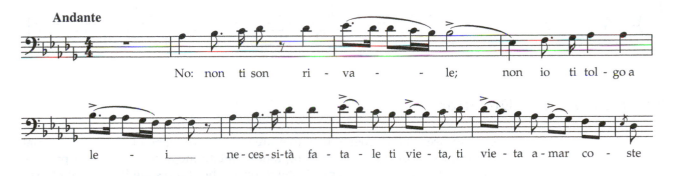

No: non ti son   ri - va - - le;   non io ti tol - go a

le -   i___   ne - ces-si-tà fa - ta - le ti vie - ta, ti vie - ta a-mar co - ste

LISTENING

EXERCISE 10.4 Dictation

The following short progressions either expand the tonic or are cadential motions. Each contains embellishing tones. Notate the outer voices and provide roman numerals; label any embellishing tones. The choices are PT (passing tone), CS (chordal skip), APT (accented passing tone), N (neighbor note), S (suspension), and APP (appoggiatura).

A.   B.

C.   D.

EXERCISE 10.5 Dictation

You will hear short progressions that are *either* expansions of tonic *or* cadential motions: each contains embellishing tones. Notate the outer voices and provide roman numerals; label any embellishing tones. The choices are PT (passing tone), CL (chordal leap), APT (accented passing tone), N (neighbor note), S (suspension), and APP (appoggiatura).

A.   B.   C.

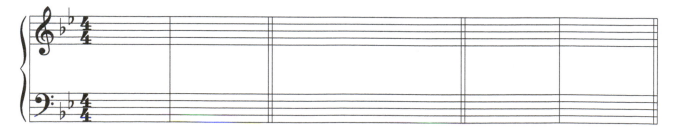

E. F.

E. F.

EXERCISE 10.9 Embellished Paradigms

You will hear short paradigms that either expand the tonic or are cadential progressions. Refer to the list of paradigms in Chapter 9. Each has from one to three accented embellishing tones. Notate the outer voices, and provide roman numerals and figured bass.

A. B. C. D. E.

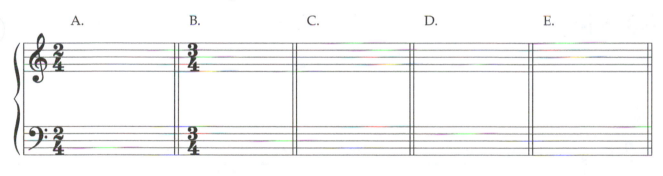

F. G. H. I.

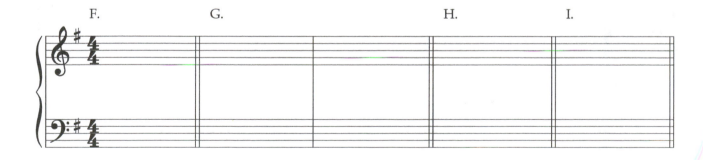

EXERCISE 10.10 Dictation

Each of the following longer four-voice examples contains from two to five embellishing tones. Notate the outer voices and provide roman numerals.

A.

B.

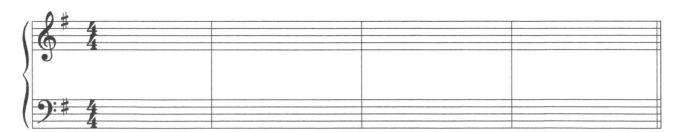

C.

EXERCISE 10.11 Dictation from the Literature

Notate the bass and florid soprano of the two examples from Mozart's string quartets. Analyze with roman numerals and label the embellishing tones.

A. Mozart, String Quartet in G major, K. 80, *Adagio*

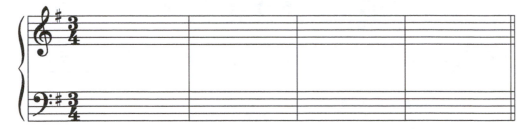

B. Mozart, String Quartet in G major, K. 156, *Presto* (but played *Moderato*)

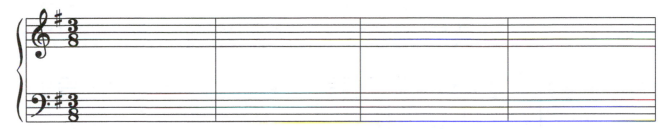

PLAYING

EXERCISE 10.12 Adding Embellishing Tones

Study the given counterpoint and look for opportunities to add passing tones and suspensions. Particularly appropriate spots are marked with asterisks (*). Play the resulting embellished two-voice counterpoint. Next, add inner voices to create a four-part texture. Analyze your work by labeling harmonies and suspensions.

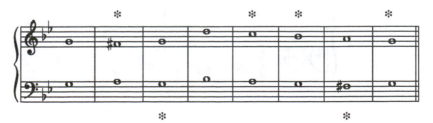

EXERCISE 10.13 Adding Suspensions to Harmonic Paradigms

Provided is a series of harmonic paradigms in four voices. Play each two times, the first time as written without suspensions, and then, following the figured bass, with the suspensions.

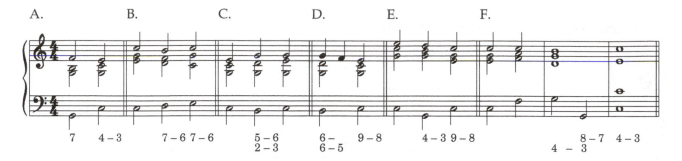

EXERCISE 10.14 Sing and Play

Play the bass and tenor voices with the left hand while singing the upper voice. Analyze.

EXERCISE 10.15 Adding Suspensions to a Figured Bass

Realize the following figured bass in four voices. Then, add at least two suspensions in appropriate places (it is possible to insert approximately 6 suspensions). Analyze.

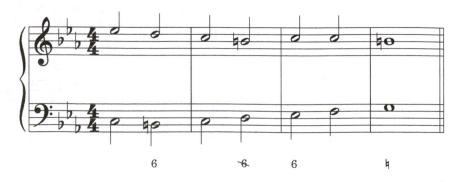

EXERCISE 10.16 Suspensions in Context

The following example illustrates the most common upper-voice suspensions. Play as written (in keyboard style) and in the parallel minor. Then transpose to G major and E major and their parallel minors. Be able to sing either outer voice or the alto while playing the other voices.

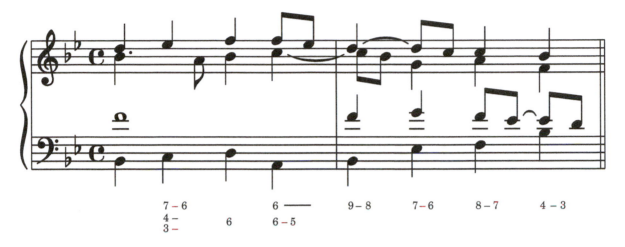

EXERCISE 10.17 Figured Bass

Realize the figured bass in four voices. Analyze. You may write out the soprano voice.

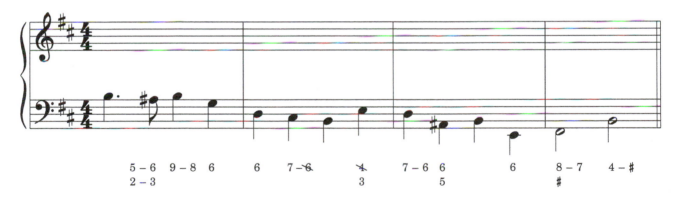

CHAPTER 11

Six-Four Chords, Revisiting the Subdominant, and Summary of Contrapuntal Expansions

SINGING

These exercises address not only material from the current chapter (including six-four chords and IV as prolonging chord), but also all concepts we have covered before, including contrapuntal expansions, the phrase model (T–PD–D–T), and embellishing tones.

EXERCISE 11.1 Melodies

Sing the following melodies using scale degrees or solfège. Analyze.

A.

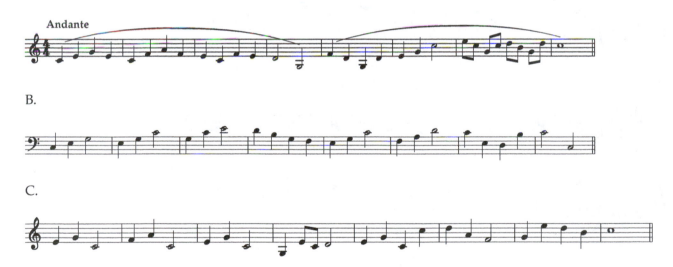

B.

C.

D. Mozart, *Le Nozze di Figaro* (*The Marriage of Figaro*), act 1, no. 9

E. Mozart, "Despina's Duet," from *Cosi fan tutte,* act 2

Pren-de - rò___ quel bru - net - ti - no che più le - pi - do mi par.___

Ed in - tan - to io col___ bion - di - no vo un po ri - de-re e bur - lar

LISTENING

EXERCISE 11.2 Notation of Bass Lines

Notate the bass lines below the given upper voices. Determine the chords implied by the given voices before listening to the example. Add a first- and second-level harmonic analysis.

A.

B.

C.

D.

E.

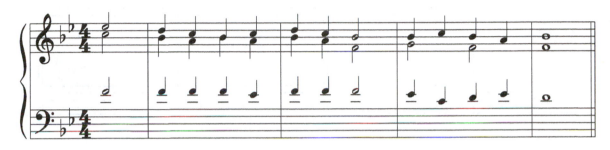

EXERCISE 11.3 Two-Voice Dictation

Notate the two voices and, based on the harmonic implications of these voices (bass and soprano), analyze using roman numerals.

A.

B.

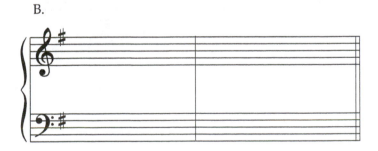

C.

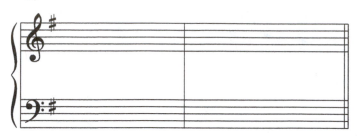

D.   E.

EXERCISE 11.4 Two-Voice Dictation: 2 + 2 = 4

You will hear the outer-voice counterpoint for one beat, immediately followed by the added inner voices, their combination resulting in four-voice harmony. You are to notate the outer voices only, using both their counterpoint and the addition of the inner voices to determine the harmonies.

A.   B.   C.

EXERCISE 11.5 Two-Voice Dictation

Notate the two voices, and add roman numerals based on the harmonic implications of the counterpoint.

A.   B.   C.

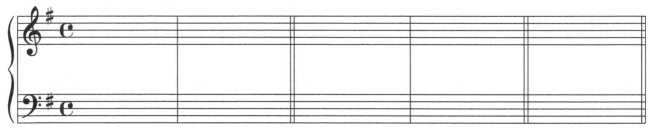

D.   E.

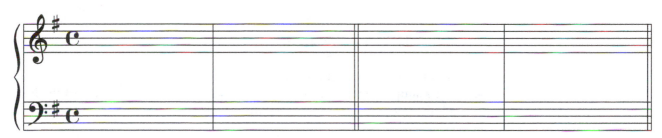

EXERCISE 11.6 Dictation

Notate outer voices and provide a two-level analysis for examples that contain six-four chords.

A.

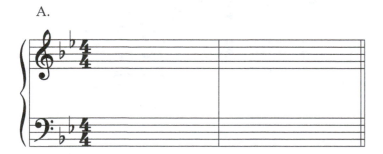

B.

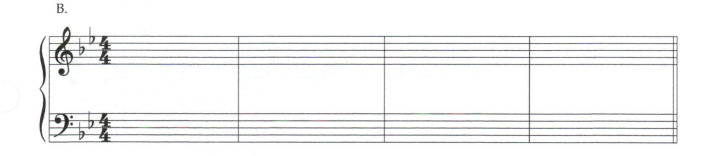

C.

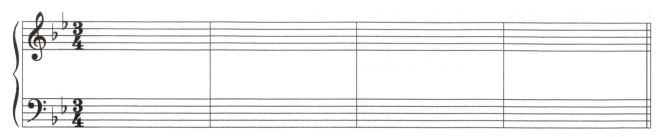

D.

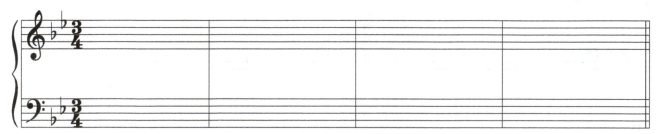

EXERCISE 11.7 Analysis and Dictation from the Literature

For Examples A and B, add the bass line beneath the given upper voices of the following examples. For Examples C–G, no upper voices are given; add the bass line. Include a first- and second-level harmonic analysis.

A. Schumann, "Die beiden Grenadier," op. 49, no. 1

B. Mozart, "Non ti fidar, o misera," from *Don Giovanni*, K. 527, act 1, scene 3

C. "Wayfaring Stranger"

D. Verdi, "Ah Si, ben mio, coll' essere," from *Il Trovatore*, act 3, scene 2

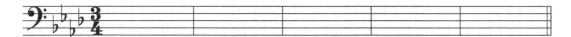

E. Mozart, Symphony in D major, K. 133, *Andante*

F. Bach, Chorale, "His Bitter Passion's Story"

G. Haydn, Piano Sonata in D major, Hob XVI.24, *Adagio*

EXERCISE 11.8 Dictation

You will hear examples in which the subdominant extends the tonic. Notate bass and soprano in Exercises A–D, and analyze with roman numerals and figured bass. Notate only the bass and analyze for Exercise E.

A.

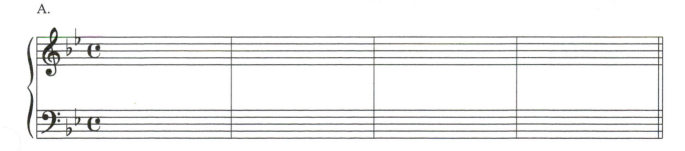

B.

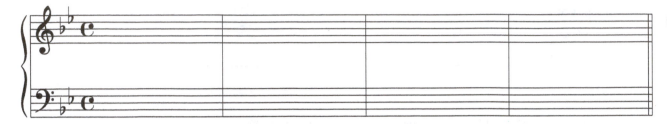

C.

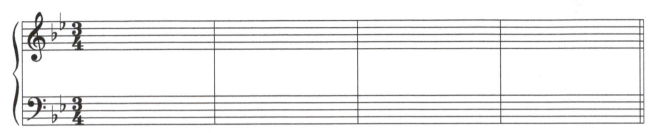

D.

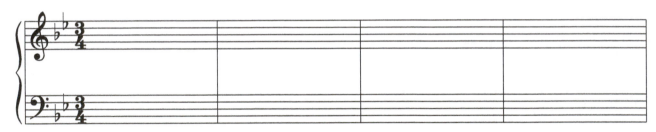

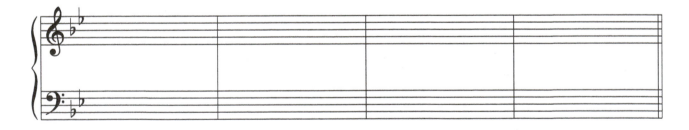

E. "Red River Valley"

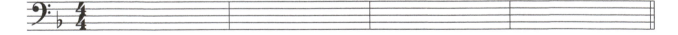

EXERCISE 11.9 Six-Four Chord Dictation

Identify the types of six-four chords in the progressions you will hear. Your choices are passing (P), pedal (PED), arpeggiating (ARP), and cadential (CAD).

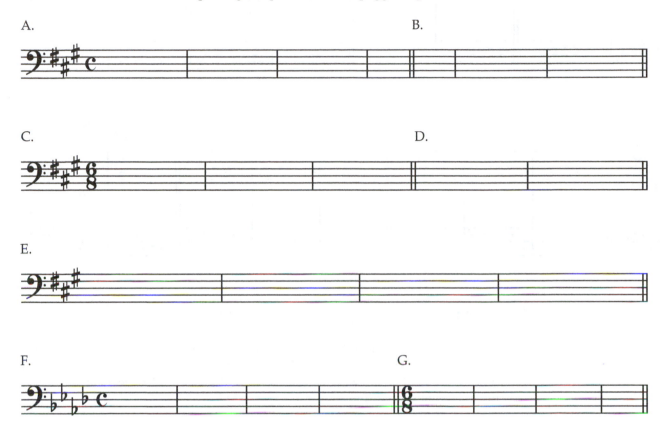

EXERCISE 11.10 Paradigm Speed Drills

This exercise requires quick recognition of basic contrapuntal expansions. Notate outer voices and provide roman numerals. Examples A–F contain a single expansion of tonic. Examples G–L contain two or more expansions of tonic. All examples are either in G minor or B♭ major.

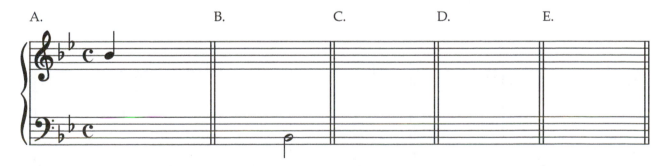

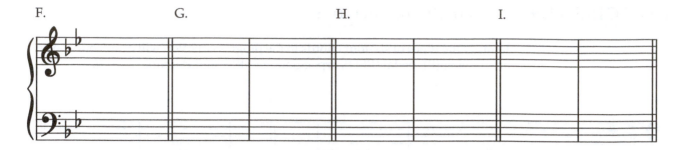

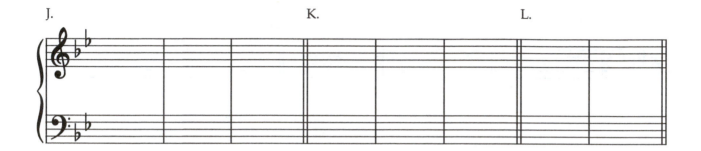

EXERCISE 11.11 Dictation of Complete Progressions

This exercise is similar to Exercise 11.10. However, each excerpt contains not only one tonic expansion but also a cadential progression (i.e., the PD–D or PD–D–T portion of the phrase). Notate outer voices, and provide a two-level analysis. Use the following procedure.

Step 1. Label events:

    a. cadence type _____ includes cadential $^6_4$ chord? _____

    b. PD type _____

    c. tonic expansion type:

        passing (bass scale degrees either $\hat{1}$–$\hat{2}$–$\hat{3}$ or $\hat{3}$–$\hat{2}$–$\hat{1}$)
        neighboring ($\hat{1}$–$\hat{7}$–$\hat{1}$, $\hat{1}$–$\hat{2}$–$\hat{1}$, $\hat{3}$–$\hat{4}$–$\hat{3}$)
        chordal skip ($\hat{1}$–$\hat{3}$)

Step 2. Notate bass and add roman numerals.
Step 3. Notate the soprano.

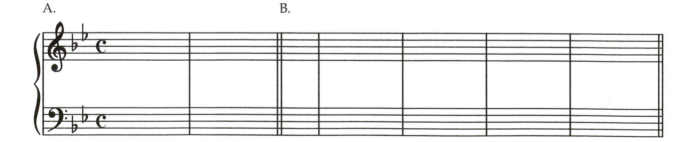

C.   D.

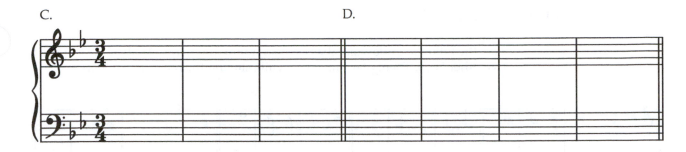

E.   F.

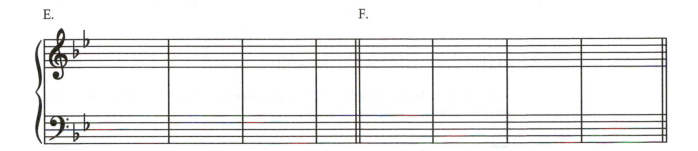

PLAYING

EXERCISE 11.12 Six-Four Chords in Context

Realize each figured bass in four voices, and then transpose to keys up to and including two sharps and two flats. Analyze each example.

A.   B.   C.   D.

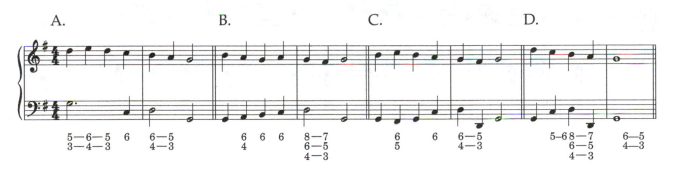

EXERCISE 11.13 Unfigured Bass

The following unfigured bass incorporates six-four chords. Realize it in four-voice keyboard style. Analyze; be aware of six-four chords.

EXERCISE 11.14 Sing and Play

Play the following two-voice (bass and soprano) fragments. Analyze. Transpose to two other keys. Then, play one voice while singing the other and switch.

EXERCISE 11.15 Figured Bass from the Literature

Sing the melody from Beethoven's song, then realize the figured bass in keyboard style in order to accompany yourself.

EXERCISE 11.16 Illustrations

In four voices, play the following progressions. You may write out a bass line to assist in your preparation.

A. A progression in E minor, $\frac{4}{4}$, that

    1. expands the tonic with a passing six-four chord
    2. closes with a cadential six-four chord and PAC
    3. contains a 4–3 suspension

B. A progression in C minor, $\frac{4}{4}$, that considerably expands the tonic using the following chords in any order:

    1. a diminished seventh chord
    2. a passing V_3^4
    3. a descending bass arpeggiation incorporating iv^6

C. A progression in B minor, $\frac{6}{8}$, that

   1. contains one bass suspension
   2. contains a passing six-four chord and one chordal leap
   3. closes with a cadential six-four chord

INSTRUMENTAL APPLICATION: REDUCTION AND ELABORATION

EXERCISE 11.17 Reduction

Reduce the textures in the given excerpts. Analyze, verticalize (into a four-voice homophonic texture), and then perform each example as follows. If you are a pianist, simply play your four-voice realization. If you are a melodic instrumentalist, arpeggiate each example. If necessary, refer to the discussion in Chapter 8 for a detailed procedure. Play each reduction in the key in which it is written; then transpose to one other key of your choice.

A. Mozart, Symphony in D major, K. 95, Trio

B. Mozart, Symphony in A major, K. 114, Trio

EXERCISE 11.18 Elaboration

Elaborate the following four-voice homophonic examples and the figured bass by arpeggiating in strict ascending four-voice chords that maintain proper voice leading between chords. Then embellish your solution by adding changes in contour and embellishing tones. Refer to the discussion in Chapter 8 for a detailed procedure.

A.

B.

5 — 6 — 5   5 — 6 — 7   4   6   6   6 — 5
3 — 4 — 3   3 — 4 — 5   3   4 — 3

CHAPTER 12

The Pre-Dominant Refines the Phrase Model

SINGING AND PLAYING

EXERCISE 12.1 Performing

The following arpeggiations create progressions that incorporate pre-dominant seventh chords. Sing them and/or play them on an instrument. Listen to how often harmonies change; then analyze the progressions with roman numerals.

A.

B.

EXERCISE 12.2 Sing and Play

The following examples contain pre-dominant seventh chords. Play the lower three parts while you sing the upper part (soprano). Then, play each example in the parallel minor. Finally, transpose to one other major key and its parallel minor; analyze.

A.   B.

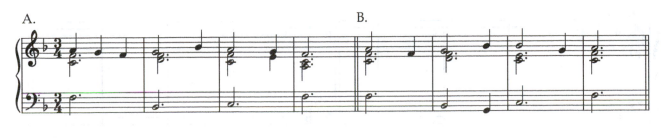

C.

EXERCISE 12.3 Performing

The following arpeggiations create progressions that incorporate EPMs and expanded pre-dominants. Listen to how often harmonies change; then analyze the progressions with roman numerals and either sing or play them on your instrument. (If you play the examples, you must transpose them to one other key of your choice.)

A.

B.

C.

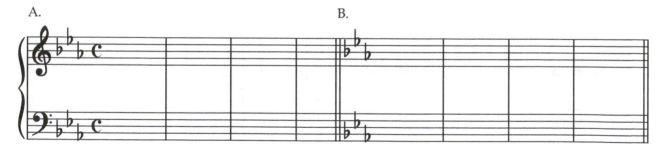

LISTENING

EXERCISE 12.4 Notating Outer Voices

Notate the bass and soprano for the given chorale-style exercises. Provide a two-level harmonic analysis.

A.   B.

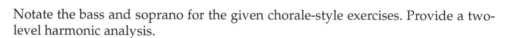

C.

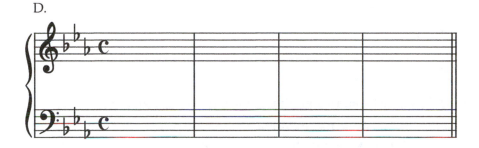

D.

EXERCISE 12.5 Phrases from the Literature

Notate the *bass* for each example from the literature, and provide a two-level harmonic analysis.

A. Chopin, *Grand valse brillante*, op. 34, no. 1
B. Schubert, Piano Sonata in C minor, op. posth., D. 958, *Allegro*
C. Haydn, Piano Sonata no. 36 in C major, Hob XVI.21, *Allegro*
D. Mozart, Symphony no. 24 in B♭ major, K. 182, *Andantino grazioso*
E. Mozart, Symphony no. 33 in B♭ major, K. 319, *Minuetto*
F. Mozart, Symphony no. 26 in E♭ major, K. 184, *Andante*
G. Mozart, String Quintet in C major, K. 515, *Andante*
H. Schumann, *Davidsbundlertänze*, op. 6, no. 10

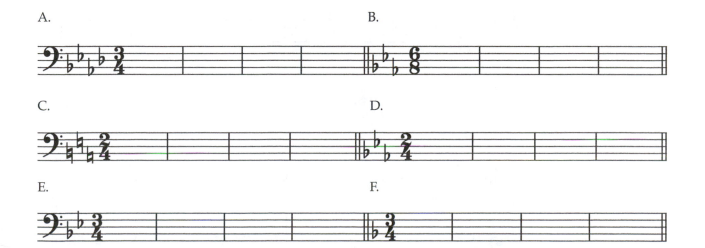

G.

H.

EXERCISE 12.6 Dictation

Listen to each complete phrase four times (a few pitches are given).

- First playing: focus on the underlying harmonic progression. Keep the meter in mind, noting the progression from tonic (usually expanded) to predominant and dominant within the phrase. Add roman numerals and the bass of the harmonic changes that occur after the tonic expansion.
- Second playing: notate the bass line for the tonic expansion and any structural melodic notes (e.g., the first pitch and the two or three pitches involved in the cadence).
- Third playing: complete the melody.
- Fourth playing: try to reserve this playing for checking your work.

A.

Beat within
measure: 1   3

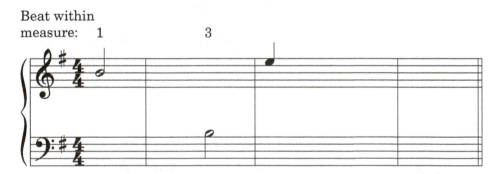

B.

C.

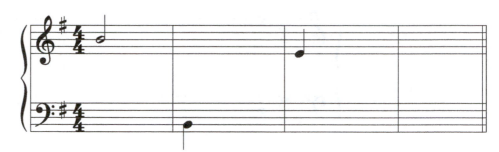

EXERCISE 12.7 Figurated Textures

This exercise incorporates a melody over an embellished accompaniment. Notate the bass and provide roman numerals.

A.

B.

C.

EXERCISE 12.8 Dictation

Listen to each complete phrase four times (a few pitches are given).

- First playing: focus on the underlying harmonic progression. Keep the meter in mind, noting the progression from tonic (usually expanded) to predominant and dominant within the phrase. Add roman numerals and the bass of the harmonic changes that occur after the tonic expansion.
- Second playing: notate the bass line for the tonic expansion, and any structural melodic notes (e.g., the first pitch and the two or three pitches involved in the cadence).
- Third playing: complete the melody.
- Fourth playing: try to reserve this playing for checking your work.

A.

B.

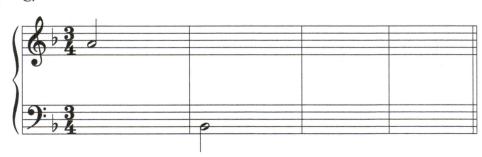

C.

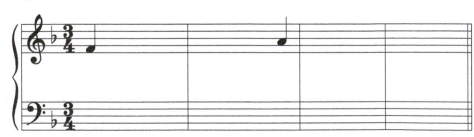

D.

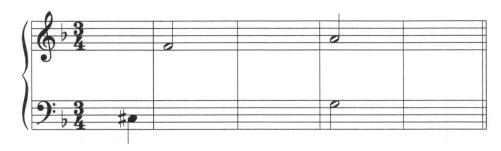

EXERCISE 12.9 Figurated Textures

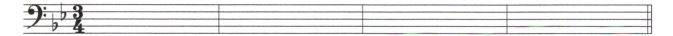

This exercise incorporates a melody over an embellished accompaniment. Notate the bass and provide roman numerals.

A.

B.

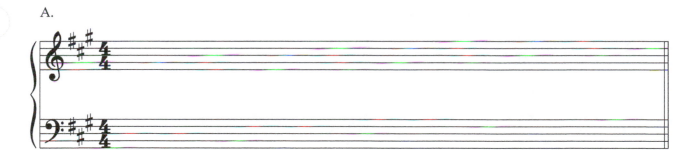

EXERCISE 12.10 Dictation of Pre-Dominant Seventh Chords

Notate outer voices and provide roman numerals for the examples that contain pre-dominant sevenths.

A.

B.

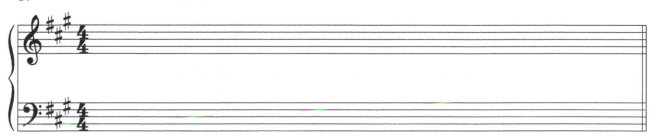

C.

EXERCISE 12.11 Bass Dictation from the Literature

Notate the bass line and provide roman numerals; focus on the type of pre-dominant seventh used.

A. Beethoven, "Rule Britannia," *Fünf Variationen* in D major, WoO 79

B. Schumann, "Auf einer Burg" ("In a Castle"), *Liederkreis*, op. 39, no. 7

C. Haydn, Piano Sonata in E major, Hob XVI.37, *Allegretto*

D. Mozart, "Rex tremendae majestatis," *Requiem*, K. 626

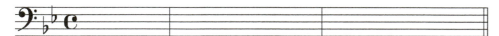

E. Handel, Chamber Sonata no. 22, *Adagio*

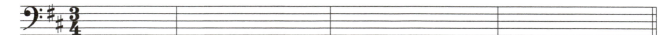

EXERCISE 12.12 Bass-Line Dictation from the Literature

The following examples contain pre-dominant seventh chords, expanded pre-dominants, contrapuntal cadences, and EPMs. Notate the bass lines and provide a first- and second-level analysis.

A. Mendelssohn, Concerto for Violin, op. 64, *Allegro, molto appassionato*

B. Marcello, Sonata no. 9 for Harpsichord in A major

C. Bach, Chorale: "Nun Lob', Mein Seele', den Herren"

D. Haydn, Symphony in F♯ minor, "Farewell," Hob I.45, *Allegro*

E. Corelli, Trio Sonata in C major, op. 2, no. 3, *Adagio*

F. Bach, "Aus Liebe will mein Heiland Sterben," from *St. Matthew Passion*, BWV 244 (note treble clef)

EXERCISE 12.13 Variation and Contrapuntal Expansion of a Harmonic Model

You will hear contrapuntal expansions of a T–PD–D–T harmonic progression. The model bass line will be fleshed out in variations that maintain the metric placement of the given harmonies implied by the bass notes. Complete the following tasks:

1. Notate the bass and soprano voices of the contrapuntal chords that embellish the given harmonic structure.
2. Provide a two-level harmonic analysis. Your harmonic vocabulary now includes I, I⁶, IV⁶, V, V⁶, V⁷, V⁶₅, V⁴₃, V⁴₂, vii°⁶, vii°⁷, vii°⁶₅, and vii°⁴₃, and the pre-dominants ii, ii⁶, ii⁷, ii⁶₅, ii⁴₃, IV, IV⁶, IV⁷, IV⁶₅. Don't forget EPMs and contrapuntal cadences.

Model A:

Variation 1   Variation 2

Variation 3

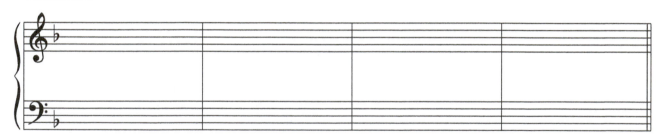

Variation 4

Model B:

Variations 1–4 are 2 measures in length.
Variations 5–6 are 4 measures in length.

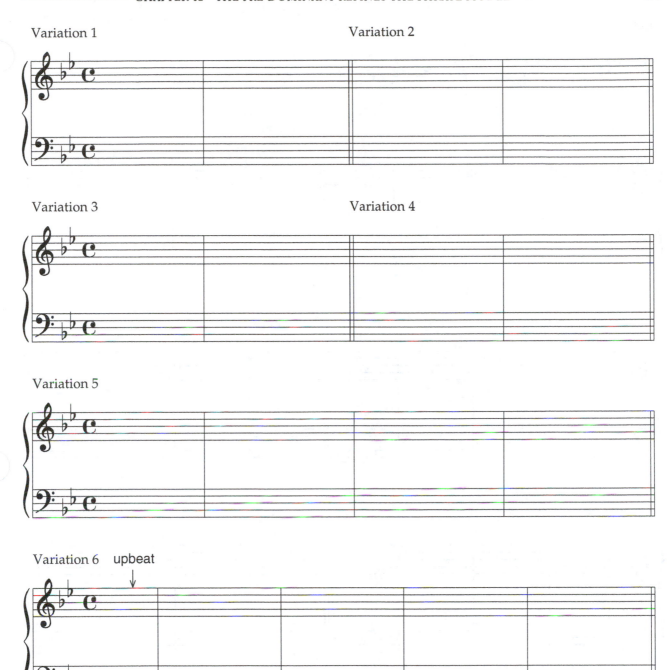

Model C:

Variation 1   Variation 2

Variation 3   Variation 4

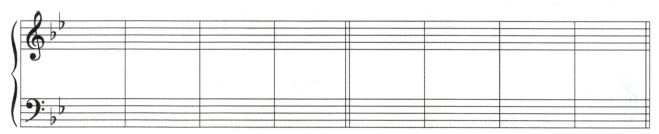

Variation 5   Variation 6

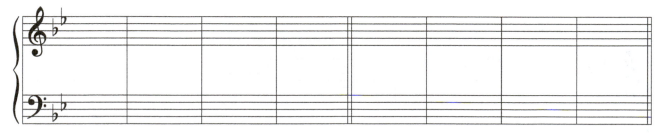

EXERCISE 12.14 Dictation

Listen to each phrase four times. On the first playing, focus on the underlying harmonic progression. Keep the meter in mind, noting the changes from tonic to pre-
dominant to dominant within the phrase. Then add roman numerals and the bass
of the harmonic changes that follow the tonic expansion. On the second playing,
notate the rest of the bass line and structural melodic notes. On the third playing,
complete the melody. Check your work on the fourth playing.

A.

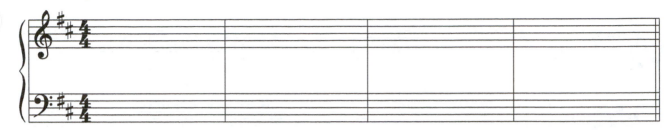

B.

C.

D.

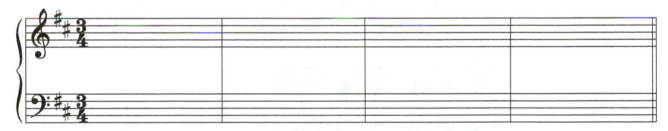

E.

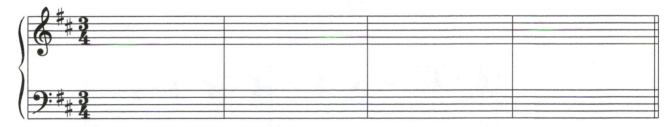

F.

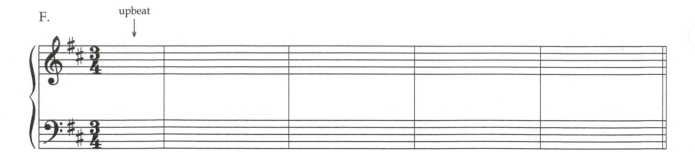

PLAYING

EXERCISE 12.15 Model Progressions Using Pre-Dominant Seventh Chords

Play the following four-voice models as written and in major and minor keys up to and including two sharps and two flats. Be able to sing either outer voice while playing the other three voices. Circle the seventh of each pre-dominant seventh chord, then draw a line to its preparation and resolution pitches. Provide roman numerals with inversions, for exercises C and D.

A.

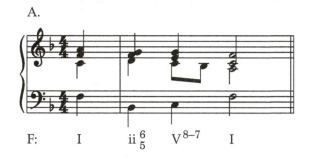

$$\text{F:} \quad \text{I} \qquad \text{ii}^{6}_{5} \quad \text{V}^{8-7} \qquad \text{I}$$

B.

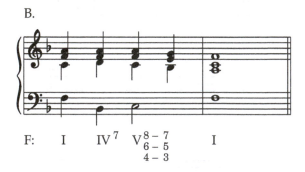

$$\text{F:} \quad \text{I} \qquad \text{IV}^{7} \quad \text{V}^{8-7}_{6-5}_{4-3} \qquad \text{I}$$

C.   D.

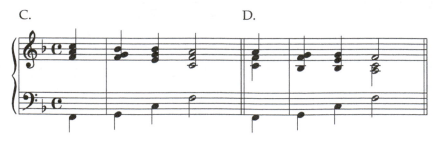

EXERCISE 12.16 Embedded Phrase Model and Contrapuntal Cadences

The following progressions feature weak T–PD–D–T functions. Play each in major and minor keys up to and including two sharps and two flats. Be able to sing either outer voice while playing the other three voices.

A.

B.

C.

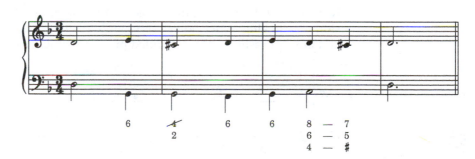

EXERCISE 12.17 Soprano and Bass Harmonization

Harmonize each of the following soprano and bass scale degree fragments in four-voice keyboard style. Each fragment includes an EPM—use inversions of PD and/or D chord to weaken the cadential motion. Play at the keyboard in two keys of your choice.

Soprano fragments:

A. $\hat{3}$–$\hat{2}$–$\hat{1}$

B. $\hat{3}$–$\hat{4}$–$\hat{4}$–$\hat{3}$

C. $\hat{1}$–$\hat{2}$–$\hat{3}$–$\hat{4}$–$\hat{3}$–$\hat{2}$–$\hat{1}$

Bass fragments:

D. $\hat{8}$–$\hat{6}$–$\hat{7}$–$\hat{8}$

E. $\hat{1}$–$\hat{4}$–$\hat{4}$–$\hat{3}$

F. $\hat{1}$–$\hat{4}$–$\hat{2}$–$\hat{1}$

PLAYING AND SINGING

EXERCISE 12.18 Figured Bass Recitative

Sing the following melody from one of Handel's operas. You must determine the key from the context since there is no key signature. Then, realize the figured bass. Finally, be able to accompany your singing with your figured bass realization.

Handel, "Ye Worshippers," from *Judas Maccabeus*, HWV 63, act 2, no. 49

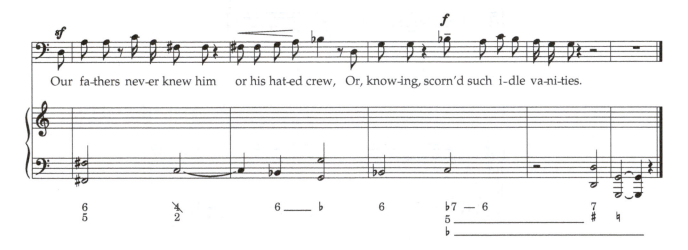

EXERCISE 12.19 Figured Bass

Realize the following figured bass in four voices. Be able to analyze the progression and to sing either outer voice while playing the three other voices. Bracket and label phrases, EPMs, expanded pre-dominants, and contrapuntal cadences.

INSTRUMENTAL APPLICATION

EXERCISE 12.20 Reduction

These embellished examples—all taken from Bach's solo violin and cello works—differ from previous reductive examples, in that compound melody is involved; that is, more voices are implied than there are instruments playing. Analyze, verticalize (into a three- or four-voice homophonic texture), and then perform each example as follows: If you are a pianist, simply play your four-voice realization. If you are a melodic instrumentalist, arpeggiate each example. If necessary, refer to the discussion in Chapter 8 for a detailed procedure.

Play each reduction in the key in which it is written; then transpose to one other key of your choice. The sample solution presented shows how Corelli's *Vivace* can be verticalized to create four voices.

Sample solution:

Corelli Violin Sonata, op. 5, no. 2, *Vivace*

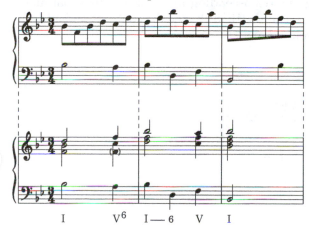

I   V⁶   I — 6   V   I

A. Bach, Violin Partita in D minor, BWV 1004, Gigue

B. Bach, Violin Sonata in C major, BWV 1005, *Allegro*

continue to authentic cadence in d minor

C. Bach, Violin Sonata in A minor, BWV 1003, Fuga

1.

2.

EXERCISE 12.21 Elaboration

Elaborate the following figured basses and scale degree melodies (with roman numerals) by first arpeggiating in strict ascending four-voice chords that maintain proper voice leading between chords. Then change the contours and add embellishing tones to create a compound melody.

Sample:

Given:

Elaboration:

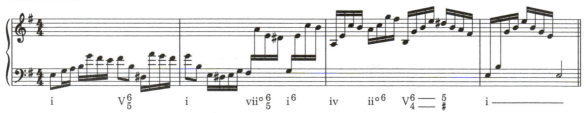

A.

B.

EXERCISE 12.22 Instrumental Application: Reduction and Elaboration

Analyze, verticalize (into a three- or four-voice homophonic texture), and then perform each example as follows: If you are a pianist, simply play your homophonic realization. If you are a melodic instrumentalist, arpeggiate each example. If necessary, refer to the discussion in Chapter 8 for a detailed procedure. Play each reduction in the key in which it is written, then transpose to one other key of your choice.

The sample solution shows how Corelli's vivace can be verticalized to create four voices.

Sample solution:

Corelli, Violin Sonata, op. 5, no. 2, *Vivace*

A. Bach, *Gavotte en Rondeau*, Violin Partita in E major, BWV 1006

B. Bach, Cello Suite no. 1 in G major, BWV 1007

1.

2.

C. Bach, Violin Sonata in A minor, BWV 1003, *Allegro*

continue pattern to AC or HC

The Submediant: A New Diatonic Harmony, and Further Extensions of the Phrase Model

SINGING

EXERCISE 13.1 Melodies That Imply the Submediant

The following melodies create progressions that incorporate the submediant. Sing them. For Exercises D–H, play the given bass notes on the piano as you sing. Figured bass symbols will allow you to add two voices in the right hand to complete the harmonies.

A.

B.

C. Mozart, *Die Zauberflöte* (*The Magic Flute*), K. 620, act 1

D. Schubert, "Wandrers Nachtlied," op. 4, no. 3, D. 224

Langsam, Mit Ausdruck (Lento con espressione)

Der   du von dem Him - mel bist,   al - les Leid   und Schmer - zen stillst,   den,

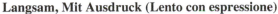

$$\begin{matrix} 6 \\ 5 \end{matrix} \qquad 7$$

E. R. Schumann, "Tragödie," op. 64, no. 3

F. R. Schumann, "Wenn ich in deine Aguen seh'," op. 48, no. 4, from *Dichterliebe*

G. Handel, "I Know That My Redeemer Liveth," from *Messiah*

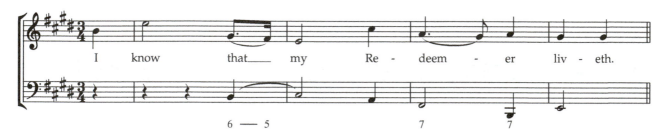

H. Bach, *Wachet Auf*, BWV 140

LISTENING

EXERCISE 13.2

Each of the following progressions contains at least one instance of a submediant harmony. Identify the type of cadence for each excerpt (note that an excerpt
may end with a deceptive V–vi motion).

Locate the submediant and identify its function:

- Is it a "bridge" in a descending-thirds motion?
- Does it start a descending-fifths motion?
- Does it substitute for tonic in a deceptive motion?
- Is it the PD chord?

Provide roman numerals for each chord (one roman numeral for each line given).

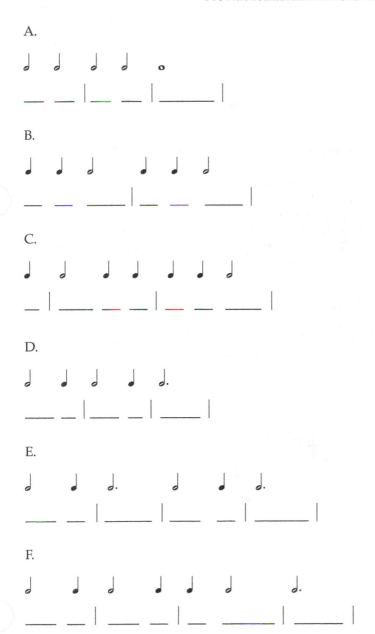

G. Mozart, "Voi, che sapete," from *The Marriage of Figaro*

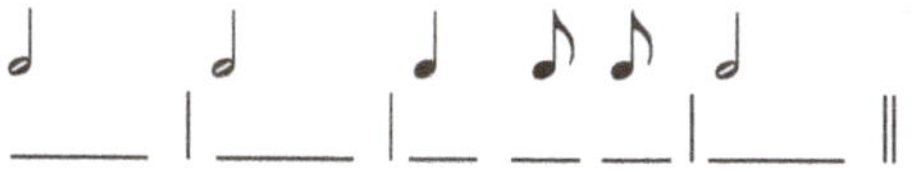

♩   ♩   ♩   ♪ ♪   ♩
___ | ___ | __ _ _ | __ ‖

H. Mozart, Symphony in B♭, K. 22, *Allegro*

o   o   o   o   o   o   o   o   o
___ | ___ | ___ | ___ | ___ | ___ | ___ | ___ | ___ ‖

I. Mozart, First quintet, from *The Magic Flute*

♩ ⅜ ♩ ⅜   ♩.   ♩ ♩ ♩   o   ♩ ⅜ ♩ ⅜   ♩.   ♩ ♩ ♩   ♩ ⅜ ⅜ ⅜
__ __ | __ __ | __ __ | ___ | __ __ | __ __ | __ __ | __ ‖

EXERCISE 13.3 Bass-Line Dictation

Notate bass lines of the progressions that contain the submediant harmony; provide roman numerals.

Since this exercise continues to develop tonal memory, begin by listening and memorizing before notating pitches. Focus on the deeper-level harmonic functions. For example, since a tonic prolongation will often begin the exercise, ask yourself how long tonic is prolonged before it yields to a new harmonic function.

Do not focus on details (such as the type of contrapuntal chords used to expand the tonic) until the last hearing, during which time you can refine your answer. Always begin with the large picture, which should include questions such as "How long is the excerpt?" "Is it a progression, a prolongation, or both?" and "Where does the tonic prolongation end?"

A.   B.

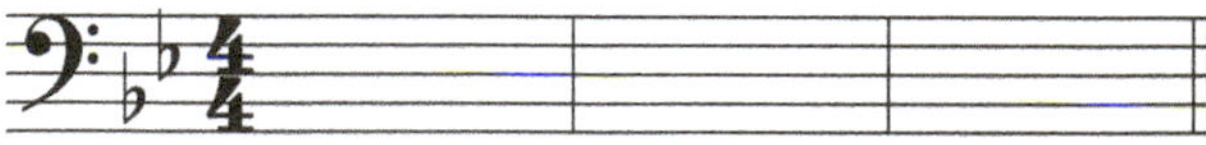

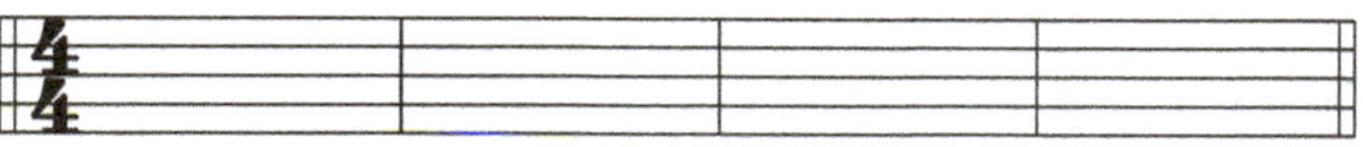

C. 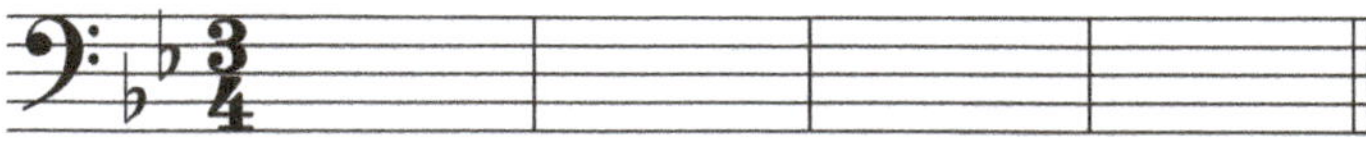   D.

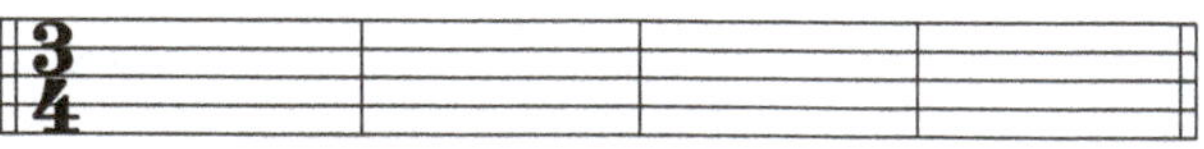

EXERCISE 13.4 Outer-Voice Dictation

Notate bass and soprano voices of progressions that include the submediant harmony. A few pitches are provided. Analyze using two levels.

E.

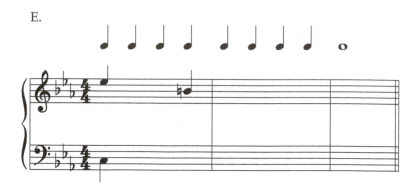

EXERCISE 13.5 Analysis and Listening

The bass lines are omitted from the following literature excerpts. Based on listening and with the assistance of the upper voices, notate the missing voice and add roman numerals.

A. Schubert, Impromptu in G♭ major, op. 90, D. 899

B. Haydn, Symphony no. 104 in D major, "London," Hob I.102, *Andante*

C. Haydn, String Quartet in E♭ major, "Fantasia," op. 76, no. 6, Hob III.80, *Adagio*

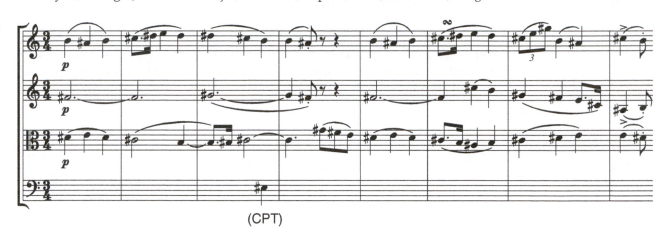

(CPT)

D. Mascagni, "O Lola," from *Cavalleria Rusticana*, scene 1

stentando

por - ta; _____   Se per te mo - jo e va - do in pa - ra di - so,
ev - er, _____   *Yet would I seek   your love,   though it de -stroy   me*

portando

Non c'en-tro se __ non ve-do   il tuo bel vi - - so
Suf-fe r the pain _ and sor-row   if you were near   me!

EXERCISE 13.6 Dictation of Embellished Excerpts
Using the Submediant

Notate the bass of each example that contains one or two appearances of the submediant. Provide roman numerals, and label the harmonic function for each statement of the submediant.

A.

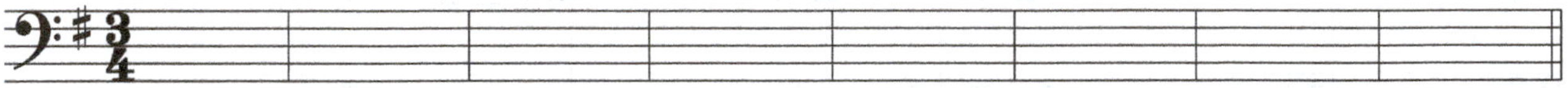

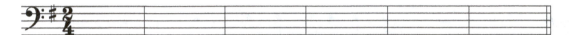

B. (Contains intro.)

C. (Contains intro.)

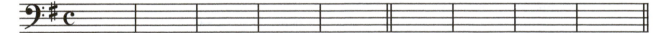

D.   E.

F.

EXERCISE 13.7 Dictation

Notate the bass and soprano and provide roman numerals. Label the function for each occurrence of the submediant harmony. Your choices are bridge between T and PD, PD, or part of the step-descent bass.

A.   ♩ = 108

B.

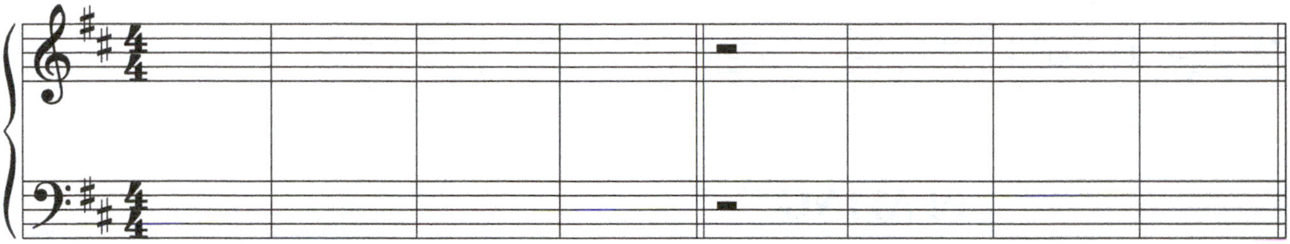

C.

D.

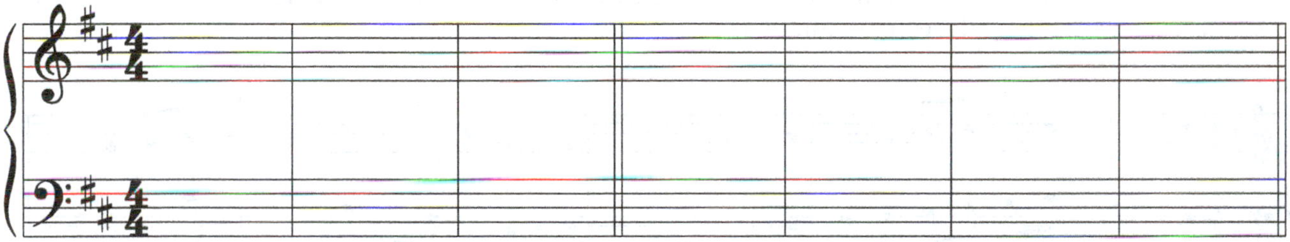

E.

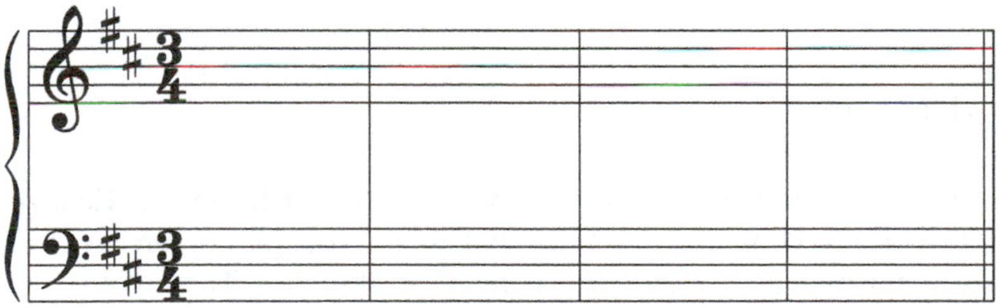

EXERCISE 13.8 Dictation from the Literature

Notate the bass and provide roman numerals. You need not notate repeated pitches.

A. Bach, "Ermuntre dich, mein schwacher Geist," *Christmas Oratorio*, no. 12, BWV 248

Andante

(V / V)

B. Carissimi, "Plorate, filii Israel," from *Jepthe*

Andante

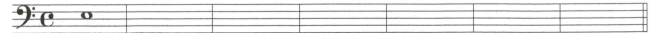

C. Schubert, "Am Bach im Frühling" ("To the Brook in Springtime"), D. 361

Andante

PLAYING

EXERCISE 13.9 Figured Bass

Realize the following figured bass in four-voice keyboard style. Include a two-level harmonic analysis.

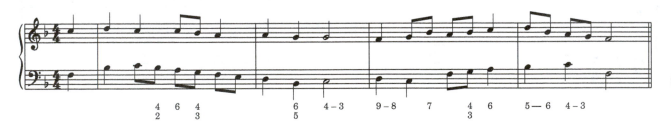

EXERCISE 13.10 Contrapuntal Models

The following outer-voice models incorporate the submediant harmony. Realize each model in four-voice keyboard style. Note that when you play Exercise D in minor, the nonfunctional passing v^6 chord contains $\flat\hat{7}$ in the bass. This avoids the augmented second between $\sharp\hat{7}$ and $\flat\hat{6}$.

Be able to sing either of the outer voices while playing the other three voices. Transpose each exercise to A major and F major and their parallel minors. Be aware of parallels in Exercise E.

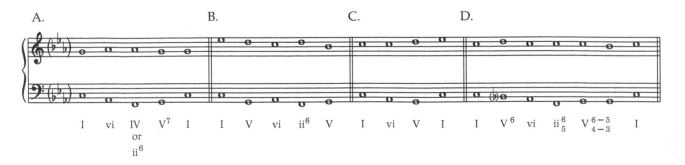

E.

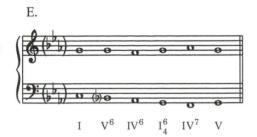

I   V⁶   IV⁶   I₄⁶   IV⁷   V

EXERCISE 13.11 Figured Bass Using the Submediant

Realize and analyze the exercise in four-voice keyboard style. Be able to discuss the effects of the repetition of any harmonic patterns in the exercise, and label the numerous passing figures.

EXERCISE 13.12 Sing and Play

Play the bass and alto voice while singing the soprano voice. Analyze.

EXERCISE 13.13 Figured Bass and Singing

Sing the following melodies. Next, realize the figured basses in four voices as you sing.

A. Bach, " Jesu, der du meine Seele," Cantata no. 78, BWV 78

B. Handel, "Let All the Angels of God Worship Him," *Messiah*, HWV 56

EXERCISE 13.14 Harmonizing the Ascending Scale

Combining two or more harmonic paradigms creates longer progressions. One such progression is a complete stepwise octave ascent. We will learn one harmonization for the ascending soprano and one for the ascending bass.

Study the figures and realize in four voices. Paradigms are bracketed. Be able to sing either outer voice while playing the other three voices.

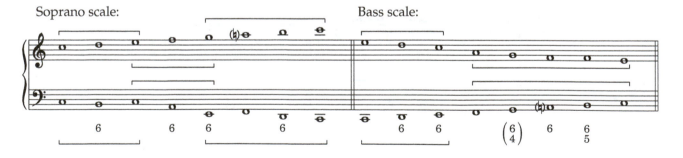

EXERCISE 13.15 Step-Descent Basses

Realize the following contrapuntal models in four voices. Be able to sing either outer voice while playing the other three. Transpose to C and B minor.

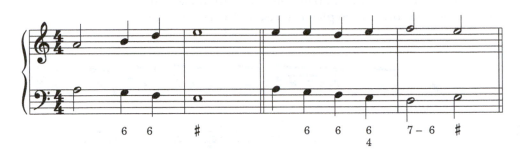

EXERCISE 13.16 Figured Bass

Create a good soprano line and add inner voices; you may write out the soprano. Analyze, and be able to sing the bass while playing the other three voices.

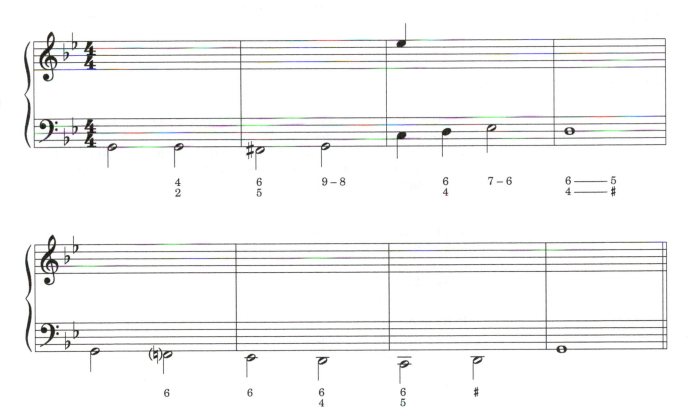

EXERCISE 13.17 Embellishment

Now create an embellished piece from the figured bass you realized in Exercise 13.16. Below is one realization of mm. 1–2 of Example 13.16, followed by common embellishments used in Baroque keyboard music. Choose one that you like or develop your own. Then play Exercise 13.16 in the embellished style.

EXERCISE 13.18 Illustrations

Complete one of the two following illustrations in a meter of your choice (tasks need not appear in the order given). *Hint*: Study each carefully, for you might save time by combining one or more tasks (e.g., the following four individual tasks can be made into a single contrapuntal expansion of tonic: a suspension, an EPM, a bass arpeggiation, and a six-four chord).

1. In D minor:
    a. VI in a bass arpeggiation
    b. a direct step-descent bass V
    c. at least two suspensions
    d. a contrapuntal expansion using $ii^{\varnothing4}_{2}$
    e. a $ii^{\varnothing6}_{5}$ in the final half cadence

2. In B minor:
    a. a lament bass that descends to $\hat{4}$
    b. a six-four chord
    c. at least one suspension
    d. a deceptive progression
    e. a iv^{7} in the final cadence

The Mediant, the Back-Relating Dominant, and a Synthesis of Diatonic Harmonic Relationships

SINGING

EXERCISE 14.1 Arpeggiating the Mediant

The following arpeggiations create progressions that incorporate the mediant. Sing them and analyze the progressions with roman numerals.

A.

B.

C.

EXERCISE 14.2 Arpeggiating the Back-Relating Dominant

The following arpeggiations create progressions that incorporate the back-relating dominant. Sing them and analyze the progressions with roman numerals.

A.

B.

C.

EXERCISE 14.3 Duet

The following duet contains examples of the mediant and the subtonic (VII) in minor (as V/III). Be able to sing either voice part, then, with your partner sing the duets. Switch parts. Its is a good idea to practice these as sing-and-play exercises before meeting with your partner. (Fingerings are given, should you wish to play the piece.)

LISTENING

EXERCISE 14.4 Dictation

For the following progressions that feature III, notate the bass and analyze. (Remember, III is often preceded by its dominant, V/III.)

A.

B.

C.

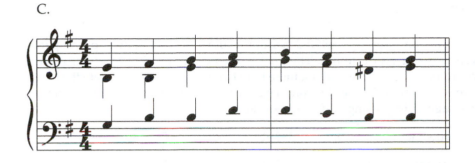

D.

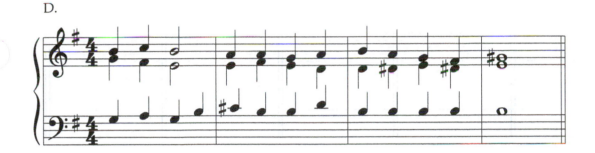

EXERCISE 14.5 The Mediant in Context: Two Voice Becomes
Four Voice

You will hear the outer-voice counterpoint for one beat, immediately followed
by the added inner voices, their combination resulting in four-voice harmony.
Notate the outer voices only, using both their counterpoint and the addition of
the inner voices to deduce the harmonies. Exercises are in $\frac{4}{4}$ meter and either D
minor or F major.

A.   B.   C.

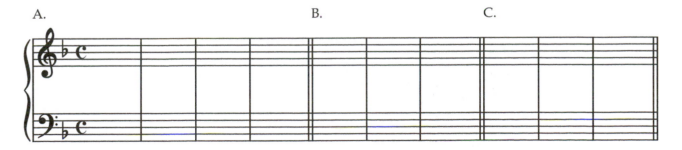

D.   E.

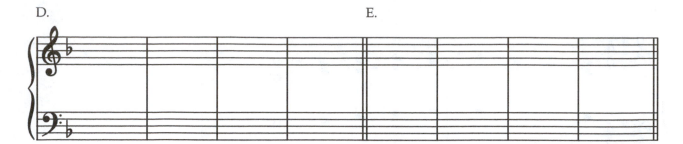

EXERCISE 14.6 Aural Snapshots

You will hear numerous unmetered harmonizations of three-note soprano paradigms in G major and E minor. The goal is fluency: to be able to identify each three-chord paradigm in one but not more than two playings and to notate the outer voices and provide a first- and second-level analysis. There are only two types of soprano fragments: passing and neighboring.

Passing forms include: $\hat{3}$–$\hat{2}$–$\hat{1}$; $\hat{1}$–$\hat{2}$–$\hat{3}$; $\hat{5}$–$\hat{4}$–$\hat{3}$; $\hat{3}$–$\hat{4}$–$\hat{5}$

Neighboring forms include: $\hat{1}$–$\hat{7}$–$\hat{1}$; $\hat{1}$–$\hat{2}$–$\hat{1}$; $\hat{3}$–$\hat{4}$–$\hat{3}$

A.   B.   C.   D.   E.

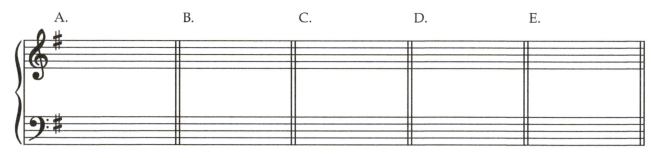

F.   G.   H.   I.

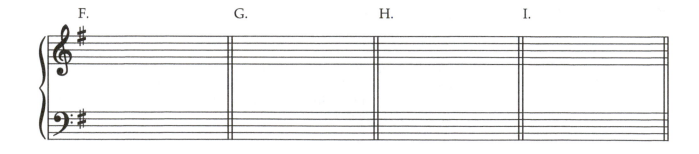

EXERCISE 14.7 Combining Snapshots

The following exercises combine two or three short paradigms (for a total of six to nine chords). Notate the outer voices and provide a two-level harmonic analysis. As with Exercise 14.6, the goal here is fluency, but this time you may hear each example up to three times. Expect to hear both tonic expansions and complete progressions (T–PD–D–[T]). All exercises are in $\frac{3}{4}$ and either in G major or E minor.

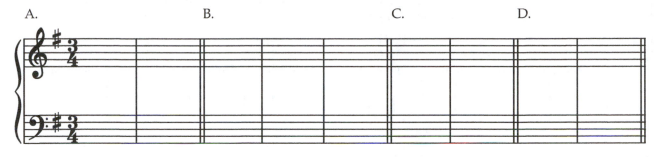

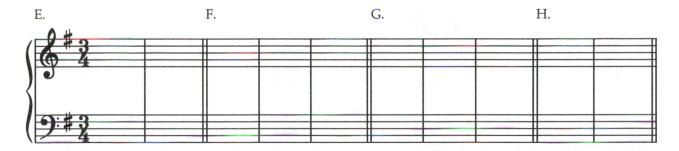

EXERCISE 14.8 Dictation

For the following progressions that feature III, notate the bass and analyze. (Remember, III is often preceded by its dominant [V/III].)

A. Wagner, "Bridal Chorus," from *Lohengrin*, act 3, scene 1

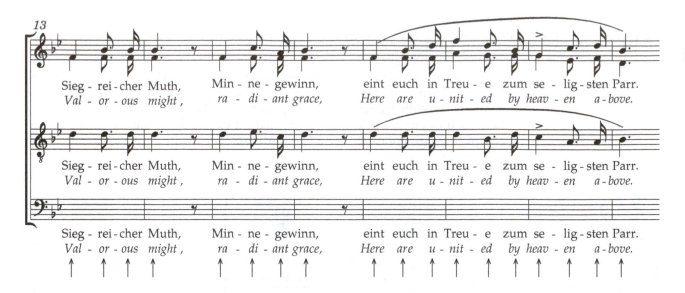

Sieg - rei - cher Muth,   Min - ne - gewinn,   eint euch in Treu - e zum se - lig - sten Parr.
Val - or - ous might,   ra - di - ant grace,   Here are u - nit - ed by heav - en a - bove.

Sieg - rei - cher Muth,   Min - ne - gewinn,   eint euch in Treu - e zum se - lig - sten Parr.
Val - or - ous might,   ra - di - ant grace,   Here are u - nit - ed by heav - en a - bove.

Sieg - rei - cher Muth,   Min - ne - gewinn,   eint euch in Treu - e zum se - lig - sten Parr.
Val - or - ous might,   ra - di - ant grace,   Here are u - nit - ed by heav - en a - bove.

B. Beethoven, Piano Sonata no. 25 in G major, op. 79, *Andante*

C. Schubert, Impromptu in A♭ major, op. 90, D. 899, no. 4

EXERCISE 14.9 Analysis and Dictation

Analyze the following examples with a two-level analysis. All the examples are missing some or all of their bass lines; notate them. Mozart wrote the violin sonata at the age of 7.

A. Mozart, Symphony no. 35 in D major, K. 385, Menuetto

B. Mozart, Violin Sonata in D major, K. 7, *Adagio*

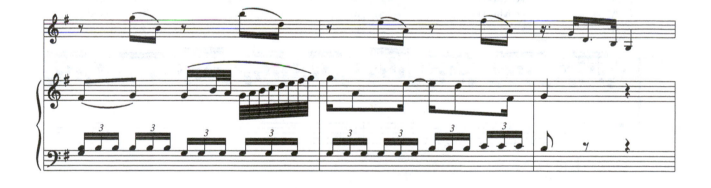

C. Brahms, "Da unten im Tale" ("Down in the Valley There"), *Deutsche Volkslieder*, WoO 33, no. 6

D. Schubert, "Ave Maria," D. 839

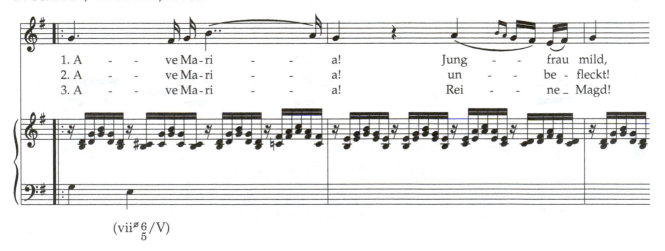

$$(\text{vii}^{\varnothing}{}^{6}_{5}/\text{V})$$

EXERCISE 14.10 Analysis and Dictation

Analyze the following examples with a two-level analysis. All the examples are missing some or all of their bass lines; notate them.

A. Handel, "I Know That My Redeemer Liveth," from *Messiah*, HWV 56

I know that __ my Re - deem - er liv - eth,

B. Tchaikovsky, "June," *The Seasons*, op. 37b, no. 6, *Andante cantabile*

EXERCISE 14.11 Dictation

The following six exercises contain the upper voices of progressions that include various functions of III and VI. Notate the bass and choose one example to subject to two-level analysis. Begin by bracketing short, complete progressions. For example, a tonic expansion may be followed by a PD–D that may be followed by a deceptive motion. There may be more than a single motion to the cadence. Study this sample chord progression.

I   vii°⁶   I⁶   ii⁶   V   vi   IV   vii°⁶   I   iii   IV   V   I

T ———— EPM w/deceptive motion   another EPM   mediant leads to cadence

T ————————————————————————————————— PD   D   T

A.

B.

C.

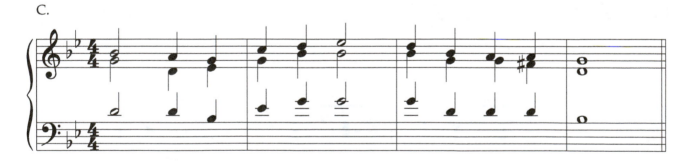

D.

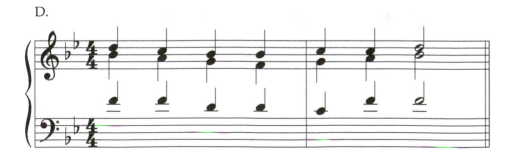

E.

F.

EXERCISE 14.12 Dictation

Notate the outer voices of the following homophonic examples that contain back-relating dominants. Provide a first- and second-level analysis. A few notes are given.

A.

B.

C.

D.

E.

EXERCISE 14.13 Analysis and Dictation

Analyze the following examples with two-level analysis. All the examples are missing some or all of their bass lines; notate them.

A. Rossini, "Una voce poco fa," from *Il Barbiere di Siviglia (The Barber of Seville)*, act 1, scene 9

cor -   fe-ri - to è già,   e ⎯ Lin - Dor ⎯   fu che il pia-gò.   Sì,   Lin -

E: V_3^4/ii

do - ro — mio — sa - rà, lo. giu - ra - i, la — vin - ce rò,

B. Haydn, "Es vollbracht," *The Seven Last Words*, op. 51, no. 6, Hob III.55

EXERCISE 14.14 Dictation

Listen to the embellished exercises for flute with piano accompaniment. Notate the bass line of the piano and provide a roman numeral analysis.

A.

upbeat

B.

upbeat

EXERCISE 14.15 Variation and Expansion

Each of the following models is followed by a series of variations and expansions that elaborate each model's basic progressions. Notate the outer voices and analyze each of the expansions.

Model A:

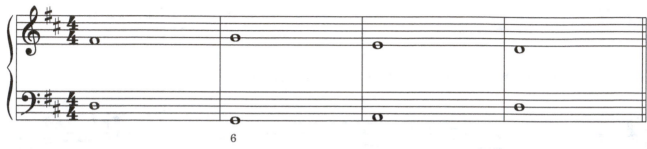

Variation 1

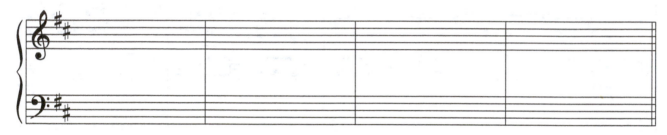

Variation 2

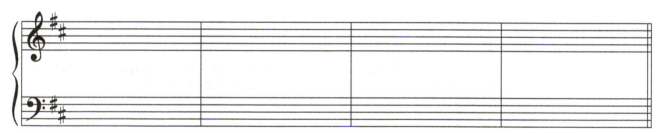

Variation 3

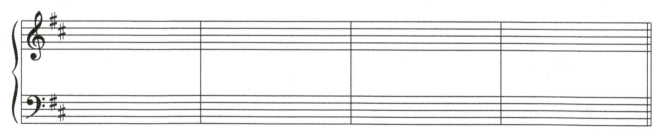

Variation 4

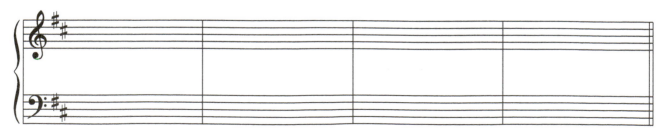

Model B:

Variation 1

Variation 2

Variation 3

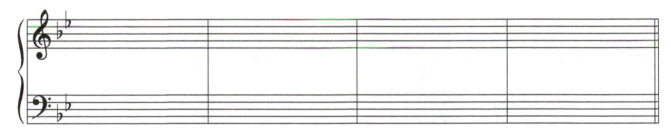

Variation 4

PLAYING

EXERCISE 14.16 Multiple Harmonizations

Harmonize the following melodic fragment in three different ways. Include at least one statement of the submediant or mediant in each harmonization. You may wish to set this melody in major and its relative minor.

EXERCISE 14.17 Figured Basses

The following exercises contain mediant harmony and/or back-relating dominants. Realize the figured bass in four-part keyboard style, and provide a two-level analysis. Play each at the keyboard; try to sing either outer voice while playing the other three voices. Transpose each to any two other keys (Exercises A and D should be in major only, and Exercise C should be in minor only).

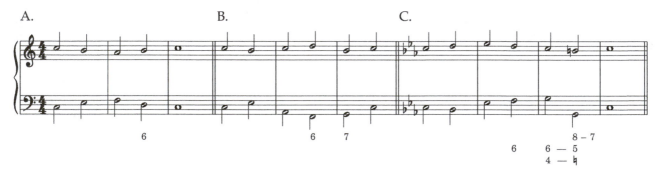

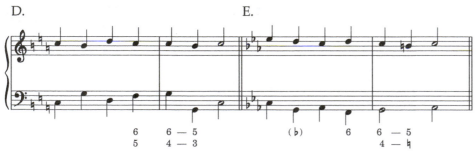

EXERCISE 14.18 Figured Bass

Realize and analyze the following figured bass.

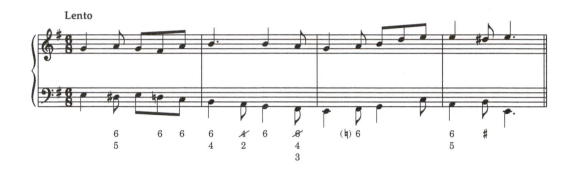

EXERCISE 14.19 Figured Bass and Back-Relating Dominants

Realize the following figured bass. Explain the function of each dominant harmony.

EXERCISE 14.20 Expansions of a Harmonic Model

The following harmonic models present a four-measure tonic–pre-dominant–dominant–tonic progression. Expand each stage as required by the instructions. Analyze your work.

A.

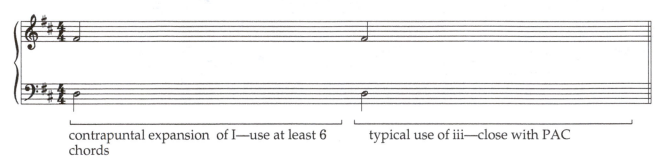

contrapuntal expansion of I—use at least 6 chords   typical use of iii—close with PAC

B.

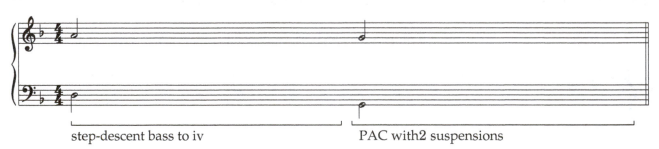

step-descent bass to iv   PAC with 2 suspensions

EXERCISE 14.21 Outer-Voice Progressions

Play the outer-voice counterpoint examples and transpose each to at least two keys. Analyze.

EXERCISE 14.22 Continuation of Embellished Textures

Play the first half of the exercise as written. Complete the exercise by realizing the figured bass and continuing the embellishing pattern. Add appropriate embellishing tones.

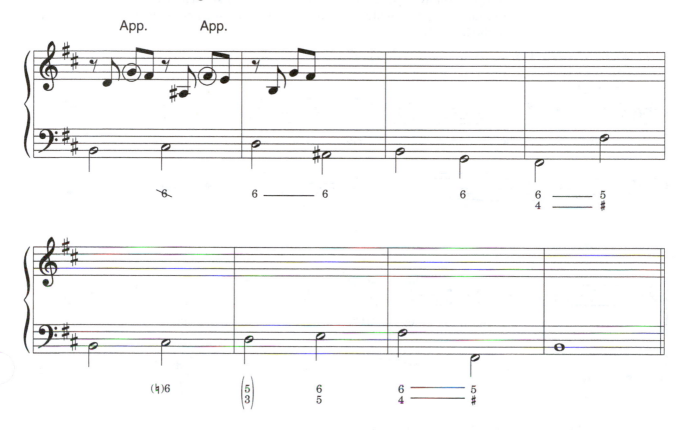

EXERCISE 14.23 Descending-Scale Harmonization

We now harmonize descending soprano scales (ascending scales were presented in Chapter 13). Study each model and realize it according to the figured bass. Note that the mediant appears in setting the descending line $\hat{8}$–$\hat{7}$. Be able to sing the scale while playing the other voices. Transpose each to another key of your choice.

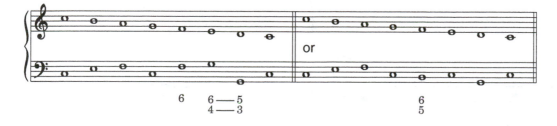

PLAYING AND SINGING

EXERCISE 14.24 Figured Bass and Singing from the Literature

Sing the following melodies and determine their key. Then, realize the figured bass in four voices and analyze. Finally, combine singing and realizing the figured bass at the keyboard.

A. Handel, "What Do I Hear," from *Saul*, HWV 53, act 1, scene 3

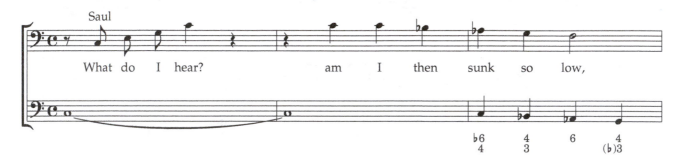

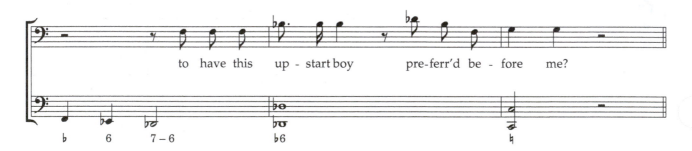

B. Stradella, "Pietà, Signore!" ("Have Pity, Lord"), S11-27 (by Fétis)

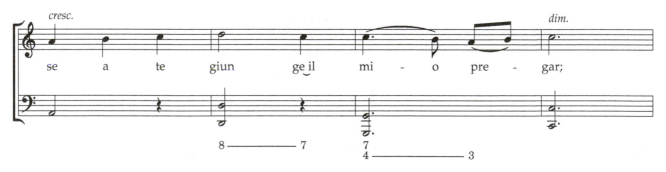

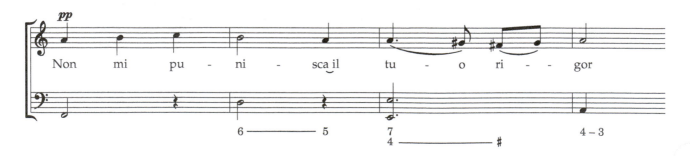

C. Torelli, "Tu lo sai quanto t'amai" ("You Know How Much I Love You")

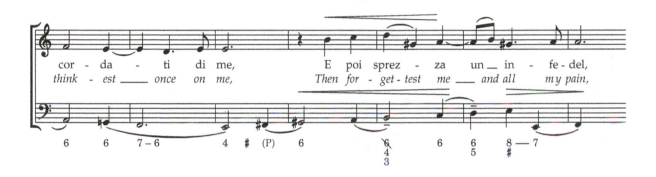

INSTRUMENTAL APPLICATION

EXERCISE 14.25 Reduction

The following excerpts illustrate the melodic, contrapuntal, motivic, and harmonic techniques we have developed beginning in Chapter 5. These techniques include the phrase model and the three structural harmonic functions of T–PD–D as well as the various harmonies that work within the phrase model (e.g., iii and vi). Further, these excerpts illustrate the techniques composers used to prolong any of these structural harmonies (e.g., contrapuntal elaborations, including passing and neighboring chords).

Study the embellished literature excerpts in order to determine their harmonic and contrapuntal unfolding; then reduce them to their essential four-voice SATB chorale texture using good voice leading to connect each harmony. Perform each excerpt as follows: If you are a pianist, simply play your realization. If you are a melodic instrumentalist, arpeggiate each. If necessary, refer to the discussion in Chapter 8 for a detailed procedure. Play each reduction in the key in which it is written; then transpose to one other key of your choice.

Sample solution: Corelli, Church Sonata, op. 3, no. 5, *Allegro*

i   V⁶   i⁵⁻⁶   V⁶₅/III   III   IV   V

A. Corelli, Chamber Sonata in C major, op. 2, no. 3, Preludio, *Largo*

B. Corelli, Chamber Sonata in B minor, op. 4, no. 12, Giga

C. Handel, Concerto Grosso, *Alexander's Feast*, *Andante, non presto*

EXERCISE 14.26 Embellishment

Elaborate the given figured basses (with soprano) by first arpeggiating in strict ascending four-voice chords that maintain proper voice leading between chords. Then change the contours and add embellishing tones to create a compound melody.

A.

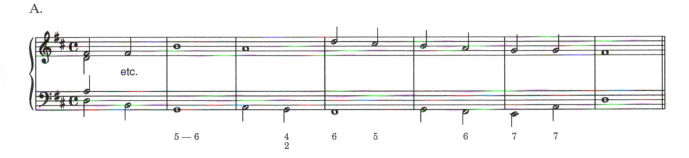

B.

CHAPTER 15

The Period

SINGING

EXERCISE 15.1 Melodies from the Literature

The following melodies are (for the most part) cast as periods. Study each melody, then sing it. Be able to label the period type.

A. Mozart, Piano Concerto no. 27 in B♭ major, K. 595, *Allegro*

B. Haydn, Symphony no. 100 in G major, Hob I.100, *Presto*

C. Haydn, Symphony no. 104 in D major, Hob I.104, *Allegro*

D. Mozart, Horn Concerto in E♭, K. 380

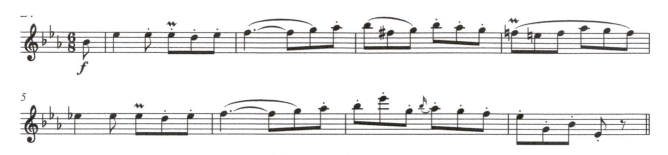

E. Mozart, Violin Sonata in F major, K. 377, Variation VI

F. Mozart, *Die Zauberflöte* (*The Magic Flute*), K. 620, *Andante*

G. Beethoven, Violin Concerto in D major, op. 61, *Allegro ma non troppo*

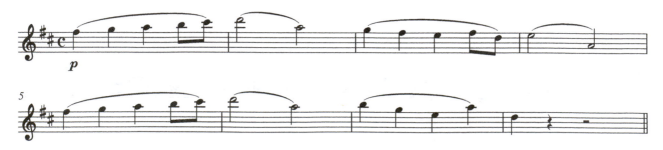

H. Mozart, Violin Sonata in C major, K. 403

I. Schumann, "An den Sonnenschein," op. 36, no. 4

O Son - nen- schein, o Son - nen- schein! wie__ scheinst du mir in's Herz hin- ein, weckst

drin - nen lau - ter Lie - bes- lust, dass__ mir so en - ge wird die Brust.

J. Haydn, Symphony no. 83 in G minor, *Vivace*

K. Mozart, Violin Sonata in F major, K. 377, Variation V

L. Mozart, Piano Sonata no. 8 in A minor, K. 310, *Presto*

M. Beethoven, Six Variations on "Nel cor più non mi sento," from Paisiello's opera *La Molinara*, WoO 70, Theme

N. Beethoven, Piano Sonata no. 27 in E minor, op. 90

Nicht zu geschwind und sehr singbar vorzutragen

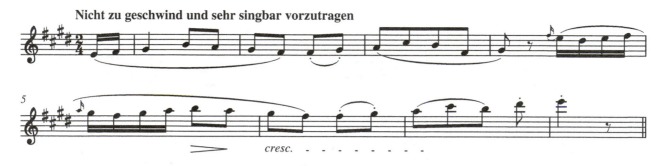

O. Mozart, Symphony no. 14 in A major, K. 114, *Allegro moderato*

Variation 1

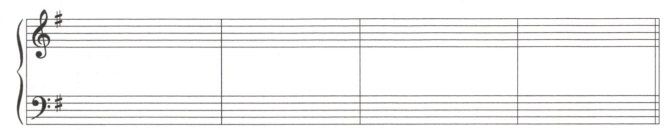

Variation 2

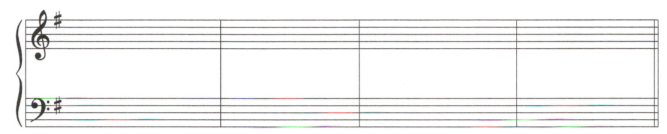

Variation 3

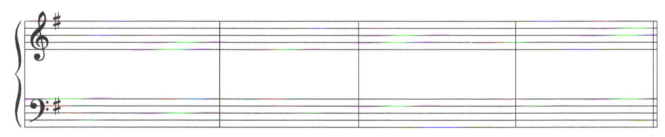

Variation 4

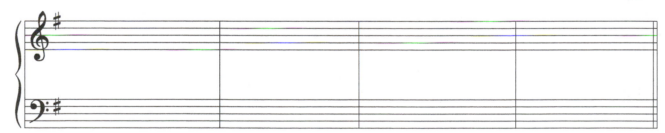

EXERCISE 15.9 Variation and Contrapuntal Expans
a Harmonic Model

You will hear the contrapuntal expansions of a per͏   ͏en
will be fleshed out in variations that maintain the m͏   ͏en
harmonies implied by the bass notes (there are two exceptions͏   ͏l-
lowing tasks:

1. Notate the bass and soprano voices of the contrapuntal chords that e͏
   ish the given harmonic structure.
2. Provide a two-level harmonic analysis. Your harmonic vocabulary now
   cludes I, I⁶, IV⁶, V, V⁶, V⁷, V_5^6, V_3^4, V_2^4, vii°⁶, vii°⁷, vii°$_5^6$, and vii°$_3^4$,
   pre-dominants ii, ii⁶, ii⁷, ii$_5^6$, ii$_3^4$, IV, IV⁶, IV⁷, IV$_5^6$, and the new harmonies
   and iii (and VII in minor).

Model period:

Beware: Two of the variations do NOT follow the model!

Variation 1

Variation 2

Variation 3

Variation 4

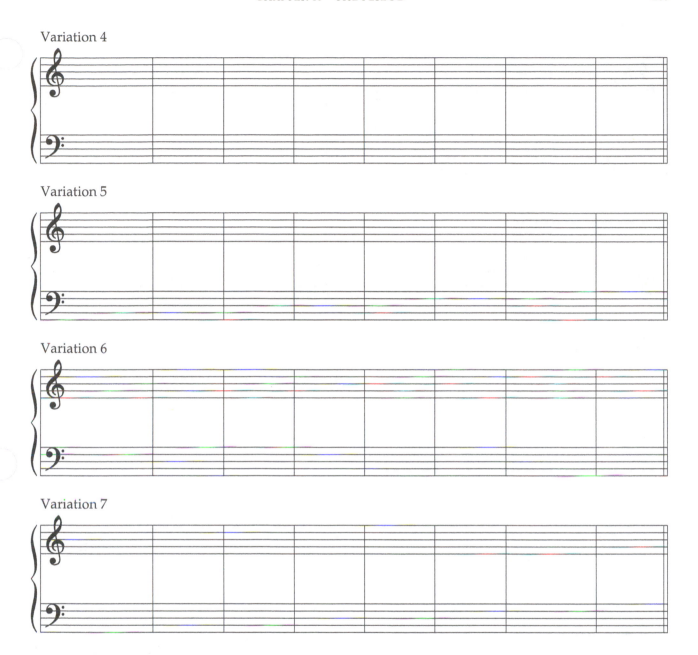

Variation 5

Variation 6

Variation 7

EXERCISE 15.10 Variation and Contrapuntal Expansion of a Harmonic Model

You will hear contrapuntal expansions of a I–V–I harmonic progression. The model bass line given will be fleshed out in variations that maintain the metric placement of the given harmonies implied by the bass notes. Complete the following tasks:

1. Notate the bass and soprano voices of the contrapuntal chords that embellish the given harmonic structure.
2. Provide a two-level harmonic analysis. Your harmonic vocabulary now includes I, I^6, IV^6, V, V^6, V^7, V$^6_5$, V$^4_3$, V$^4_2$, vii^{o6}, vii^{o7}, vii$^{o6}_5$, and vii$^{o4}_3$, the pre-dominants ii, ii^6, ii^7, ii$^6_5$, ii$^4_3$, IV, IV^6, IV^7, IV$^6_5$, and the new harmonies vi and iii (and VII in minor).

Model (single phrase):

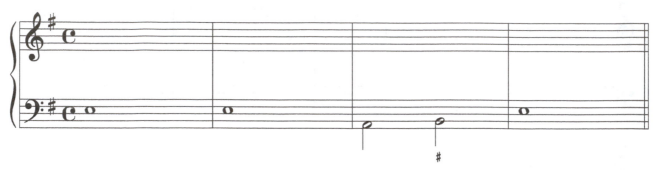

Variation 1

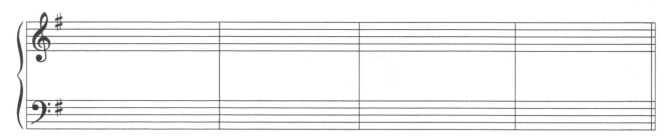

Variation 2

Variation 3

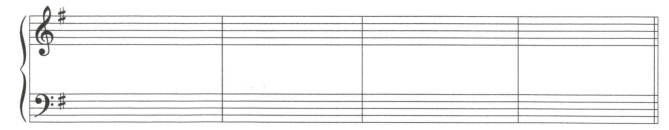

PLAYING

EXERCISE 15.11 Sing and Play: Improvising Period Structures

Two antecedent phrases follow that lack a consequent.

1. Sing and play these phrases. (If you have trouble with the accompaniments as given, you may play block chords in the right hand.)
2. Determine the period type you want. Design a tonal plan and cadence for the second phrase.
3. Improvise/work out a consequent phrase that closes on the tonic to create a period. Improvise both a parallel and a contrasting consequent. Be prepared to perform your periods in class.

A. Beethoven, "Ich liebe dich" ("I Love You"), WoO 132

B. Mendelssohn, "Wenn sich zwei Herzen scheiden" ("When Two Hearts Separate"), op. 99, no. 5

EXERCISE 15.12 Figured Bass and Singing

Accompany your singing of Mozart's melody by realizing the figured bass.

Mozart, "Ein Mädchen oder Weibchen" ("A Maiden or a Little Wife"), from *Die Zauberflöte*, K. 620, act 2, scene 6

so ein sanf - tes Täub - chen wär Se - lig - keit für mich,
tur - tle - doves to - geth - er, We'd share a hap - py life!

INSTRUMENTAL APPLICATION AND IMPROVISATION

EXERCISE 15.13 Improvisation of Antecedent and Consequent Phrases

We will use the following phrases from the literature to create periods. Depending on their shape and harmonic implications, they will function as *either* antecedent phrases or consequent phrases in a two-phrase period. Your compositional choices include PIPs, CIPs, and CCPs.

If you are not a pianist, find an accompanist to provide a harmonic setting for each tune. You will need to play the given phrase and your newly created antecedent or consequent phrase for your accompanist in order for him/her to be able to hear the implied harmonies and be able to accompany you. If you are a pianist, add either full chords or just a bass voice to accompany yourself.

A.

B. Beethoven, "An den Fernen Geliebten," op. 75, no. 5

Einst wohn - ten sü - sse Ruh und gold - ner _ Frie - den in mei - ne Brust,

C. Mendelssohn, "Wenn sich zwei Herzen scheiden"

1. Wenn sich zwei Her - zen schei - den, die sich der - einst ge _ liebt,
1. When themselves two hearts, separate who each other once loved

D. Schumann, "Volksliedchen," from *Children's Pieces*, op. 68

Wenn ich früh in den Gar - ten geh', in mei - nem _ grü - nen Hut,

E. Mozart, Symphony no. 12, in G major, K. 110

F. Haydn, String Quartet in E♭ major, op. 64, no. 6, Trio

G. Jean Baptiste Loeillet, Sonata in G minor, op. 2, no. 2

H. Beethoven, "Urians Reise um die Welt," op. 52, no. 1

Wenn   je – mand ei – ne   Rei – se thut,   so kann   er   was ver – zäh – len.

I. Haydn, String Quartet in D major, op. 64, no. 5, Finale

J. Mozart, Symphony in D major, K. 97, Trio

CHAPTER 16

Other Small Musical Structures: Sentences, Double Periods, and Modified Periods

SINGING

EXERCISE 16.1 Sentences and Period from the Literature

Sing the following melodies using scale degree numbers.

A. Corelli, Concerto Grosso in C major, op. 6, no. 10, Minuetto

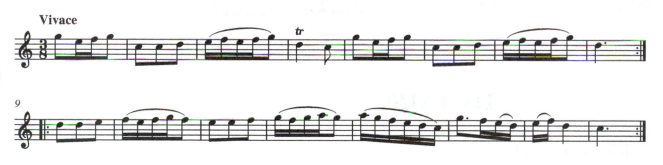

B. Mozart, "Batti, batti, o bel Masetto," from *Don Giovanni*, act 1

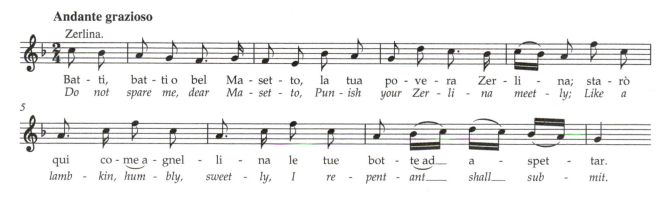

Andante grazioso

Zerlina.

Bat - ti,   bat - ti o bel Ma - set - to,   la tua po - ve - ra Zer - li - na;   sta - rò
Do   not   spare me, dear Ma - set - to, Pun - ish your Zer - li - na   meet - ly;   Like a

qui   co - me a - gnel - li - na le tue bot - te ad___ a - spet - tar.
lamb - kin, hum - bly, sweet - ly, I re - pent - ant___ shall___ sub - mit.

C. Mozart, "Non siate ritrosi," from *Cosi fan tutte*, act 1

D. Beethoven, Violin Sonata no. 4 in A minor, op. 23

LISTENING

EXERCISE 16.2

You will hear several examples cast as sentence structures or double periods. Notate the bass lines, the grid for which is provided in each case. Begin by identifying cadences, then flesh out the specific harmonic changes. Analyze with two levels.

A. Haydn, String Quartet, in F major op. 3, no. 5, *Andante cantabile*

B. Haydn, String Quartet in D minor, op. 42, *Andante ed innocentemente*

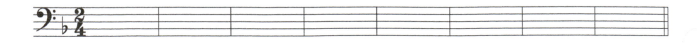

C. Bach, Menuet I, Partita no. 1 in B♭ major

D. Haydn, Symphony no. 91 in D major, "The Clock," Menuetto

E. Mozart, Symphony no. 40 in G minor, K. 550, *Allegro molto* (in 2)

EXERCISE 16.3 Aural Analysis of Periods

Provide a formal diagram and label for each period.

A. Mozart, Piano Sonata in A major, K. 331, *Andante grazioso*

B. Rameau, "La Villageouise," Suite in E minor, *Pièces de clavecin*, 1724

C. Mozart, "In diesen heil'gen Hallen," *Die Zauberflöte*, K. 620, act 2, scene 3

D. Schumann, "Erster Verlust," from *43 Pieces for Children*

E. Mozart, Piano Sonata in D major, K. 576, *Allegro*

F. John Stanley, Solo in D, op. 1, no. 1, Minuet

EXERCISE 16.4 Bass-Line Notation of Sentences

Notate the bass and provide roman numerals for the following phrases cast in sentence structure.

A. Felice Giardini, *Six Duos for Violin and Cello*, no. 2, *Allegro* (harmonic rhythm at the dotted quarter)
B. Marcello, Sonata in A minor, no. 8, Minuetto ($\frac{3}{4}$, usually two harmonic changes per measure)
C. Bach, Sonata in B minor, BWV 1030, *Andante* (slow $\frac{4}{4}$, eighth-note bass motion)

A.

B.   C.

PLAYING AND SINGING

EXERCISE 16.5 Reduction

Sing the following excerpts from Mozart's *The Marriage of Figaro*. Accompany your singing with your reduction. Be able to discuss each excerpt's phrase, period, or sentence structure.

A. Mozart, "Non so più cosa son', cosa faccio," from *Le Nozze di Figaro* (*The Marriage of Figaro*), K. 492, act 1, scene 3

ghiac-cio,   o-gni don - na can-giar di co - lo - re,   o-gni don - na mi fa   pal-pi - tar,

B. Mozart, "Dove sono" ("Where Are They"), from *Le Nozze di Figaro* (*The Marriage of Figaro*), K. 492, act 3, scene 8

Do - ve so - no   i bei mo - men - ti,   di   dol - cez - za   e

di __ pia - cer, __ do - ve an - da - ro i gin - ra men - ti

di quel. lab - bro men - ro - gner, di quel lab - bro men - ro - gner!

EXERCISE 16.6 Harmonization

Choose three of the following melodies and determine possible harmonizations and period types. Harmonic changes usually occur once per measure. Accompany yourself with your harmonization.

A. Foster, "Old Folks at Home"

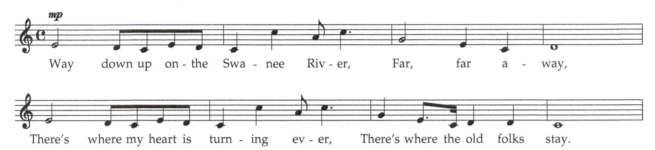

B. "Auld Lang Syne"

C. "Red River Valley"

D. "Home on the Range"

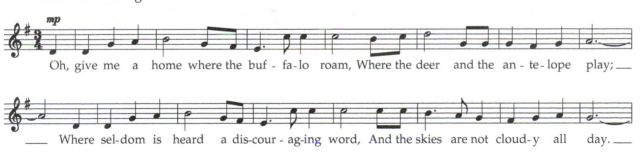

KEYBOARD, ANALYSIS, SINGING, AND COMPOSITION

EXERCISE 16.7 Period Criticism

The given melody is in period form; there are three different figured bass harmonizations below the melody. Sing the melody and provide roman numerals for each of the harmonizations. Then accompany your singing by realizing each of the figured basses in turn. Which do you like best, and why? Are there portions of the figured basses that you particularly like? Create your own distinct figured bass setting by combining material from the three figured basses into a new setting.

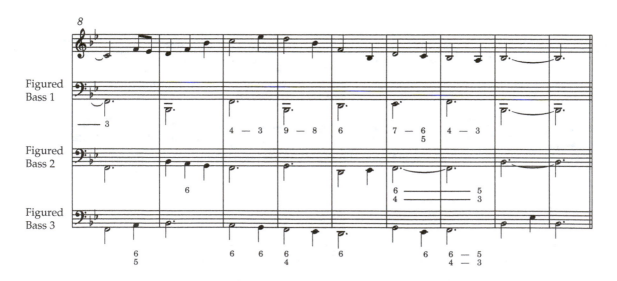

INSTRUMENTAL APPLICATION

EXERCISE 16.8 Improvising Sentence Structures

Given are the openings of potential sentences (i.e., the a portion of the overall a-a'-b entirety). Study the given examples, which demonstrate ways to develop the given material.

Example 1:

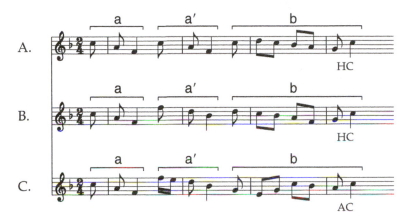

Example 1 presents a falling triad (a), which is literally repeated (a') and developed in the b area by leading to a HC. Example 1B shows how a' can be transposed to IV. Example 1C adds a decorative PT to a', and the b closes with an AC.

Example 2:

Example 2 presents a melodically fluent structure in which a begins on $\hat{1}$ and leads to $\hat{2}$, a' moves from $\hat{2}$ to $\hat{3}$; b reverses the contour and returns by step to $\hat{1}$.

Transfer the given melodic fragments onto a sheet of manuscript paper. This material will function as the "a" section of varied sentence structures; analyze each example using roman numerals. Then compose suitable material to create complete sentences (i.e., you will write the a' and b sections to follow the given a sections).

A.   B.   C.   D.

CHAPTER 17

Harmonic Sequences

SINGING

EXERCISE 17.1 Arpeggiating Sequences

Sing the following arpeggiated sequences. Identify each sequence.

A.

B.

C.

D.

EXERCISE 17.2 Arpeggiating Seventh-Chord Sequences

Using solfège syllables or scale degree numbers, sing each of the following sequences (as written and in the parallel minor) and label each sequence.

A.

B.

EXERCISE 17.3 Singing and Playing

Sing the following melodies as you play the sequences. Identify each sequence. Some examples require you to continue the pattern without the aid of the score. Lead these to an authentic cadence.

A. Mozart, "Solche hergelaufne Laffen," *The Abduction from the Seraglio*, K. 384, act 1

B. Handel, Sonata for Flute and Continuo in A minor, *Allegro*

C. Vivaldi, Violin Sonata in D minor, op. 2, no. 3

D. Brahms, Romance in F major, op. 118, no. 5 (modified), *Andante*

E. Mozart, String Quartet in G major, K. 80, Trio
    Continue the pattern for the second violin and viola parts.

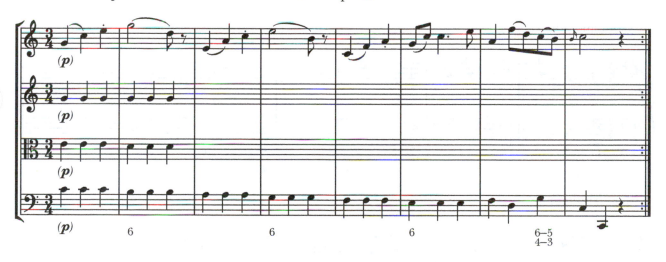

F. Vivaldi, Violin Sonata in G minor, op. 2, no. 1

G. Vivaldi, Violin Sonata in E minor, op. 1, no. 2

EXERCISE 17.4 Singing, Playing, and Improvising

Play the lower voices of the following sequences while singing the soprano tune. Continue each sequence and cadence, based on the given pitches. For Example E, you must continue the sequence and cadence without the aid of figured bass. For Examples F and G, you must create your own four-voice models and embellishment, and continue the sequence and cadence.

A. Major and minor

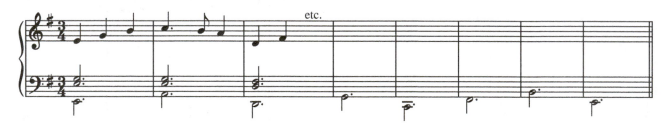

B. Major and minor

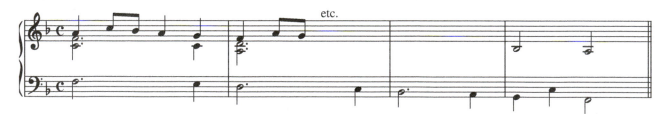

C. Major only

D.

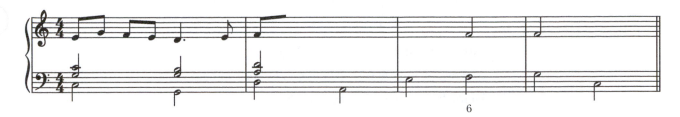

E.

F.   G.

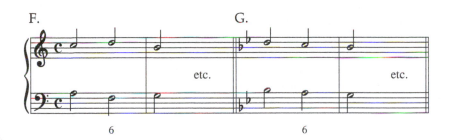

LISTENING

EXERCISE 17.5 Identifying Sequences

Listen to and label the root-position sequences; identify with a sequence label. Follow these guidelines when listening.

1. Determine whether or not the sequence ascends or descends overall.
2. If the sequence descends:
    a. Listen to the bass to determine whether the copies descend by second or third overall.
    b. Note that the D3 sequence usually has a stepwise descending soprano, while the D2 sequence usually has a "sawtooth" motion in the soprano that moves in contrary motion with the bass.
3. If the sequence ascends:
    a. Listen to the bass to determine whether the model has (+5/−4) or (−3/+4) motion.
    b. Note that the A2 (+5/−4) sequence has bigger leaps in the bass and usually has a "sawtooth" motion in the soprano that moves in contrary motion with the bass.
    c. The A2 (−3/+4) sequence typically has a soprano that sounds like 5–6 motion in the model, and the soprano note will repeat as it starts the next copy. Listen for a repeating soprano note.

A._____ B._____ C._____ D._____

E._____ F._____

G. Mozart, Symphony in A major, K. 134 _____

H. Mozart, String Quartet in G major, K. 80, Trio _____

I. Heinichen, Sonata for Oboe and Bassoon, *Allegro* _____

EXERCISE 17.6 Aural Identification of Sequences

This exercise is the same as textbook Exercise 17.5, but now six-three variants are added to the D2 (–5/ +4) and D3 (–4/ +2), and A2 (–3/ +4) sequences. Follow these listening guidelines:

1. Determine whether the sequence ascends or descends. This step reduces sequential possibilities by 50 percent.
2. Listen to the bass to determine which one of the two remaining sequence types is played. Focus on the repetitions of the model. For example, in a descending sequence, does the bass descend by third or second? It is slightly more difficult to distinguish between the two ascending sequences given that both ascend by second. Focus on whether you hear minimal harmonic movement; if so, it is the ascending A2 (–3/ +4) sequence. If you hear a hopping bass, then it is the A2 (+5/–4) sequence.

A. _____   B. _____   C. _____

D. _____   E. _____   F. _____

EXERCISE 17.7 Sequence Dictation

Label the sequence type and notate the bass and the soprano. Pay close attention to the model, since it determines the repetitions. Make sure that the counterpoint is logical and that pairs of intervals are consistent.

A.   B.

C.

D.   E.

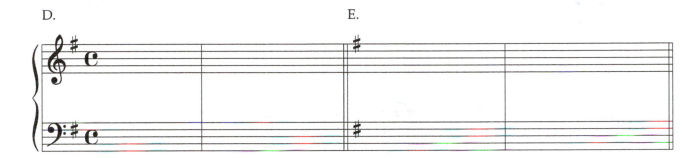

EXERCISE 17.8 Analysis and Notation of Sequences

The incomplete scores of excerpts follow; the bass lines are missing. Identify the sequence type and notate the bass line in each of the excerpts.

A. Quantz, Trio Sonata in G minor, *Allegro*

B. Chopin, Mazurka in F major, op. 68, no. 3, BI 34, *Allegro, ma non troppo*

C. Corelli, Concerto Grosso in C major, op. 6, no. 10, Corrente
   Notate only the downbeat bass notes.

D. Corelli, Violin Sonata in F major, op. 5, no. 10, *Largo*

EXERCISE 17.9 Analysis and Notation of Sequences

Provided are the incomplete scores of excerpts; the bass lines are missing. Identify the sequence type and notate the bass line in each of the excerpts.

A.

B.

C.

D. Mozart, Violin Sonata in A major, K. 526, *Molto allegro*

EXERCISE 17.10 Bass-Line Notation

Each of the following six phrases includes a sequence. As you listen, focus on the three basic components of phrases that contain sequences: tonic expansion, sequence, and cadence. Notate the bass line and provide a second-level harmonic analysis. (Remember that only the first and last chords of a sequence receive roman numerals.) Identify and label each sequence type.

A.

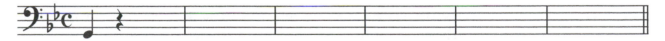

B.

C.

D.

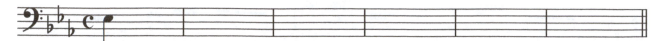

E.

F. Handel, Concerto Grosso in B minor, op. 6, no. 12, HWV 330, *Allegro*: F♯ minor $\frac{4}{4}$; quarter note = 108. The sequence begins after two measures of music. Notate only the bass line of the sequence.

EXERCISE 17.11 Sequences with Seventh Chords

These examples contain the four types of triadic sequences and D2 sequences with seventh chords. Notate the bass lines of the sequential passages from the literature on a separate sheet of manuscript paper, and label the sequence type.

A. Cimarosa, Concerto for Oboe (adapted by A. Benjamin): $\frac{3}{8}$; dotted quarter = 50

B. Corelli, Violin Sonata in B minor, op. 3, no. 4, *Adagio*: $\frac{3}{8}$; eighth note = 96

C. Handel, Concerto Grosso, op. 3, no. 2: quarter note = 96

D. Mozart, Violin Concerto no. 3: alla breve; half note = 60

E. Handel, "He Gave His Back to the Smiters," *Messiah*: $\frac{4}{4}$; quarter note = 69

F. Mozart, Serenade in C minor, K. 388, *Andante*: $\frac{3}{8}$; eighth note = 96

G. Corelli, Violin Sonata in D major, op. 4, no. 4: $\frac{4}{4}$; quarter note = 96

EXERCISE 17.12 Aural Identification of Sequences Within Phrases

Notate the bass of the incomplete scores and provide a roman numeral analysis. Bracket and label sequences.

A.

B. Write only two bass notes per measure (the other pitches are accompanying arpeggiations).

C.

EXERCISE 17.13 Analysis and Notation

The following sequences from the literature are missing some notes in Exercises A and B and the complete bass line in C. Listen to and study each sequence; then, identify each sequence and notate the bass line.

A. Mozart, Piano Sonata in F major, K. 332, *Allegro*
   Consider this excerpt to be in C minor. What rhythmic device is employed in mm. 64 and 65?

62

B. Chopin, Etude in G♭ major, op. 25

V^6/V

C. Haydn, Piano Sonata no. 44 in B♭ major, Hob XVI.29, *Moderato*

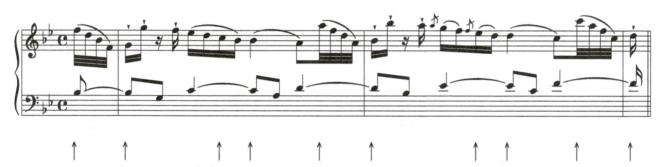

EXERCISE 17.14 Analysis and Notation

The following sequences from the literature are missing bass lines. Listen to and study each sequence; then, identify each sequence and notate the bass line.

A. Geminiani, Violin Sonata in G minor, op. 1, no. 12, *Allegro*
Notate only the bass pitches that occur on the beat.

19

♭   #6   6   ♭   ♭7   #   7

B. Bach, *Allemande*, English Suite no. 3 in G minor, BWV 808

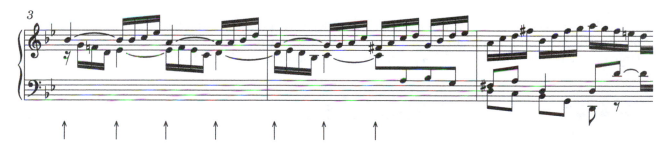

C. Corelli, Concerto Grosso in F major, op. 6, no. 2, *Allegro*

EXERCISE 17.15 Notation of Sequences

You will hear several D2 (−5/+4) sequences with and without sevenths. If the sequence contains sevenths, determine whether it is alternating or interlocking. Notate the bass.

A.   B.

C.   D. Handel, "Pena tiranna io sento," from *Amidigi di Gaula*, act 1, *Largo*

E. Schumann, "Ich will meine Seele tauchen" ("I Want to Delve My Soul"), *Dichterliebe*, op. 48, no. 5

You will hear the entire song, which is composed of two large phrases. Each phrase may in turn be divided into two subphrases. What type of larger musical structure do the two large phrases create? Each large phrase begins unusually with a pre-dominant harmony, $ii^{\varnothing 7}$, rather than the tonic.

$ii^{\varnothing 7}$ V

EXERCISE 17.16 Expansion of Basic Progressions

You will hear two basic chord progressions; each is followed by elaborated versions that include contrapuntal expansions and sequences. Notate the bass and the soprano and include roman numerals. In a sentence or two, describe the way the tonic is expanded.

Model A:

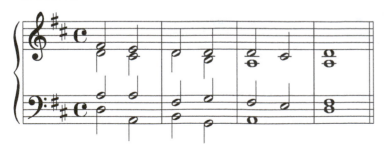

Variation 1

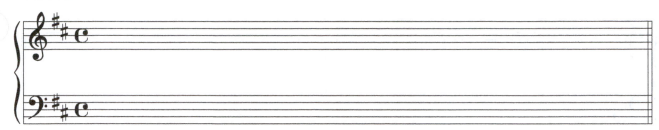

Variation 2

Variation 3

Variation 4

Model B:

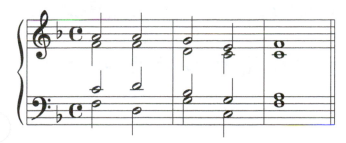

Variation 1 (3 mm.)　　　　　　　　　　Variation 2 (3 mm.)

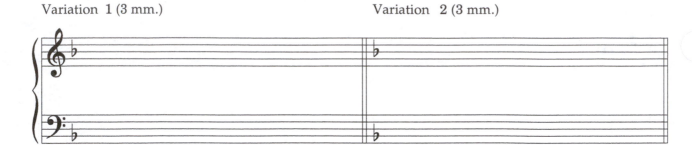

Variation 3 (3 mm.)　　　　　　　　　　Variation 4 (4 mm.)

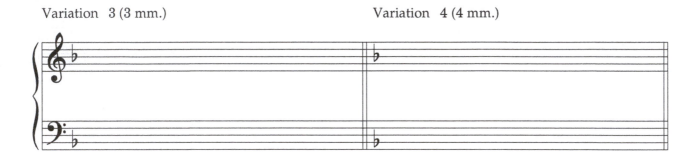

EXERCISE 17.17 Analysis and Notation

The following sequences from the literature are missing part of their bass lines. Listen to and study each sequence; then identify each sequence and notate the bass line.

A. Tchaikovsky, Symphony no. 4, op. 36, *Andantino in modo di canzona*

B. Corelli, Concerto Grosso in F major, op. 6, no. 12, Gigue, *Allegro*

PLAYING

EXERCISE 17.18 Singing and Playing

Play each of the following sequence models in four voices and in major and minor keys up to two sharps and two flats. Be able to sing either outer voice while playing the remaining three voices.

A.

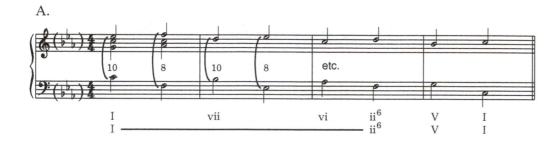

B.

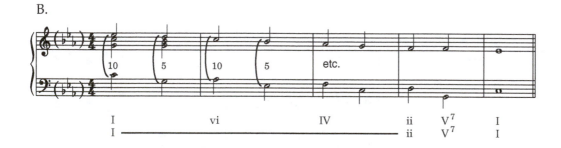

C.

D. major only

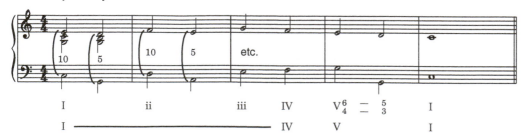

EXERCISE 17.19 Sequences with Six-Three Chords

Identify and play each of the sequence models below in major and minor keys up to and including two sharps and two flats. Voicings are given for the model. Be able to sing either outer voice while playing the other three voices.

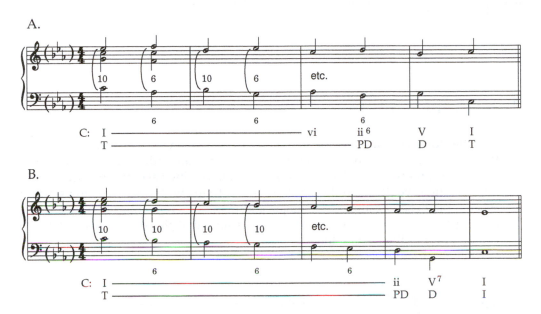

A.

B.

EXERCISE 17.20 Illustrations

Complete the following.

A. In D minor and a meter of your choice:

1. Establish tonic (approximately 2 mm.). Include one suspension.
2. Use a descending sequence that leads to a HC (approximately 2–3 mm.).
3. Begin again on tonic; use any rising sequence to lead to a cadential six-four chord. Close with a PAC. The result will be an interrupted period (whether it is parallel or contrasting is up to you).

B. In E minor and a meter of your choice.

1. Establish tonic; use a voice exchange (approximately 2 mm.).
2. Use a D3 (–4/+2) sequence to lead to a PD and an IAC.
3. Begin again on tonic; use an A2 (–3/+4) sequence to lead to iv.
4. Close with a PAC; include one suspension. The result will be a sectional period (whether it is parallel or contrasting is up to you).

EXERCISE 17.21 Figured Bass

Realize the following figured bass in four voices. Label all sequences. Be able to sing the bass while playing the upper voices. You may write out your soprano.

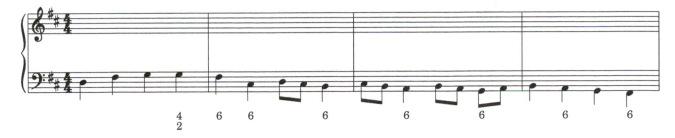

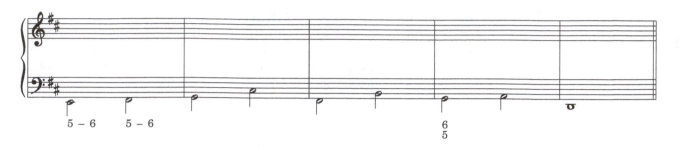

5 – 6   5 – 6   6
                                                          5

EXERCISE 17.22 Seventh Chords

Play the following models for the D2 (–5/+4) sequences with seventh chords. Preparation and resolution of the chordal sevenths are indicated by dotted lines and arrows, respectively. The first model has alternating sevenths, the second has interlocking sevenths, and the third alternates triads with first-inversion seventh chords. Play each example in C major and C minor—remember how to use the leading tone in minor-mode sequences and note that the first chord of letter B should also use the leading tone.

A.

B.

C.

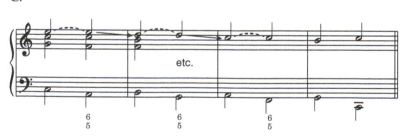

EXERCISE 17.23 Figured Bass

Realize the figured bass in four voices; a few given soprano pitches will guide your upper line. Sing the bass voice while playing the upper parts. Analyze.

INSTRUMENTAL APPLICATION

EXERCISE 17.24 Embellishing Sequences

The small number of common-sequence types reappear through the common-practice period and continue to this day because composers have found countless ways to mold and embellish them to suit the specific needs of their compositions. In this exercise we both review and embellish sequences. In Example A1, a D2 (–5/+4) sequence with six-three chords is implied by the figured bass, then realized in four voices in Example A2. Example A3 uses compound melody to elaborate the sequence. Example A4 fills the thirds in the outer-voice counterpoint by adding passing tones; this structure is embellished by the added voices in Example A5.

Composers often distribute the pitches between individual instruments, adding embellishments that tie the voices together. The examples from Corelli and Bach show how three- and four-voice homophonic models can be embellished by simple figures that comprise passing, neighboring, and chordal skipping motions. Study the models, then embellish the homophonic sequence given. Lead each to an authentic cadence.

A.

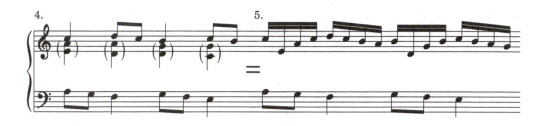

B1. A2 (−3/+4)

B2. Corelli Trio Sonata in C major, op. 4, no. 1, *Allegro*

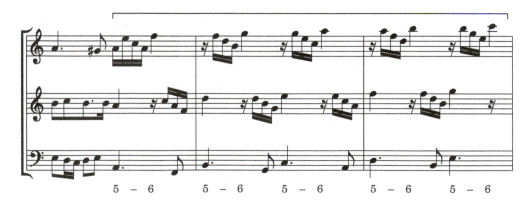

C1. D2 (−5/+4) with $\frac{6}{3}$ chords

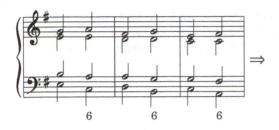

C2. Bach, Prelude in G major, BWV 902

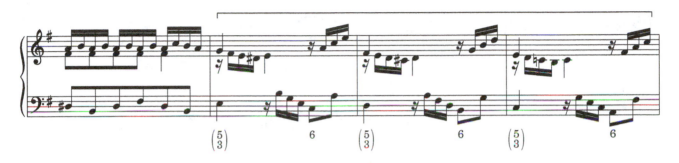

D1. D2 (−5/ +4)

etc.

D2. Corelli Concerto Grosso in F major, op. 6, no. 12, Giga

EXERCISE 17.25 Improvising and Elaborating Sequences

One student plays the given bass while the second student arpeggiates the required chords based on the bass and the figures. Ascend on the first chord and descend on the second. Play in the parallel mode and transpose to two other keys. Finally, players should reverse voices.

A. Duets (or one pianist)

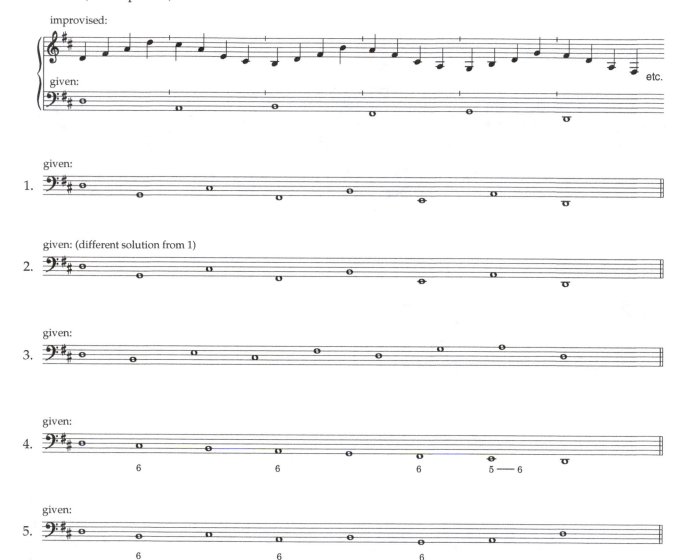

B. Figurated Duets
Add embellishing tones to your melodic lines. Begin with chordal leaps and passing tones (see Example 1). Feel free to add combinations of these embellishing tones as well as neighbors and suspensions. Try to balance the faster motion between voices, a procedure called *complementation*.

given:

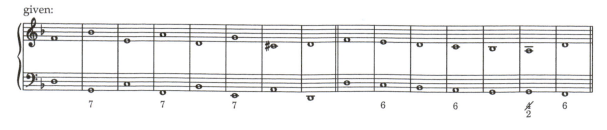

Example1:

EXERCISE 17.26 Reduction of Sequences

Determine the sequence type in the given examples, and reduce the texture to three or four voices, which you will play as either vertical sonorites on the piano or arpeggiations on a melody instrument. A sample solution is provided, which contains three sequences.

Sample solution:

A. Corelli, Concerto Grosso no. 10 in C major, Corrente

B. Corelli, Chamber Sonata in C major, op. 4, no. 1, Preludio

Applied Chords

SINGING

EXERCISE 18.1 Arpeggiating Applied Chords

Using solfège syllables or scale degree numbers, sing or play on your instrument the following progressions that incorporate applied chords. Label all applied chords, and circle their chordal thirds (temporary leading tones) and sevenths.

A. Major only

B.

C. Once without sharps in parentheses, once with

D.

E. Minor only

EXERCISE 18.2 Arpeggiating Applied Dominant Substitutes

Using solfège syllables or scale degree numbers, sing or play on your instrument the following progressions that incorporate applied dominant substitute chords. If you play these on your instrument, be able to transpose each to one other key.

A. Major only

B. Minor only

EXERCISE 18.3 Melodies from the Literature that Contain Applied Dominants

Sing the following melodies, each of which implies one or more applied chords.

A. Mozart, Symphony no. 38 in D major, "Prague," K. 504, *Presto*

B. Schubert, Symphony no. 8 in B minor, "Unfinished," D. 759, *Allegro moderato*

C. Beethoven, Piano Sonata in G major, op. 49, no. 2, Tempo di Menuetto

D. Schubert, "Trout" Quintet, D. 667, *Andantino*

E. Schubert, "Frühlingssehnsucht," D. 957, no. 3
Play the bass while singing; analyze.

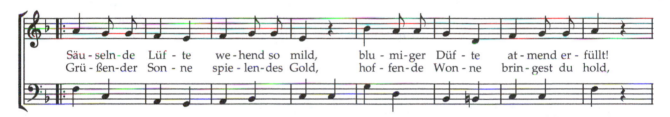

Säu - seln - de Lüf - te we - hend so mild, blu - mi - ger Düf - te at - mend er - füllt!
Grü - ßen - der Son - ne spie - len - des Gold, hof - fen - de Won - ne brin - gest du hold,

F. Schubert, "Der Alpenjäger," op. 13, no. 3

Auf ho - hem Ber - ges - rü - cken, wo fri - scher al - les

grünt, ins Land hin - ab - zu - bli - cken, das ne - bel - leicht_ zer - rinnt,

G. Handel, "Dove sei amato bene?" from *Rodelinda*

Do - ve se - i a - ma - to be - ne? Vie - ni, l'al - ma a con - so-
Where now art thou, my own be - loved one? Come, con - sole me; my heart ___ is

lar,_____ a con - so - lar!
sore,_____ my heart is sore.

H. Fanny Hensel Mendelssohn, "Gondelied," *Allegretto*

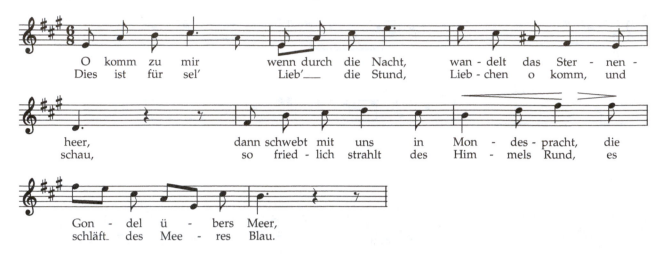

O komm zu mir wenn durch die Nacht, wan - delt das Ster - nen -
Dies ist für sel' Lieb'___ die Stund, Lieb - chen o komm, und

heer, dann schwebt mit uns in Mon - des - pracht, die
schau, so fried - lich strahlt des Him - mels Rund, es

Gon - del ü - bers Meer,
schläft. des Mee - res Blau.

EXERCISE 18.4 Applied-Chord Sequences from the Literature

Using solfège or scale degree numbers, sing the following harmonic patterns, which incorporate applied-chord sequences. Label all applied chords, and identify their chordal thirds and sevenths. Play left-hand pitches in Exercises D and E.

A.

B.

C.

D. Mozart, "Solche hergelaufne Laffen," from *Abduction from the Seraglio*, act 1

müßt ihr früh___ auf - ste-hen, müßt ihr früh___ auf -

ste - hen, ich hab auch Ver-stand, ich hab auch Ver -

stand, ich hab auch Ver-stand, ich, ich hab_auch Ver-stand.

E. Mozart, "Ich gehe doch rate ich dir," from *Abduction from the Seraglio*, act 2

Es ist um die Au-gen ge-sche-hen, es ist um die Au-gen ge-sche-hen,

LISTENING

EXERCISE 18.5 Aural Comparison of Progressions with and without Applied Chords

You will hear four pairs of short progressions; the first progression of the pair (the model), is diatonic, and the second adds applied chords that embellish the first progression. Listen to the model and write out the roman numerals. Then listen to the second example, which contains one applied chord. For each applied chord you hear, write "V" beneath the harmony and follow it with an arrow that leads to the diatonic chord that is being tonicized. For example, if the first progression you hear is I–V–I, but the second contains an applied chord between the tonic and the dominant, you would write I–V⤸V–I.

A. model: _____ _____ _____

              _____ _____ _____

B. model: _____ _____ _____ _____

              _____ _____ _____ _____ _____

C. model: _____ _____ _____

              _____ _____ _____

D. model: _____ _____ _____

              _____ _____ _____ _____

EXERCISE 18.6 Applied-Chord Progressions

Each of the following progressions contains one applied chord. Notate the bass and soprano lines and provide roman numerals.

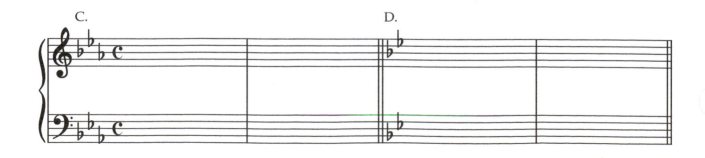

EXERCISE 18.7 Notation of Chromatic Tones

Notated diatonic progressions are provided to which applied chords will be added. Notate appropriate pitches and roman numerals that reflect these added applied harmonies.

Listening tip: Remember, a chromatically raised pitch functions as the temporary leading tone to the next chord (i.e., it becomes $\hat{7}$), and a chromatically lowered pitch usually functions as the seventh of the chord that descends to the third of the following chord. The chromaticism often appears in an outer voice.

A.   B.

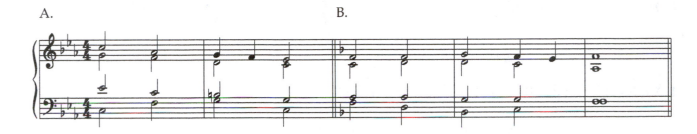

C. Note the parallel fifths between bass and tenor in m. 1. Added applied chords are often used as voice-leading correctives that eliminate such fifths and octaves.

EXERCISE 18.8 Notation of Chromatic Tones

Applied chords will be added to the diatonic progressions. Notate appropriate pitches and roman numerals to reflect these added applied harmonies.

A.   B.   C.

EXERCISE 18.9 Comparison of Applied V⁷ and vii°⁷ in Short Phrases

Notate outer voices of the following progressions, and provide roman numerals.

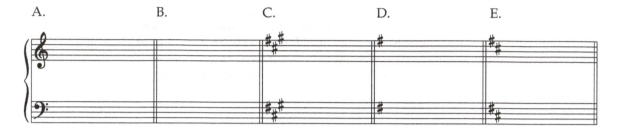

EXERCISE 18.10 Applied Sequences

Label each applied-chord sequence that you hear.

A. _____   B. _____   C. _____   D. _____

E. _____   F. _____   G. _____   H. _____

EXERCISE 18.11 Applied Chord Sequences within the Phrase Model: Analysis and Notation

The following phrases contain applied-chord sequences. The upper voices are provided.

1. Identify the sequence and notate the bass line.
2. Provide a two-level analysis of each excerpt.

A. Mozart, String Quartet in B♭ major "Hunt," K. 458 Minuetto

B. Schubert, Waltz in G major, *Twelve German Dances and Five Ecossaises*, no. 3, D. 529

C. Schubert, Waltz in A major, *Twelve German Dances and Five Ecossaises*, no. 12, D. 420

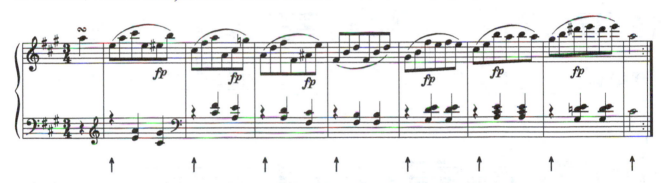

D. Beethoven, Violin Sonata no. 6 in A major, op. 30, no. 1, *Adagio molto expressivo*
    Note that there is a slightly longer tonicization of each step within the sequence.

EXERCISE 18.12 Notation of Applied-Chord Sequences

Add the missing bass voice by using your ear and the visual clues provided by the given upper voices. Label the sequence type.

D.

E.

PLAYING

EXERCISE 18.13 Brain Twister

Determine the major and (relative) minor keys for each example, and label the applied dominant or diminished seventh chord given. In four-voice keyboard style, play and resolve the applied chords; then lead each example to an authentic cadence, first in major and then in the relative minor key.

EXERCISE 18.14 Building and Resolving Applied Chords

In keyboard style, play and resolve the following applied chords. Lead each example to an authentic cadence.

A. F major and D major: V^7/IV; vii$^{\circ 7}$/ii; V^7/vi

B. B♭ major and G major: V^7/V; V^7/vi; V$^6_5$/IV

C. E minor and D minor: vii$^{\circ 6}_5$/iv; vii$^{\circ 7}$/III; vii$^{\circ 7}$/VI

D. C major and E♭ major: vii$^{\circ 6}$/ii; V$^6_5$/iii; V$^4_2$/vi

EXERCISE 18.15 Model Progressions

Play in major and minor modes as specified in keys up to and including one sharp and one flat. Be able to sing either outer voice while playing the remaining three voices. Analyze.

EXERCISE 18.16 Short Progressions

Add upper voices to the following bass lines. Include at least one applied chord in each example. Cast each example in a metric and rhythmic setting of your choice. Transpose to one other key of your choice.

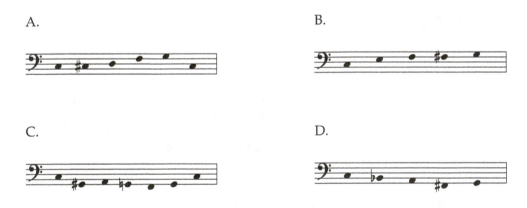

EXERCISE 18.17 Unfigured Bass

Realize the unfigured bass in four voices. Write a two-level analysis.

EXERCISE 18.18 Applied-Chord Sequences

Play the models for applied-chord sequences as written; then continue the given pattern. Analyze all progressions, and label sequence types. Be able to sing either outer voice while playing the remaining three voices. Transpose to major keys up to two flats and two sharps.

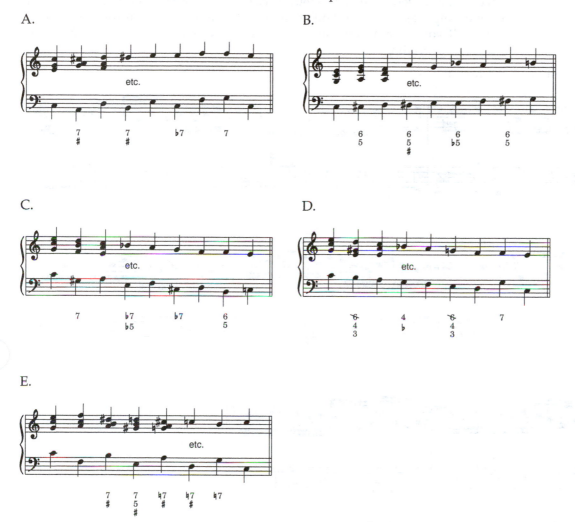

EXERCISE 18.19 Embellishing Sequences

Improvise embellished versions of any of the sequences given in Exercise 18.18. In order to include various embellishing tones (PT, NT, CL, S, or some combination of two or three of these), consider each chord as occupying one measure of $\frac{2}{4}$ or $\frac{3}{4}$. Maintain proper voice leading. Play in the key given and in one other key of your choice.

INSTRUMENTAL APPLICATION

EXERCISE 18.20 Reduction

Reduce the textures in the following excerpts to determine the type of sequence used. Analyze, verticalize (into a four-voice homophonic texture), and then perform each example as follows: if you are a pianist, simply play your four-voice realization; if you are a melodic instrumentalist, arpeggiate each example. Maintain proper voice leading.

A. Marcello, Sonata no. 8 in A minor

B. Corelli, Concerto Grosso in F major, op. 6, no. 6, *Allegro*

C. Corelli, Concerto Grosso in D major, op. 6, no. 4, *Vivace*

D. Corelli, Sonata for Violin in B♭ major, op. 5, no. 2, *Vivace*

E. Corelli, Concerto Grosso in D major, op. 6, no. 1, *Allegro*

CHAPTER 19

Tonicization and Modulation

SINGING AND PLAYING

EXERCISE 19.1 Tonicized Areas and Modulations

Sing (or play on your instrument) the following progressions using solfège or scale degree numbers. Given that the progressions contain expansions of nontonic areas, analyze each exercise before singing. Your instructor will give you analytical guidelines specific to the needs of your school's curriculum.

A.

B.

C.

D. Schubert, "Fischerweise," op. 96, no. 4, D. 881
   Play the bass while singing. Feel free to add chords with the right hand based on the figured bass.

Sing the following progressions using solfège or scale degree numbers. Each progression modulates, closing in a different tonal area and containing a pivot chord. Analyze. If you play these exercises on your instrument, transpose each to one other key.

E.

F.

G.

H.

I.

J.

K. Mozart, Symphony in G minor, K. 183, Trio

L. Mozart, Symphony in F major, K. 130, Menuetto

M. Bach, Flute Sonata in A minor, BWV 1033, Menuett II

N. Marcello, Sonata no. 2 in E minor for Cello and Basso Continuo

O. Turk, Gavotte in A major

P. Andre, Sonatina in C major

Q. Turk, Dance in G

R. De Fesch, Sarabanda for Flute in B minor

S. Schubert, "Heidenröslein," op. 3, no. 3, D. 257

T. Schubert, "Die Forelle" ("The Trout"), op. 32, D. 550

In   ei - nem Bäch - lein   hel - le,   da schoß   in   fro - her___
Fi - scher mit   der   Ru - te   wohl   an   dem   U - fer___

Eil   die   lau - ni - sche Fo - rel - le   vor - ü - ber___ wie ein   Pfeil.
stand,   und   sah's mit kal - tem   Blu - te,   wie   sich   das__ Fisch - lein   wand.

U. Handel, Concerto Grosso, op. 6, no. 2, *Allegro*

V. Handel, Concerto Grosso, op. 3, no. 2, *Allegro*

W. Mozart, Serenade in C minor, K. 388, *Allegro*

X. Schubert, "Heiss' mich nicht reden," from *Lied der Mignon*, op. 62, no. 2

Lansam (Lento)

Heiß   mich nicht re - den,   heiß___   mich schwei - gen,   denn   mein Ge - heim - nis

ist   mir Pflicht,   ich möch - te   dir___   mein gan - zes Inn - re   zei - gen, al -

lein   das Schick - sal___   will   es___ nicht.

Y. Handel, Violin Sonata in D minor

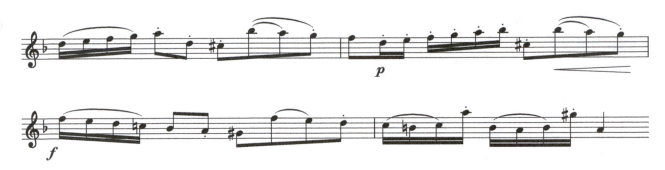

Z. Donizetti, "Regnava nel silenzio," from *Lucia di Lammermoor*, act 1

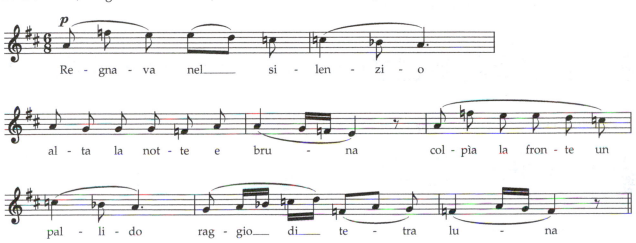

Re - gna - va nel____ si - len - zi - o

al - ta la not - te e bru - na col - pìa la fron - te un

pal - li - do rag - gio__ di__ te - tra lu - na

AA. Mozart, Piano Sonata no. 4 in E♭, K. 282, Menuetto

Allegro

BB. Bellini, "Meco all'altar di Venere," from *Norma*, act 1, scene 2

POLLIONE
legato

Me - co al - l'al - tar di Ve - ne - re e - ra A - dal - gi - sa in

Ro - ma, cin - ta di ben - de can - di - de,

spar - sa di fior la chio - ma;

CC. Schubert, "Der Kreuzzug," D. 932

Ein Mü - nich steht in sei - ner Zell am Fen - ster git - ter___ grau, viel

Rit - ters leut in Waf - fen hell, die rei - ten durch die___ Au.

DD. Corelli, Concerto Grosso in B♭ major, op. 6, no. 11

EE. Corelli, Concerto Grosso in D major, op. 6, no. 1

FF. Schumann, *Carnaval*, op. 9

GG. Durante, "Danza, danza, fanciulla gentile"

Dan - za,___ dan - za, fan - ciul - la,___ al___ mi - o can - tar, dan - za,___
Dance, O___ dance, maid - en gay, to___ the___ song that I sing; dance, O___

dan - za,___ fan - ciul - la___ gen - ti - le, al mi - o can - tar.
dance, maid - en___ gay, to___ the___ song, to the song that I sing.

HH. Bach, Suite for Unaccompanied Cello no. 2 in D minor, BWV 1008, Gigue

II. Vivaldi, Violin Concerto in D minor

JJ. Bach, Cello Suite in C major, BWV 1009

KK. Sing and play: modulating sequence

LISTENING

Hearing Modulations

When listening to a phrase, there are several ways to determine whether or not it has modulated.

1. Listen for the presence of new chromatic pitches that persist through the end of the phrase. This most likely signals a modulation.
2. If the first key is in major and the closing key is in minor (or vice versa), then a modulation has occurred. If you wish to know the specific harmonic motion of the modulation, you should be able to reduce your choices by a process of elimination. For example, if the music begins in a major key and ends in a minor key, the example probably has closed in either iii or vi. There will be exceptions, but this is the most common modulation strategy. Similarly, if the music begins in a minor key and ends in a major key, the example probably will have modulated to III (very common) or VI (less common).
3. To identify modulations in phrases that begin and end in the same mode, get a physical sense of how it feels to sing the tonic of the initial key. When the phrase ends, sing the closing tonic and compare it to the opening tonic. If the closing tonic is higher or lower than the opening tonic, a modulation has occurred. The possible tonal areas for modulation are very limited: If the opening and closing keys are major, you have likely modulated to V. If the opening and closing keys are minor, you have almost certainly moved to minor v.

EXERCISE 19.2 Hearing Modulations

1. Listen to the following progressions and determine whether or not they modulate (answer yes or no).
2. Label the mode (major or minor) that occurs at the beginning of the progression.
3. If there is a modulation, determine the mode at the end of the progression.

Does the example modulate?	Mode (M or m) of opening	Mode (M or m) of closing (if example modulates)
A. _____	_____	_____
B. _____	_____	_____
C. _____	_____	_____
D. _____	_____	_____
E. _____	_____	_____
F. _____	_____	_____

EXERCISE 19.3 Determining Goals of Modulations

Listen to the following examples and determine to what key each excerpt modulates. Use roman numerals to represent the new key. In order to do this, combine the two methods described earlier. Sing the opening tonic and determine the mode. Do the same for the closing tonic. Then ask whether the new tonic is above or below the original and if it is major or minor, which will tell you the goal of the modulation.

For example, if you begin in C major and you end in a minor key that is below C major, you have modulated to vi; if you end above C major you have modulated to iii. As you know from previous chapters, you must always listen to complete spans of music rather than focusing on individual pitches. Therefore, listen to the entire harmonic progression before you determine to where it modulates.

EXERCISE 19.4 Notation of Modulating Phrases and Pivot-Chord Location

Each short progression modulates, closing with a PAC in a new key. Before listening, determine modulatory possibilities.

   An incomplete score is given for each example. Add missing bass and soprano pitches and provide roman numerals; mark the pivot chord.

A.   B.

EXERCISE 19.5 Notation of Modulating Phrases and Pivot-Chord Location

Each short progression modulates and closes with a PAC in the new key. Before listening, determine modulatory possibilities. An incomplete score is given for each example; the Haydn example is missing its entire bass line, and Exercises C–F include only a few bass pitches.

   For Exercises A and B, add the missing bass and soprano pitches and provide roman numerals. For Exercises C–F add the bass and analyze. Mark the pivot chord in all the exercises.

A.   B.

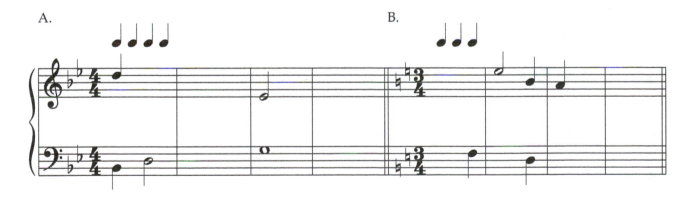

C. Haydn, String Quartet in G major, op. 64, no. 4, *Adagio*

D. Schubert, String Quartet no. 9 in G, D. 173

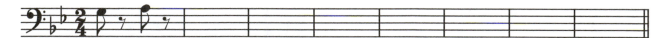

E. Kozeluch, String Quartet in A major, op. 33, no. 2, *Andante*

F. Vivaldi, Violin Sonata no. 3 in G minor, Ryom 757

EXERCISE 19.6 Notation of Modulating Phrases and Pivot-Chord Location

Each short progression modulates, closing with a PAC. Before listening, determine modulatory possibilities. An incomplete score is given for each example; the literature example is missing its entire bass line. Add missing bass and soprano pitches and provide roman numerals; mark the pivot chord.

A.

B.

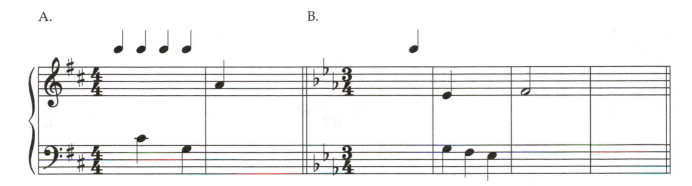

C. Johann Jacob Bach, Sonata in C minor for Oboe and Continuo

EXERCISE 19.7 Dictation of Longer Modulating Phrases

Notate the bass and soprano for Exercises A–C and the bass only for Exercises D and E. Provide a roman numeral analysis and label the pivot chord.

A.

B.

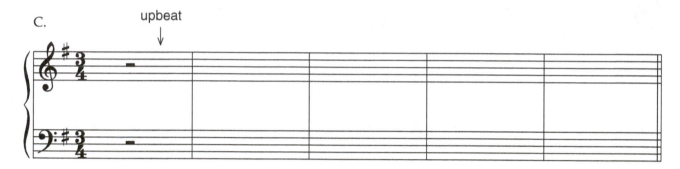

C.

upbeat

D. Handel, Concerto Grosso in C minor, op. 6, no. 8, HWV 326, *Allegro*

E. Mozart, "In diesen heil'gen Hallen," from *Die Zauberflöte (The Magic Flute)*, K. 620, act 2, scene 3

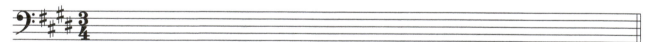

EXERCISE 19.8 Dictation of Longer Modulating Phrases

Notate bass and provide a roman numeral analysis. Label the pivot chord.

A. Haydn, String Quartet in C major, op. 54, no. 2, Hob III.58, *Adagio*

B. Schubert, Waltz in B minor, *38 Waltzes, Ländler, and Ecossaises*, D. 145

C. Beethoven, *Lustig-Traurig*, WoO 54

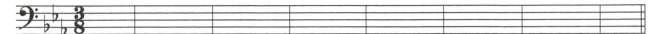

D. Haydn, String Quartet in F major, op. 74, no. 2, Hob III.70, *Allegro*

E. Chopin, Mazurka in A minor, op. 7, no. 2, BI 61

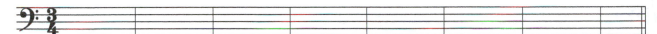

F. Haydn, Piano Sonata in C major, Hob XVI.10, Trio

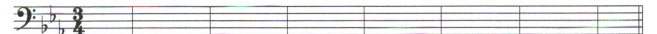

EXERCISE 19.9 Dictation: Variations of a Structural Progression

> Study each of the following models. Then listen to and notate the bass and soprano voices and provide roman numerals for the following elaborations of the model. Modulations to closely related keys will occur. Label pivot chords.

Model A:

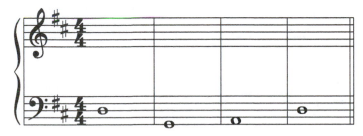

Variation 1   Variation 2

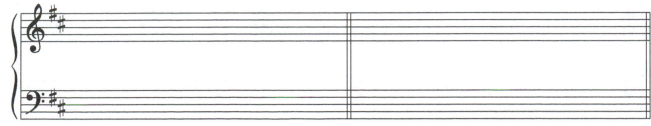

Variation 3

Variation 4

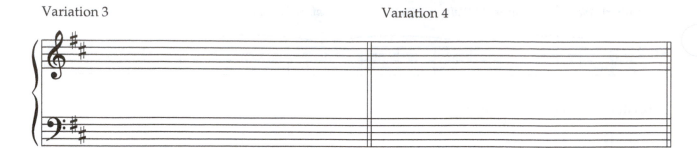

Variation 5

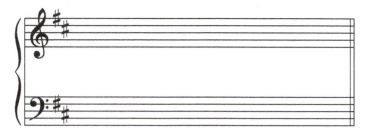

Model B:

Variation 1

Variation 2

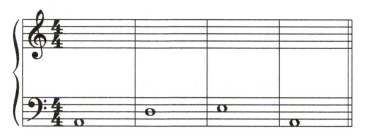

Variation 3

Variation 4

Variation 5

Model C:

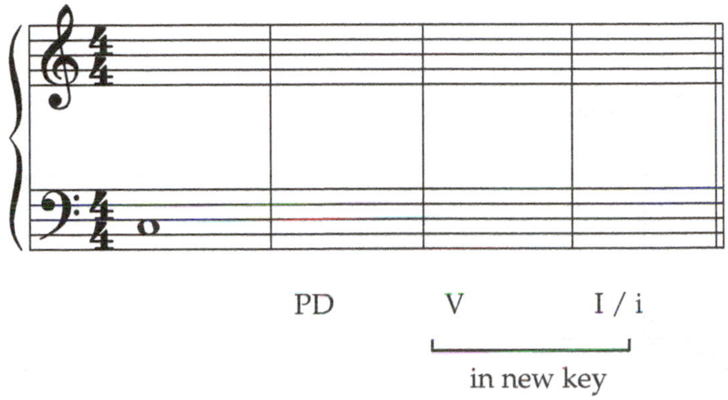

PD   V   I / i

in new key

Variation 1   Variation 2

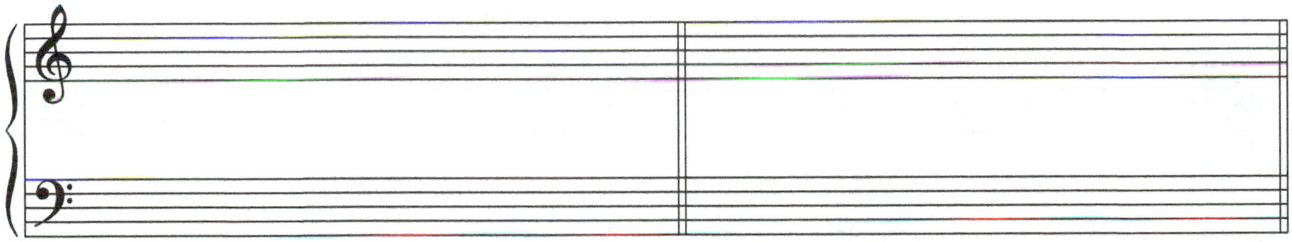

Variation 3   Variation 4

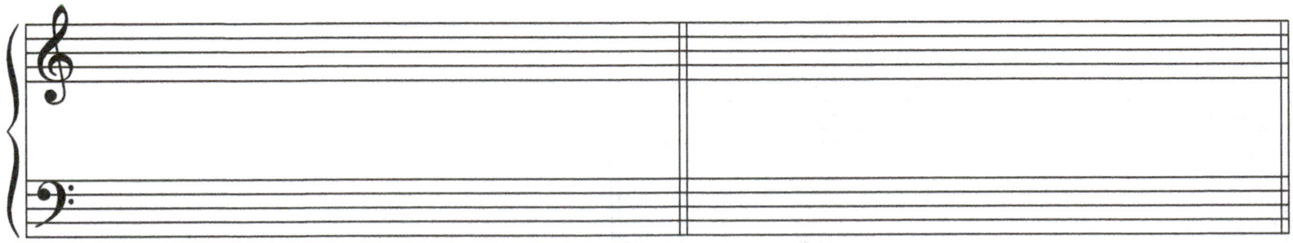

Variation 5   Variation 6

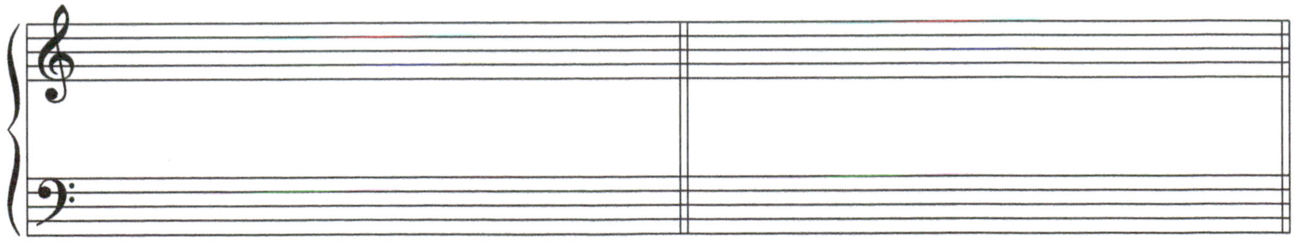

Model D:

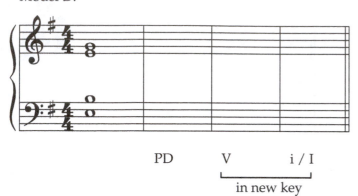

PD   V   i / I

in new key

Variation 1

Variation 2

Variation 3

Variation 4

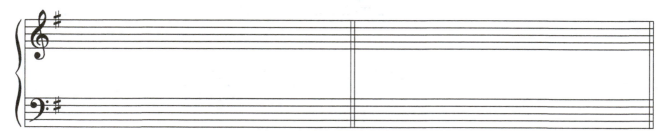

Variation 5

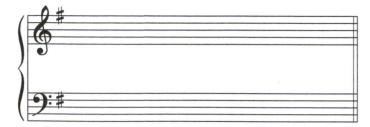

PLAYING

EXERCISE 19.10 Multiple Tonal Destinations

Given is the opening of a phrase and its continuation, which leads to three different keys. Play each progression and analyze. Be able to transpose to one other key of your choice.

1. Use roman numerals to determine the relationship of the new key to the old key.
2. Determine the pivot chord and box it, showing its roman numeral function in the original and new keys.

EXERCISE 19.11 Modulating Soprano Melodies

Determine the implied initial key and the new key of each soprano fragment. Accidentals will narrow your choices considerably, but since a diatonic melody may modulate without accidentals, there may be more than one harmonic interpretation.

Write out the bass line of the cadence and the preceding pre-dominant. Determine a possible bass for the opening of the progression. You will most likely end up in the approximate middle of the fragment, and the one or two unharmonized soprano pitches will be your modulatory pivot. Analyze and add inner voices.

A.   B.

PLAYING AND SINGING

EXERCISE 19.12 Improvising Modulating Consequents

You will now work out a modulating consequent that continues musical ideas presented in the antecedent. The result will be a parallel progressive period. Begin the consequent in the same way that the antecedent began, but insert a pivot chord approximately halfway through the consequent and cadence in the new key. Sing as you play.

A. Zumsteeg, "Nachruf" ("Farewell"), op. 6, no. 6

1. Nur ei - ne laß von dei nen-Ga - ben, ver-schwund-ne-Lie - be, _ mir_ zu - rück!
Only leave one gift   with me,   van-ished   love, re - turn to   me!

B. Mozart, "Sehnsucht nach dem Frühlinge" ("Longing for Spring"), K. 596

Fröhlich

1. Komm, lie - ber Mai, und ma - che die Bäu - me wie - der grün,
Come, dear   May,   and make   the trees   green a- gain,

C. Clara Schumann, "Cavatina," *Variations de Concert sur la Cavatine du "Pirate" di Bellini*, op. 8

Andantino

molto espressivo

sempre piano il Basso.

EXERCISE 19.13 Modulating Soprano Melodies

Sing each melody to determine the implied initial key and the new key. Accidentals will narrow your choices considerably, but since a diatonic melody may modulate without accidentals, there may be more than one harmonic interpretation.

Write out the bass line of the cadence and the preceding pre-dominant. Determine a possible bass for the opening of the progression. You will most likely end up in the approximate middle of the fragment, and the one or two unharmonized soprano pitches will be your modulatory pivot. Analyze and add inner voices.

A.   B.

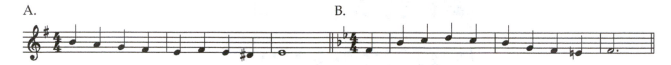

C.

D. Donizetti, *L'Elisir d'Amore*, act 1, no. 2

INSTRUMENTAL APPLICATION

EXERCISE 19.14 Improvising Consequent Phrases in Two Voices

With another melody-line player or alone at a keyboard, improvise three consequent phrases to the given antecedent phrases to create the following period types: a PIP, a PPP, and a CPP. A sample solution of a PPP is given.

A. given antecedent: added consequent forms PPP:

B.

C.

D.

E.

EXERCISE 19.15 Improvising Modulations Using Modulating Sequences

Determine the type of sequence implied by the given pattern; then continue the sequence in order to modulate to a closely related key. Close each modulation with a strong cadence in order to secure the new key. Be able to use each sequence to modulate to at least two different closely related keys.

A.

etc.

B.

etc.

C.

etc.

D.

etc.

CHAPTER 20

Binary Form and Variations

SINGING

EXERCISE 20.1 Singing Binary Forms

The following melodies are cast in binary form. Sing each example using scale degree numbers. Identify the type of binary form for each example.

A. Schubert, Minuet, D. 41

B. Mozart, Minuet, K. 104

C. Schubert, Minuet, D. 380

LISTENING

EXERCISE 20.2 Formal Listening

You will hear five short pieces, each of which is cast in binary form. You are to provide the full (two-part) label for each example. Ask yourself the following questions in order to determine the form:

1. Does the first large section cadence on the tonic (PAC or IAC)? If so, the form is **sectional**; if not, the form is **continuous**. Most binary forms are continuous, and they follow the modulatory schemes outlined in Chapter 19: In major, most pieces modulate to V; in minor, most pieces modulate to III, although modulation to minor v is fairly common too. Review the listening techniques presented in Chapter 19, and don't forget that listening is heavily dependent on educated guessing and the process of elimination. For example:

   a. If the first key is in *major* and the closing key is *major*, then most likely the modulation is to V.

   b. If the first key is in *major* and the closing key is *minor*, then most likely the modulation is to vi.

   c. If the first key is in *minor* and the closing key is *minor*, then most likely the modulation is to minor v.

   d. If the first key is *minor* and the closing key is *major*, then most likely the modulation is to III.

Hint: Usually each large section is repeated. Therefore, if you hear a chord change from the cadence to the repeat of the opening chord, then the form is continuous. It there is no change of chord, then the form is sectional.

2. If the digression opens with the same motivic material as the first half *and* there is no literal return of the opening melody in the tonic later in the second half, then the form is **simple**. If the opening material returns in tonic after the digression, then the form is **rounded**. If the motivic material from the *cadence* of the first section recurs (transposed) at the end of the second section, then the form is **balanced**.

Note: If the entire first part returns at the end of the second part, the form is rounded.

A. Haydn, String Quartet in D major, op. 76, no. 5, Menuetto
B. Boismortier, *Vivace*, from Six Duets for Bass Instruments, op. 40
C. Loeillet, Menuet in C minor. Identify each of the sequences in the digression.
D. Mozart, "Eine kleine Nachtmusik," K. 525, Menuetto
E. Beethoven, Piano Sonata no. 15 in D major, op. 28, *Andante*

EXERCISE 20.3 Bass-Line Dictation of a Binary Form

Beethoven, Piano Trio no. 8, op. 38, Trio (adapted from his septet, op. 20)
Notate the missing left-hand pitches. Provide a two-level harmonic analysis. Determine the form. What proportional structure does Beethoven employ in mm. 1–8?

EXERCISE 20.4 Aural Analysis

We now analyze without scores. Begin by studying the questions; then provide a complete formal label.

> Beethoven, "Traurig," *Lustig-Traurig,* WoO 54
> This short piece is in C minor, in $\frac{3}{8}$ meter. Repeat signs are observed.

> 1. What type of period occurs in the A section?
> 2. Notate the bass line of the first four measures on the following staff. You need notate only the "harmonic" (lowest) note of the Alberti figure, which occurs on each measure's downbeat.

EXERCISE 20.5 Aural Analysis

Study the questions that accompany each piece and provide complete formal labels.

> A. Purcell, "Ah! How Pleasant 'Tis to Love," Z. 353
>   1. Notate the opening melody (mm. 1–8) of the piece with pitch and rhythm (begin by parsing it into phrases).
>   2. The upper part of the second section of the piece is given next; notate the bass line and provide a roman numeral analysis.

A.

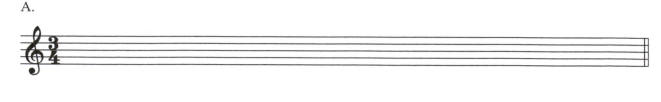

CHAPTER 21

Modal Mixture

SINGING

EXERCISE 21.1 Arpeggiating Mixture Progressions

The following arpeggiations create progressions that incorporate melodic and harmonic mixture chords. Sing them (or play them on an instrument). Listen to how often harmonies change; then analyze the progressions with roman numerals.

A.

B.

EXERCISE 21.2 Singing the Chromatic Step Descent

Sing the following progression, which involves the chromatic step descent, using solfège syllables or scale degree numbers. Improvise a consequent phrase that closes on the tonic to create a period.

EXERCISE 21.3 Sing and Play

Sing the bass melody in a comfortable octave while accompanying your singing by playing the treble chords with the right hand. Analyze.

Mozart, "O, wie will ich triumphieren," from *Abduction from the Seraglio*, act 3

denn   nun   hab   ich   vor   euch   Ruh,

denn   nun   hab   ich   vor   euch   Ruh.

LISTENING

EXERCISE 21.4 Aural Comparison of Diatonic and Mixture Progressions

Short diatonic and mixture progressions are notated here. You will hear each of the progressions performed. However, the performance of each example may not be in the order notated. If what you see is what is played, then write "OK." If what you see is played in the wrong order, write "reversed." Analyze each example.

A1.   A2.   B1.   B2.   C1.

C2.   D1.   D2.

E1.   E2.

F1.   F2.

EXERCISE 21.5 Analytical and Aural Identification of Mixture: Correction

Listen to the recording, which presents pitch differences from what is notated. Most of these differences occur on mixture harmonies. Correct the scores to conform to what is played. In addition, correct any spelling mistakes (including enharmonic errors). Analyze each progression.

A.

B.

C.

D.

E.

EXERCISE 21.6 Differentiation of Diatonic and Mixture Progressions

The following major-mode diatonic progressions are represented by roman numerals. Determine whether the roman numerals correctly represent what you hear, or whether mixture has been invoked. If what is played is what is written, write "OK." If the progressions contain mixture, then amend the roman numerals and figured bass to reflect the chromaticism. For example, given the notated progression I–vi–ii⁶–V–I, but you hear mixture on both the vi and the ii harmony, you would write "♭VI" and "ii°⁶."

A. I–ii°⁶–V⁷–I _____

B. I–vii°⁶–I⁶–IV–V _____

C. I–V–vi–ii⁶–V–I _____

D. I–vi–IV–V–I _____

E. I–iii–iv–V–vi _____

F. I–V⁶–IV⁶–V–vi _____

EXERCISE 21.7 Notating Bass and Soprano Voices

Notate the bass and soprano of each progression. Expect one or two examples of modal mixture in each progression. Analyze.

A. B.

C.

EXERCISE 21.8 Notating Bass and Soprano Voices

Notate the bass and soprano of each progression. Expect one or two examples of modal mixture in each progression. Analyze.

A. B.

C.

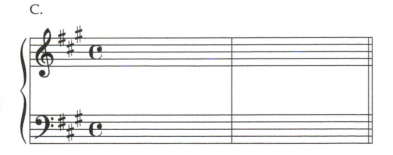

D.

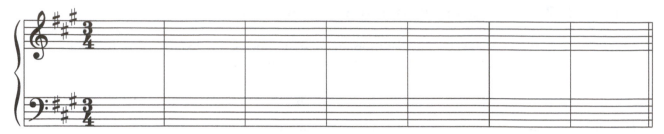

E.

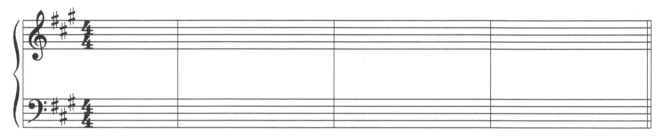

EXERCISE 21.9 Analysis and Dictation of Plagal Relations and Other Chords

Notate the bass and provide a roman numeral analysis.

A.

B.

C.

EXERCISE 21.10 Bass-Line Notation

You will hear four longer examples; the last two are from the literature. Each contains two or more instances of modal mixture. Notate the bass line of the piano accompaniment and analyze with roman numerals. The examples may modulate.

A.

B.

Andante (2 mm. intro: ♩ ♩♩**)**

C. Schubert, Impromptu in E♭ major, op. 90, D. 899

Allegro (in 1)

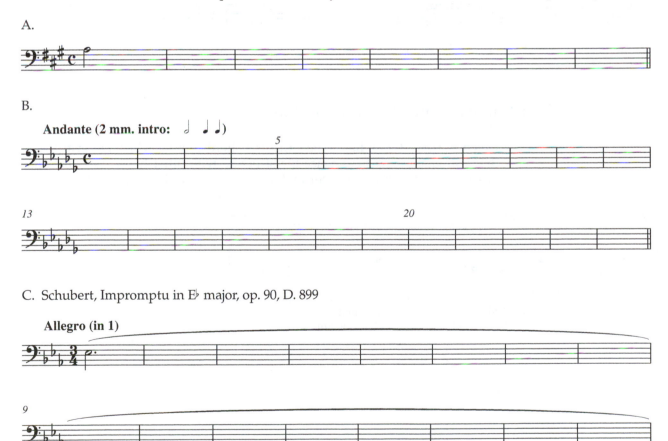

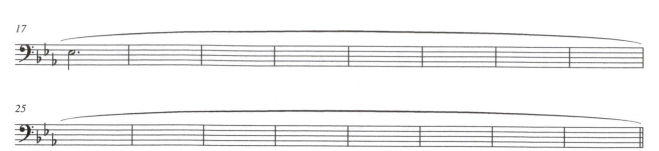

PLAYING

EXERCISE 21.11 Modal Mixture Progressions

Play the following progressions as written and in major keys up to and including three sharps.

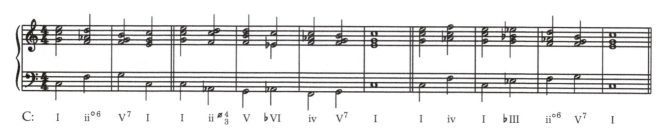

C: I   ii°⁶   V⁷   I   I   ii⌀⁴₃   V   ♭VI   iv   V⁷   I   I   iv   I   ♭III   ii°⁶   V⁷   I

EXERCISE 21.12 Expansion of Harmonic Pillars

Given is a skeleton of harmonic structural chords, under which are instructions that will enable you to enhance the structure with other harmonies, including mixture chords. Choose a meter, and play in four-voice keyboard style. Analyze.

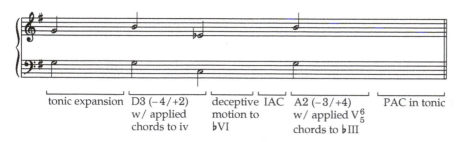

tonic expansion   D3 (−4/+2)   deceptive   IAC   A2 (−3/+4)   PAC in tonic
                   w/ applied   motion to   w/ applied V⁶₅
                   chords to iv   ♭VI   chords to ♭III

EXERCISE 21.13 Play and Sing

Sing the tune "Tiptoe thru the Tulips with Me" by Al Dubin. Then analyze the figured bass and realize in four-voice keyboard style to accompany your singing.

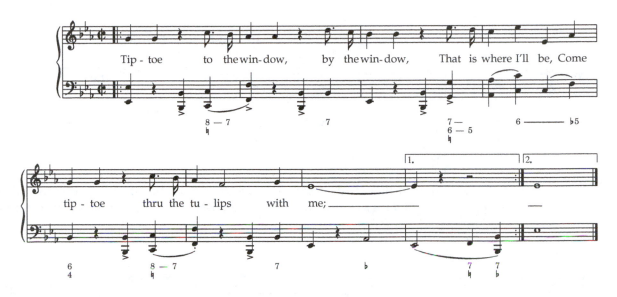

EXERCISE 21.14 Figured Bass Realization

Realize the following figured bass by adding inner voices. Analyze.

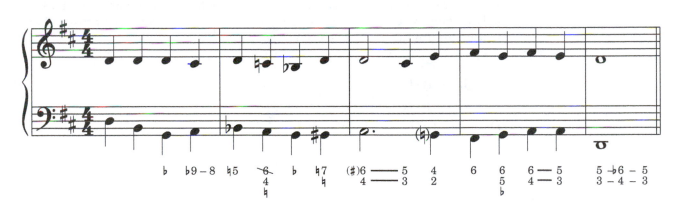

EXERCISE 21.15 Playing Mixture Progressions

Complete the following tasks.

A. Play the following progressions in four voices and in two major keys of your choice:

  1. I–ii°6–V6/5 of V–V

  2. I–♭VI–♭III–ii°6/5–V

  3. I–IV–iv–vii°7 of V–V

  4. I–I6–iv–passing V6/4–iv6–V

  5. I–♭III–V6/5 of iv–iv–V–I

B. Harmonize these soprano melodies. Include one example of mixture in each.

C. Realize the figured basses by adding upper voices.

D. Harmonize the following melody in four voices, adding as many mixture harmonies as possible; analyze. Asterisks indicate potential mixture harmonies.

EXERCISE 21.16 Plagal Relations and Other Types of Mixture

Play the progressions in major keys up to and including two sharps and flats. Be able to sing the bass while playing the other voices. *Optional:* In a broken-chord texture improvise on any two examples.

A. I–iv–ii°$^{\varnothing 4}_3$–I

B. I–iii–IV–iv–I

C. I–vi–IV–iv–cadential six-four–$^\flat$VI

D. I–V^6–V$^4_2$ of IV–IV^6–iv^6–P$^6_4$–ii°$^{\varnothing 4}_3$–I

EXERCISE 21.17 Potpourri of Mixture Progression

Play the following mixture progressions, which include step-descent bass, plagal relations, and other mixture chords as written, and in major keys up to and including two sharps and flats.

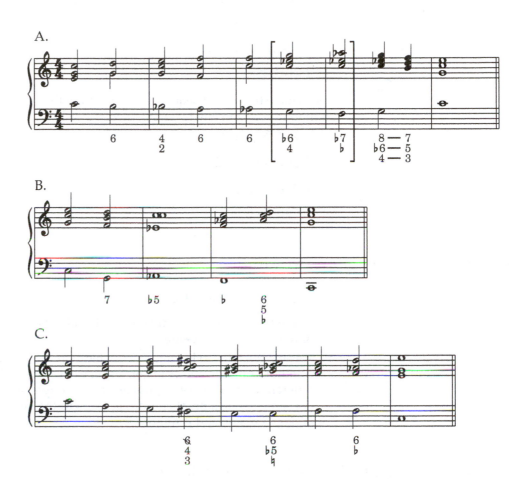

EXERCISE 21.18 Review

The following exercises review sequences, harmonization, tonicization, and modulation.

A. Harmonize each bass and soprano scale degree pattern in three different ways. Use a mix of major and minor keys. Be able to sing the given patterns while playing the other three voices.

Bass scale degree patterns:
1̂–2̂–3̂–7̂–1̂   1̂–2̂–3̂–4̂–5̂   1̂–6̂–4̂–5̂–1̂   1̂–♯1̂–2̂–3̂–4̂–♯4̂–5̂

Soprano scale degree patterns:
1̂–7̂–1̂–2̂–3̂–4̂–5̂   5̂–6̂–5̂–4̂–3̂–2̂–1̂   1̂–♭7̂–6̂–5̂–4̂–♯4̂–5̂

B. Determine the type of sequence implied from the given soprano scale degrees. Play it in four voices in any two major and minor keys. Be able to sing the given patterns while playing the other three voices.

1. $\hat{3}$–$\hat{4}$–$\hat{2}$–$\hat{3}$–$\hat{1}$–$\hat{2}$–$\hat{7}$–$\hat{1}$

2. $\hat{3}$–$\hat{2}$–$\hat{1}$–$\hat{7}$–$\hat{6}$–$\hat{5}$–$\hat{4}$

3. $\hat{5}$–$\hat{6}$–$\hat{4}$–$\hat{5}$–$\hat{3}$–$\hat{4}$–$\hat{2}$–$\hat{3}$

4. ($\hat{5}$)–$\hat{5}$–$\hat{4}$–$\hat{6}$–$\hat{5}$–$\flat\hat{7}$–$\hat{6}$

5. $\hat{1}$–$\sharp\hat{1}$–$\hat{2}$–$\sharp\hat{2}$–$\hat{3}$–$\hat{3}$–$\hat{4}$

C. Determine the type of sequence implied from the given bass scale degrees. Play it in four voices in any two major and minor keys:

1. $\hat{1}$–$\hat{6}$–$\hat{7}$–$\hat{5}$–$\hat{6}$–$\hat{4}$–$\hat{5}$–$\hat{3}$

2. $\hat{1}$–$\sharp\hat{1}$–$\hat{2}$–$\sharp\hat{2}$–$\hat{3}$–$\hat{3}$–$\hat{4}$

3. $\hat{1}$–$\hat{5}$–$\hat{6}$–$\hat{3}$–$\hat{4}$–$\hat{1}$

4. $\hat{1}$–$\hat{7}$–$\hat{6}$–$\hat{5}$–$\hat{4}$

EXERCISE 21.19 Review: Modulation

Complete the following tasks.

A. Using 8 to 10 chords, modulate from I to iii in D major, from I to V in A major, and from i to III in G minor.

B. You are given the following series of harmonies in the key of F major: F major, G minor, A minor, and B♭ major. Using each as a pivot, modulate to as many different diatonic keys as possible. For example, a C-major triad in F major (V) can become a pivot chord that leads to the keys of C major, D minor, E minor, G major, and A minor.

EXERCISE 21.20 Review: Applied Chords

Complete the following tasks at the keyboard.

A. Incorporate the progression V^7/vi to vi in the keys of D major and G minor.
B. Incorporate the progression vii°^{7}/V to V in the keys of E♭ major and A major.
C. Play a D3 sequence incorporating applied chords in the keys of B♭ major and C minor.
D. Play an A2 sequence incorporating applied chords in the key of E major.

EXERCISE 21.21 Review: Illustrations

Complete the following tasks at the keyboard.

   A. Modulate from I to V in C major; include
     1. two suspensions
     2. any sequence
   B. Modulate from i to III in E minor; include
     1. a D2 sequence
     2. a passing six-four and cadential six-four
     3. a 9–8 suspension
   C. Modulate from i to v in A minor; include
     1. a lament bass
     2. two applied chords
     3. a bass suspension

EXERCISE 21.22 Review: Figured Bass–Mixture and Applied Chords

Realize the figured bass in four voices. Analyze.

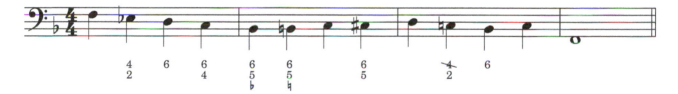

EXERCISE 21.23 Review: Unfigured Bass, Tonicization, and Modulation

Realize the unfigured bass (with given soprano) in four voices. Be able to sing either given voice while playing the other three voices. Analyze.

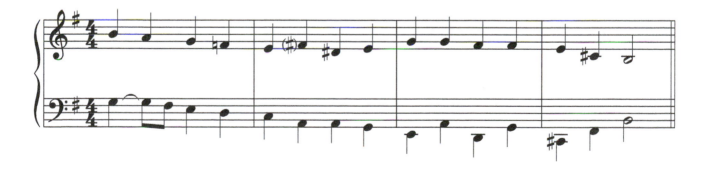

CHAPTER 22

Expansion of Modal Mixture Harmonies: Chromatic Modulation and the German *Lied*

SINGING

EXERCISE 22.1 Arpeggiating Modal Mixture Progressions

Using solfège syllables or scale degrees, sing (or play on your instrument) the following progressions, which contain chromatic pivot-chord modulations. Analyze, focusing on the location of the pivot chord. If you play the examples, be able to transpose each to at least one other key.

A.

B.

C.

EXERCISE 22.2 Sing and Play from the Literature

Sing the highest voice of the excerpts that feature modal mixture while playing the circled pitches with the left hand. Analyze.

A. Schubert, Waltz no. 2, D. 779

B. Schubert, "Suleikas Zweiter Gesang"

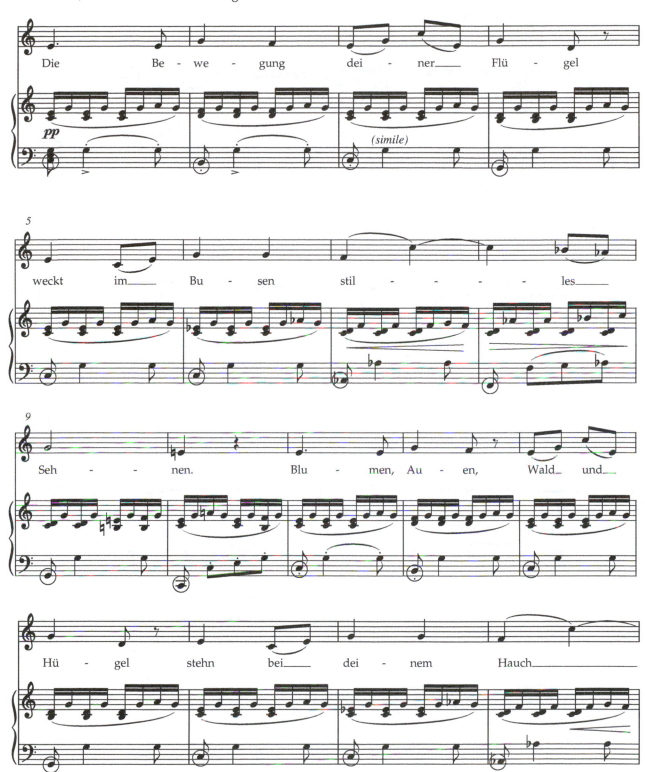

in_____ Trä - - - - - - nen,

cresc.

C. Bellini, *I Puritani*, act 1, no. 3

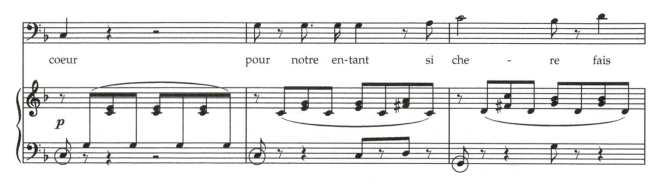

coeur   pour notre en-tant si che - re fais

p

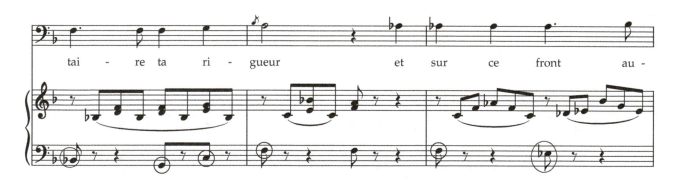

tai - re ta ri - gueur   et sur ce front au -

stè - - - re ra - mè - ne la dou - ceur

LISTENING

EXERCISE 22.3 Aural Identification of Diatonic and Chromatic Third Modulations

You will hear progressions that begin in a major key. Determine whether or not each closes in another third-related key. If it does not, write "No." If it does, provide the appropriate roman numeral for the new key (iii, ♭III, vi, ♭VI). You may wish to review the techniques for hearing modulations that were presented in Chapter 19.

A. _____   B. _____   C. _____   D. _____

E. _____   F. _____   G. _____   H. _____

EXERCISE 22.4 Aural Identification of Diatonic and Chromatic Third Modulations

This time, progressions begin in major or minor keys. Your choices include diatonic and chromatic third relations: iii, ♭III, vi, and ♭VI (in major), and III and VI (in minor).

A. _____   B. _____   C. _____

D. _____   E. _____   F. _____

EXERCISE 22.5 Analysis and Dictation

Two score examples follow, each of which modulates. The bass lines, however, are mostly missing.

1. Listen to each example, then notate the bass.
2. Provide roman numerals, circling any pivots. Watch carefully for motions to the following keys:

   • in major keys: ♭III, iii, V, ♭VI, vi
   • in minor keys: III, v, VI

A.

B.

EXERCISE 22.6 Analysis and Dictation

Two score examples follow, each of which modulates. The bass lines, however, are partially or completely missing.

1. Listen to each example, then notate the bass.
2. Provide roman numerals, circling any pivots. Watch carefully for motions to the following keys:

- in major keys: ♭III, iii, III, V, ♭VI, vi, VI
- in minor keys: III, v, VI

A.

B.

EXERCISE 22.7 Notation of Chromatic Modulations

The following examples modulate either to ♭III or ♭VI. On a separate sheet of manuscript paper, notate the bass and soprano and provide roman numerals. Remember, the standard modulatory technique establishes the initial key, employs a pivot (using a mixture chord as a pre-dominant), establishes the new key, and closes with a PAC. Exercises A and B have two sharps and are in $\frac{4}{4}$. Exercise C has one sharp and is in $\frac{4}{4}$. Exercise D has one sharp and is in $\frac{3}{4}$. Exercise E has two sharps and is in $\frac{6}{8}$.

EXERCISE 22.8 Analysis and Dictation

The following examples from the literature include chromatic modulations. Identify pivots when appropriate. Only a few bass notes are included; notate the remaining bass notes and provide roman numerals.

A. Beethoven, "Dimmi, ben mio" ("Hoffnung"), *Vier Arietten*, op. 82, no. 1

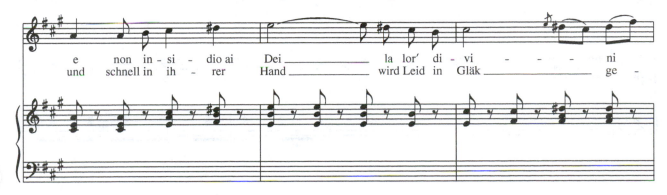

B. Wagner, *Das Rheingold*, scene 2

PLAYING

EXERCISE 22.9 Progressions Demonstrating Chromatic Third Tonicizations

Analyze and play the following progressions. Then transpose to E major and G major.

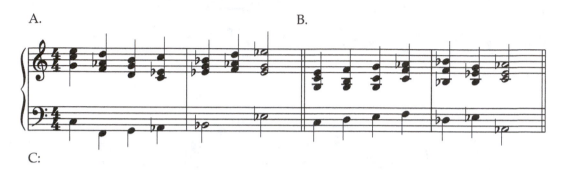

C:

EXERCISE 22.10 Soprano Harmonization

Harmonize the following soprano fragments, each of which implies a chromatic modulation. The destinations include ♭VI, ♭III, VI, and III.

EXERCISE 22.11 Figured Bass

Realize in four voices the following figured bass. Analyze. Be able to sing either outer voice while playing the remaining voices.

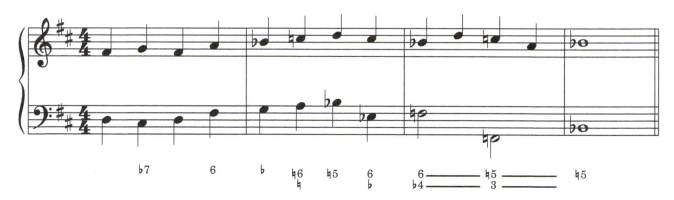

EXERCISE 22.12 Illustrations

Complete the following tasks in four voices.

 A. Given the key of D major, use iv as a pivot to tonicize ♭III.

 B. Given the key of D major, use iv as a pivot to tonicize ♭VI.

 C. Given the key of C major, use ♭VI as a pivot to tonicize ♭III.

 D. Modulate from G major to ♭III. Include two suspensions and a sequence.

EXERCISE 22.13 Pitch Reinterpretation

Follow the instructions to construct chromatic tonicizations. Each progression should contain approximately 12 chords.

 A. Modulate from D major to B♭ major; use $\hat{1}$ in the original key as the common-note pivot. Include one applied chord and two six-four chords.

 B. Modulate from F major to A♭; use $\hat{5}$ in the original key as the common-note pivot. Include one voice exchange and one pre-dominant seventh chord.

 C. Modulate from G major to E♭ major; use a common-chord pivot (it must be a mixture chord in the first key). Begin with an EPM (embedded phrase model) and include two suspensions within the progression.

 D. Modulate from C major to E major; use a common-chord pivot (it must be a mixture chord in the first key). Include a step-descent bass.

 E. Modulate from F major to A major; use $\hat{3}$ in the original key as the common-note pivot. Include an example of modal mixture in each key.

CHAPTER 23

The Neapolitan Chord (♭II)

SINGING

EXERCISE 23.1 Melodies from the Literature That Incorporate the Neapolitan

The following progressions incorporate the Neapolitan sixth chord. Sing them. Listen to how often harmonies change; then analyze the progressions with roman numerals.

A.

B.

C.

D. Schubert, Wonne der Wehmut, op. posth. 115, no. 2, D. 260

Trock - net__ nicht,   trock - net__ nicht,   Trä - nen un-glück - li-cher   Lie - be.

Trock - net__ nicht,   trock - net__ nicht,   Trä - nen un-glück - li-cher   Lie - be!

E. Mozart, String Quartet no. 15 in D minor, K. 421, *Allegro*

F. Schumann, "Ich will meine Seele tauchen," *Dichterliebe*, op. 39

G. Beethoven, Variations on "God Save the King," WoO 78

H. Bach, Mass in B minor, "Agnus Dei"
Perform as a duet or as a sing and play.

I. Vivaldi, "Et in terra pax," *Gloria*, Ryom 589
   Perform as a duet with continuo.

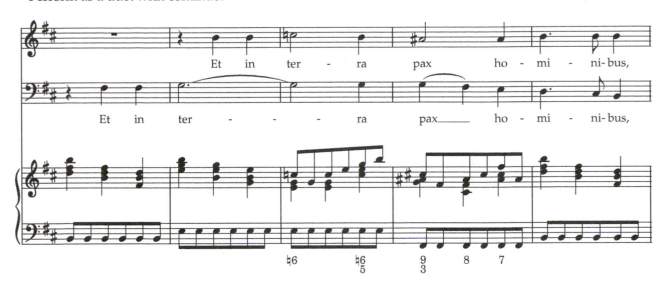

J. Beethoven, Piano Sonata in C minor, op. 10, no. 1

LISTENING

EXERCISE 23.2 Aural Comparison of ii, ii⁶, ii°⁶, and ♭II⁶

Listen to each of the following phrases, which have the following shape:

1. Either a single tonic chord or a short tonic expansion (no EPMs)
2. One of the following pre-dominant chords: ii, ii⁶, ii°⁶, ♭II⁶
3. A perfect authentic cadence (PAC)

Determine which pre-dominant chord occurs in each phrase; write the roman numeral of each pre-dominant chord on a sheet of paper. *Hint:* Each form of the supertonic is distinct:

- ♭II = major
- ii (in major keys) = minor
- ii°⁶ (in minor keys) = diminished

EXERCISE 23.3 Identifying Pre-Dominants

This exercise is identical to the previous one, except that:

1. The possible pre-dominant chords also include iv (in minor keys).
2. The possible cadences are PACs and IACs.

EXERCISE 23.4 More Pre-Dominants

The Neapolitan appears within larger musical contexts in the following examples. Listen to each example, and provide roman numerals in the blanks below the notes.

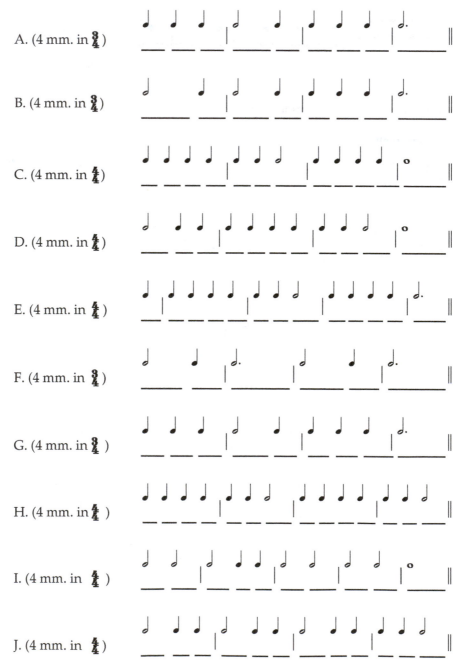

EXERCISE 23.5 Bass-Line Notation

Notate the bass voice in the following six short progressions (about six chords per progression). Include roman numerals. *Note:* Pre-dominants include ii°, ♭II⁶, iv, and iv⁶; progressions may open with an EPM.

A.   B.   C.

D.   E.   F.

EXERCISE 23.6 Bass Notation

Listen to and study each example, the upper voices for which are given. Notate the bass line and provide roman numerals for each. Arrows indicate where to notate bass notes.

A. Schubert, "Am See" ("By the Lake"), D. 124

B. Chopin, Waltz in A minor, op. 34, no. 2, BI 64

EXERCISE 23.7 Bass Notation

Listen to and study each of the following examples, the upper voices for which are given. Notate the bass line and provide roman numerals for each. Arrows indicate where to notate bass pitches.

A. Schumann, "Hör' ich das Liedchen klingen" ("I Hear the Dear Song Sounding"), *Dichterliebe*, op. 48, no. 10
This example contains a tonicization of iv.

sprin - gen   von   wil - dem Schmer - zen - drang.

B. Dvorak, *Dumka* from Piano Quintet in A major, op. 81, II

C. Schumann, String Quartet no. 3 in A major, *Assai agitato*

EXERCISE 23.8 Bass Dictation Without the Score

Determine whether the progression you hear contains a single harmonic motion or is divided into two or more subphrases. If it is divided, determine each subphrase's function (e.g., to prolong the tonic). Analyze with roman numerals; bracket and label sequences. Listen again and sing the bass and notate it. You may encounter a modulation to a closely related key.

A.

B.

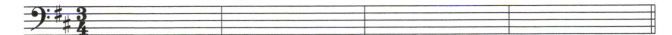

C.

EXERCISE 23.9 Notation of Progressions Incorporating the Neapolitan

Provide roman numerals and notate both the bass and soprano voices.

A.

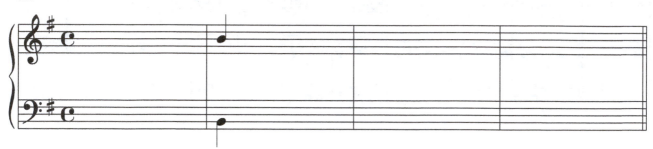

B.

C.

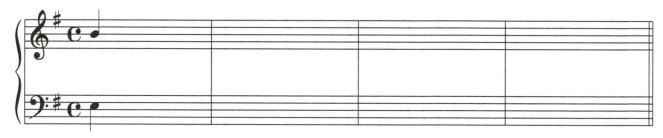

EXERCISE 23.10 Listening and Roman Numerals

Listen to the following four examples, performed with an embellished texture. Provide roman numerals for each of the examples.

A. $\frac{4}{4}$ _____ _____ | _____ _____ | _____ _____ | _____ _____

B. $\frac{6}{8}$ _____ _____ | _____ _____ | _____ _____ | _____ _____

C. $\frac{3}{4}$ _____ _____ | _____ _____ | _____ _____ | _____ _____

D. $\frac{4}{4}$ _____ _____ | _____ _____ | _____ _____ | _____ _____

EXERCISE 23.11 The Expanded Neapolitan in Homophonic Settings

Provide roman numerals and a bass line for the following examples.

A.

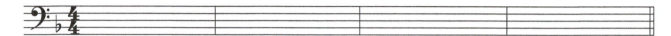

B.

C.

D.

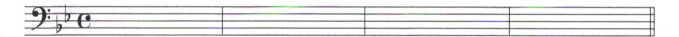

EXERCISE 23.12 Notation of Phrases Incorporating the Neapolitan

Determine whether the progression you hear contains a single harmonic motion or is divided into two or more subphrases. If it is divided, determine each subphrase's function (e.g., to prolong the tonic). Analyze with roman numerals; bracket and label the sequences. Listen again and sing the bass and notate it. You may encounter a modulation to a closely related key.

A.

B.

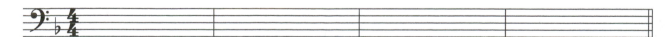

C.

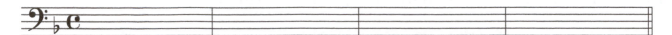

D.

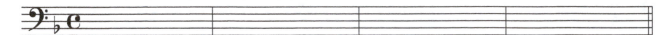

EXERCISE 23.13 Notation of Progressions Incorporating the Neapolitan

Provide roman numerals and notate both bass and soprano for Exercises A–E, each of which is four measures. Exercise F, from the literature, occupies eight measures; notate only the bass and analyze.

A.

B.

C.

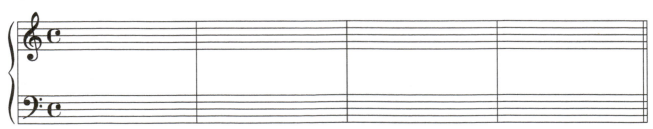

D.

E.

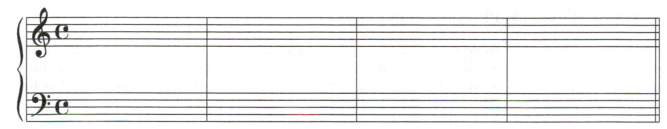

F. Vivaldi, Concerto in C major for Two Violins, Ryom 114

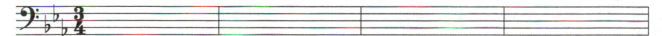

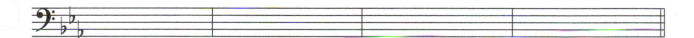

EXERCISE 23.14 The Expanded Neapolitan Embellished

Notate the bass voice and provide roman numerals for the following embellished examples of expanded Neapolitans; the last one is taken from the literature.

A.

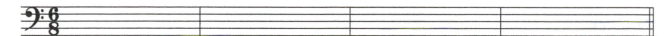

B.

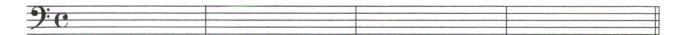

C.

D.

E. Schubert, Violin Sonata in A minor, op. posth. 137, no. 2, D. 385, Trio

EXERCISE 23.15 Phrase-Model Expansions

Study the given tonal model, which is followed by a series of variations and expansions that elaborate on the model's harmonic progression. Each variation occupies two to four measures. Notate the outer voices and analyze each of the expansions.

Phrase model A:

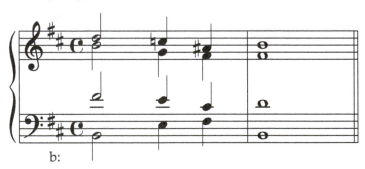

b:

Expansion 1   Expansion 2

b:

Expansion 3

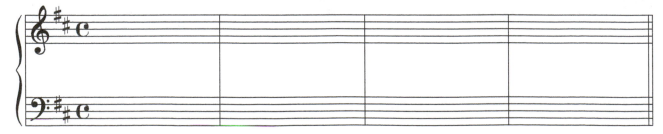

Expansion 4

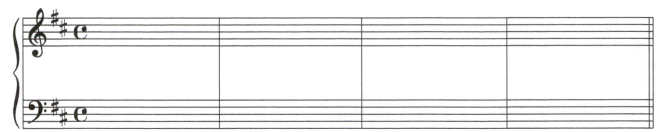

Phrase model B:

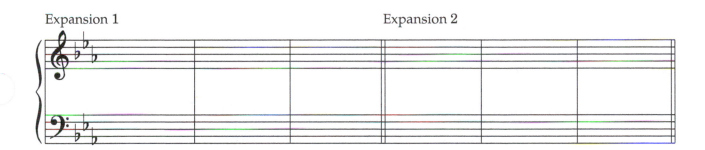

Expansion 1   Expansion 2

Expansion 3

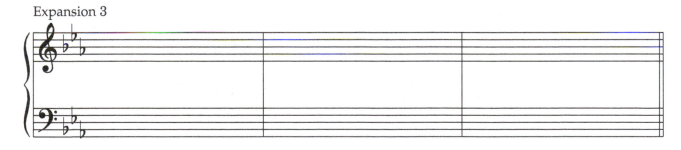

Expansion 4

Expansion 5

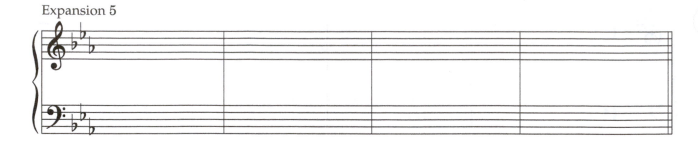

Expansion 6

PLAYING

EXERCISE 23.16   Common Neapolitan Settings

Given are four common settings of the Neapolitan sixth chord within perfect authentic cadences. Play each setting; then transpose the settings to minor keys (up to and including three sharps and three flats).

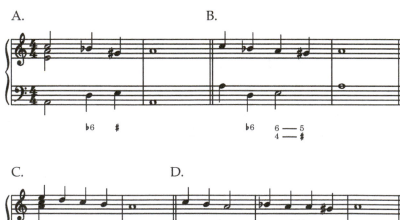

EXERCISE 23.17 Expanded Neapolitan Progressions

Given are three common contexts in which the Neapolitan is expanded. Be able to describe each context. Play in four-voice keyboard style, then transpose each to one other key of your choice.

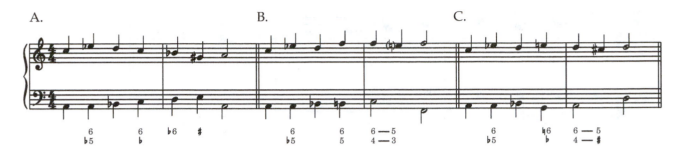

EXERCISE 23.18 Melody Harmonization

Harmonize the short soprano melodies in two different ways, one of which must include an example of ♭II⁶. *Hint*: Both settings may not need to be in minor. Feel free to include applied harmonies and mixture. Analyze.

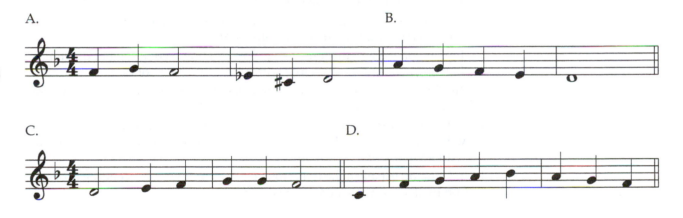

EXERCISE 23.19 Figured Bass

Realize in four voices and analyze the following figured bass using two levels. Be able to sing the bass while playing the upper voices.

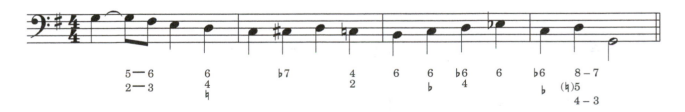

EXERCISE 23.20 Unfigured Bass

Complete the unfigured bass with soprano in four voices. Be aware of expansions of ♭II. Analyze.

EXERCISE 23.21 Illustrations

Complete the illustrations in the order described.

- A. In D minor: expand the tonic, include ♭II⁶, lead to V with an applied diminished seventh chord; close with a HC.
- B. In A minor: use a D2 (−5/+4) sequence with alternating pre-dominant sevenths that leads to ♭II⁶; close with a PAC.
- C. In F major: expand the tonic using a descending bass arpeggiation; tonicize iii using a ♭II⁶ in that key; close with a PAC in the key of iii.
- D. In C major: establish the tonic; tonicize ♭III; move to a cadential six-four chord, close with a PAC.
- E. In G minor: establish the tonic; tonicize III; include an A2 (−3/+4) sequence with applied chords that leads to VI; use ♭II⁶ as the pre-dominant; lead to V with a vii°⁷/V and close with a PAC.
- F. In D major: establish the tonic; tonicize ♭VI; continue a descending arpeggiation to ♭II; close with a PAC in D major.

EXERCISE 23.22 Figured Bass

Realize the following figured bass in four voices; analyze by using two levels. Not all suspensions may be able to be prepared. You may write in a few soprano pitches.

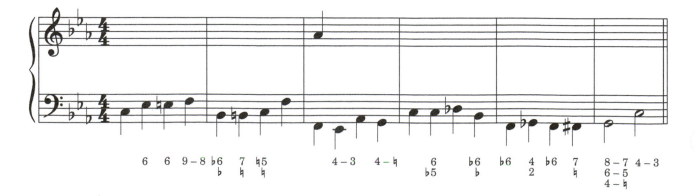

EMBELLISHMENT AND REDUCTION

EXERCISE 23.23 Embellishment

This exercise can be performed as follows: solo keyboard player, solo melodic instrumentalist, two instrumentalists (one plays the bass, the other adds the upper voices). Based on harmonic implications of the outer voices, add inner voices to the unfigured bass in the following manner:

- Arpeggiate from the bottom to the top of the chord (i.e., bass, tenor, alto, and soprano).
- Make sure the voice leading works from chord to chord (i.e., consider what you play to be linear versions of a homophonic progression).
- Consider the arpeggiations to unfold in eighth notes, such that the given quarter notes now become half notes (i.e., four eighth notes to a half note).
- In a freer texture, add passing tones and chordal leaps between alto and soprano voices, maintaining the half-note harmonic rhythm.

Follow this procedure:

1. This example moves through several keys, each of which is defined by a cadence that includes the Neapolitan harmony. Find cadences; then work from the beginning of phrases to understand the tonal motions within each phrase.

2. Intervals and accidentals are very helpful in determining harmonies. For example:

   a. A perfect fifth usually indicates a root-position harmony, a sixth usually indicates a first-inversion harmony. A diminished fifth contracts and usually moves to a root-position triad. An augmented fourth expands and usually moves to a first-inversion triad.

   b. Chromatically raised pitches indicate applied chords (they represent the temporary leading tone).

EXERCISE 23.24 Reduction

The following examples contain the Neapolitan harmony. Reduce the texture by verticalizing it into four voices. Play each reduction in the key in which it is written; then transpose to one other key of your choice. Instrumentalists who play single-line instruments will simply arpeggiate each of the harmonies (using proper voice leading).

A. Schubert, Violin Sonata in A minor, "Arpeggione," D. 821, *Allegro moderato*

B. Vivaldi, Concerto in E minor, F. XI, no. 43

CHAPTER 24

The Augmented Sixth Chord

SINGING

EXERCISE 24.1 Arpeggiating Augmented Sixth Chords

Using solfège or scale degrees, sing (or play on your instrument) the following progressions, which incorporate the augmented sixth chord. Analyze the harmonic progressions in each example. The harmonic rhythm is generally one chord per measure. Exercise A has been analyzed for you. If you play the exercises on your instrument, transpose to one other key of your choice.

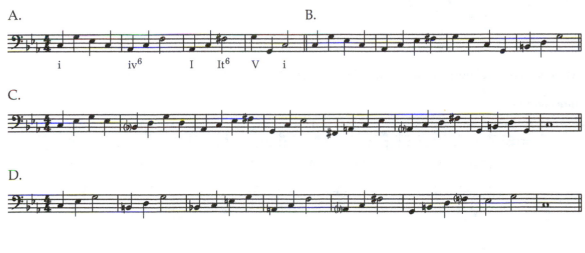

EXERCISE 24.2 Singing Augmented Sixth Chords Versus V⁷

Using scale degrees or solfège, sing (or play on your instrument) the following progressions, which incorporate enharmonic use of the augmented sixth chord. Be able to identify the starting and ending keys for each exercise.

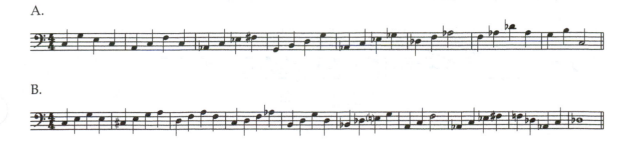

EXERCISE 24.3 Singing Augmented Sixth Chords from the Literature

Sing the following melodies. Be able to accompany yourself by playing the given bass pitches. For Exercise D use the given roman numerals to guide your bass pitches.

Extra credit: Use your right hand to play one or two pitches of the missing chord members.

A. Mozart, "Ach Belmonte! Ach, mein Leben!" from *The Abduction from the Seraglio*, act 2

B. Mozart, "Welcher Wechsel herrscht in meiner Seele," from *The Abduction from the Seraglio*, act 2

C. Mozart, "Verraten, Verspottet," from *Cosi fan tutte*, act 2

D. Schubert, String Quartet no. 13 in A minor, "Rosamunde," op. 29, D. 804

i   ii⁶   V   i   V   i   iv⁶ It⁶   V

LISTENING

Hearing Augmented Sixth Chords

The French augmented sixth chord is the easiest to identify because of its distinctive sound. Not only do its two tritones create an exotic effect, but they also often create a major-second clash in the inner pitches. It is more difficult to distinguish the Italian from the German augmented sixth chord because they sound so similar. A starting point is to recognize that the It^6 is the simplest of the three chords and thus will sound less full than the others; the Ger_5^6 contains four distinct pitches and sounds like a complete dominant seventh chord (the significance of which we will take up soon). The resolution of the It^6 and Ger_5^6 chords will usually betray their nationality: The Italian sixth moves directly to V, but the Ger_5^6 usually resolves first to a cadential six-four chord.

EXERCISE 24.4A Aural Detection of Augmented Sixth Chords

These progressions may or may not use the augmented sixth chord as a pre-dominant. Mark "Y" (yes) or "N" (no), depending on whether or not you hear an augmented sixth.

A. _____   B. _____   C. _____   D. _____   E. _____   F. _____   G. _____   H. _____

EXERCISE 24.4B Identifying Pre-Dominants

Listen to the examples and in the given answer blanks label the chord used as a pre-dominant; your choices are: iv, ii°⁶, ♭II⁶, or +6 (specify type of +6; remember that the It^6 moves directly to V and the Ger_5^6 moves to a cadential six-four).

A. _____   B. _____   C. _____   D. _____   E. _____   F. _____   G. _____   H. _____

I. _____   J. _____   K. _____   L. _____   M. _____   N. _____   O. _____

EXERCISE 24.5 Bass-Line Notation of Augmented Sixth Chords

Notate the bass and analyze the following examples with pre-dominant harmonies that include the augmented sixth chord. Focus first on the underlying chord progression and the type of pre-dominant. One way to distinguish supertonic harmonies (including ♭II) from augmented sixth harmonies is that the bass of supertonic harmonies ascends to V but the bass of the augmented sixth descends to V. Thus, once you have determined the bass's motion, you need only distinguish between ii and ♭II.

A.

B.

C.

D.

E.

EXERCISE 24.6 Bass-Line Notation of Augmented Sixth Chords

Notate the bass and analyze the following examples with pre-dominant harmonies that include the augmented sixth chord. Focus first on the underlying chord progression and the type of pre-dominant.

A.

B.

C.

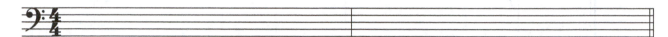

D.

E.

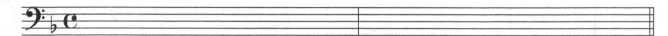

EXERCISE 24.7 Bass-Line Notation from the Literature

The following excerpts include the upper voices. Notate the basses and include roman numerals.

A. Schubert, "Wehmut" ("Melancholy"), op. 22, no. 2, D. 772

B. "Lamento di Magdalena"

C. Haydn, String Quartet in E♭ major, op. 76, no. 6, Hob III.80, *Allegretto*

EXERCISE 24.8 Longer Dictation

Notate the bass and soprano of the four-measure examples and analyze. Exercises C and D modulate.

A.

B.

C.

D.

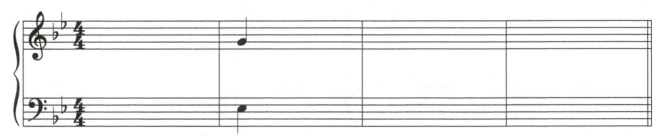

EXERCISE 24.9 Bass-Line Dictation from the Literature

The following excerpts include the upper voices. Notate the basses and include roman numerals.

A. Schubert, "Die Liebe hat gelogen" ("Love Has Lied"), op. 23, no. 1, D. 751

Die Lie - be hat ge-lo - gen, die Sor - ge la - stet schwer, be-

B. Gluck, "Sweet Affection, Heavenly Treasure," Trio from *Orpheus and Eurydice,* act 3, no. 50

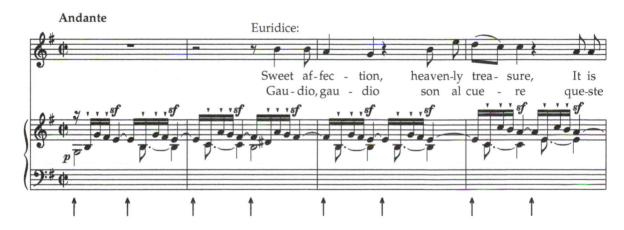

Sweet af-fec - tion, heaven-ly trea - sure, It is
Gau - dio, gau - dio son al cue - re que-ste

Orpheus:

bliss to feel _ thy chain, _   it is bliss to _ feel _ thy chain. Sweet af-
pe - nedell'_ a - mor, _   que-ste pe - ne _dell'_ a - mor. Tu, a-

fec - tion,   how much pleas - sure   Thou dost bring   to tem - per pain, _
mo - re,   qual pia - ce - re   mi - schi fra   af - fan -   no tal, _

EXERCISE 24.10 Dictation of Embellished Examples

Notate the bass lines of each of the following phrases and analyze with roman numerals.

A.   begins with upbeat

B.   **Allegretto**

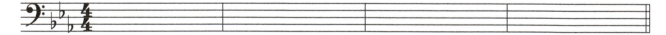

C.   **Lento**

D. Haydn, String Quartet in B♭ major, op. 50, no. 1, Hob III.44, *Adagio non lento*

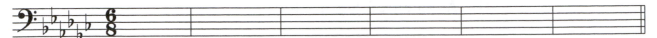

E. Gluck, "Sorrowing Mortal," from *Orpheus and Eurydice,* act 1, no. 23

Lento

EXERCISE 24.11 Dictation of Expanded ♭VI and Conversion to Augmented Sixth

Notate the bass and soprano lines for each excerpt except the last one, where you will notate only the bass (do not notate repeated pitches). Analyze.

A.

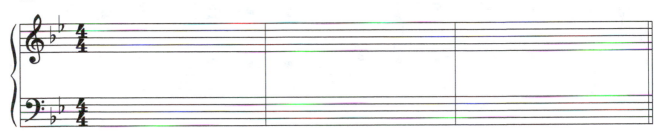

B.

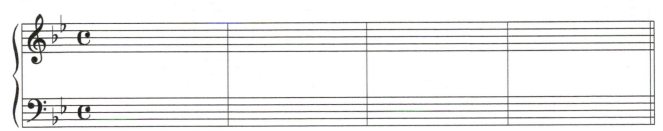

C.   notate upbeat

EXERCISE 24.12 Dictation of Modulations Featuring the Augmented Sixth Chord

Each of the four modulating phrases contains a prominent augmented sixth chord. You are given the upper voices in the first two exercises; notate only the bass and analyze. Notate both soprano and bass for Exercises C and D. Analyze using two levels.

A.

B.

C.

D.

EXERCISE 24.13 Aural Examples from the Literature

Notate the bass for each of the following examples. Analyze.

A. Haydn, Piano Sonata no. 38 in F major, Hob XVI.23, *Adagio*

B. Beethoven, String Quartet no. 3 in D major, op. 18, no. 3, Minore

C. Gluck, "His Moving Elegies," from *Orpheus and Eurydice*, act 2, no. 27
    This example begins on V. What harmony is prolonged over this example?

EXERCISE 24.14 Dictation

The following progressions contain expanded pre-dominants and enharmonic reinterpetation of augmented sixth chords. Notate bass and soprano; analyze. Possible expansions are as follows:

- $iv \rightarrow P_4^6 \rightarrow iv^6$
- $iv^6 \rightarrow P_4^6 \rightarrow ii^{\circ 6}$
- $iv \rightarrow P_4^6 \rightarrow +6$
- $Ger_5^6 \rightarrow P_4^6 \rightarrow Ger^{\circ 7}$
- $iv^6 \rightarrow P_4^6 \rightarrow \flat II^6$

A.

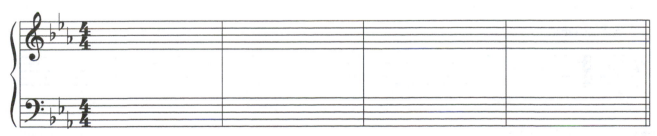

B.

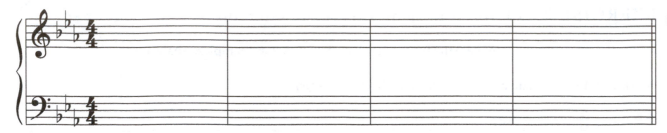

C.

D.

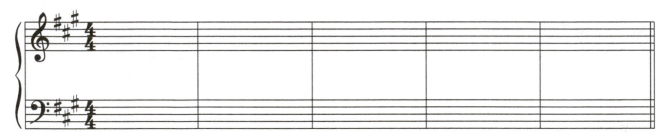

EXERCISE 24.15 Aural Examples from the Literature

Notate the bass and provide roman numerals for each of the following examples.

A. Haydn, Piano Sonata in D major, Hob XVI.33, *Adagio*

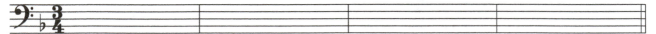

B. Schubert, Waltz in C minor, *Wiener Deutsche*, no. 6, D. 128
   This example is slightly longer (12 mm.), but the bass line should be easy to follow. What is the chromatic pre-dominant chord that leads to the final cadence?

Allegro molto

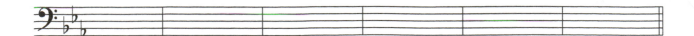

C. Schumann, Waltz in A minor, *Albumblätter,* op. 124, no. 6

Allegro

EXERCISE 24.16 Two-Voice Dictation

Notate the florid two-voice counterpoint. Include a harmonic analysis.

A.

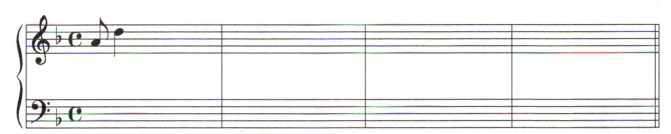

B.

C.

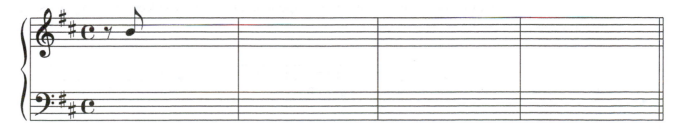

PLAYING

EXERCISE 24.17 Augmented Sixth Chord Models

Play the four-voice augmented sixth chord models as written and in minor and major keys up to and including two sharps and two flats.

EXERCISE 24.18 Figured Bass

Realize the two figured basses, each of which contains a bass descent.

A.   B.

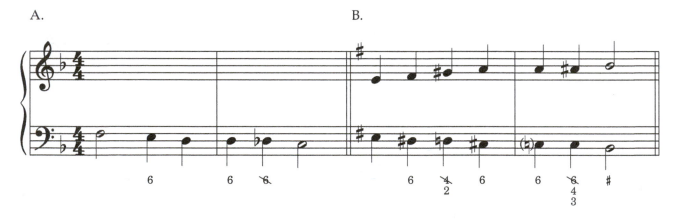

EXERCISE 24.19 Review: Unfigured Bass

The following unfigured bass and soprano contains sequences, applied chords, modulations, mixture, and the Neapolitan. Play in four voices and analyze using two levels.

PLAYING AND SINGING

EXERCISE 24.20 Figured Bass

Add the inner voices to the given soprano, bass, and figures. Analyze using two levels. Be able to sing the bass while you play the other voices.

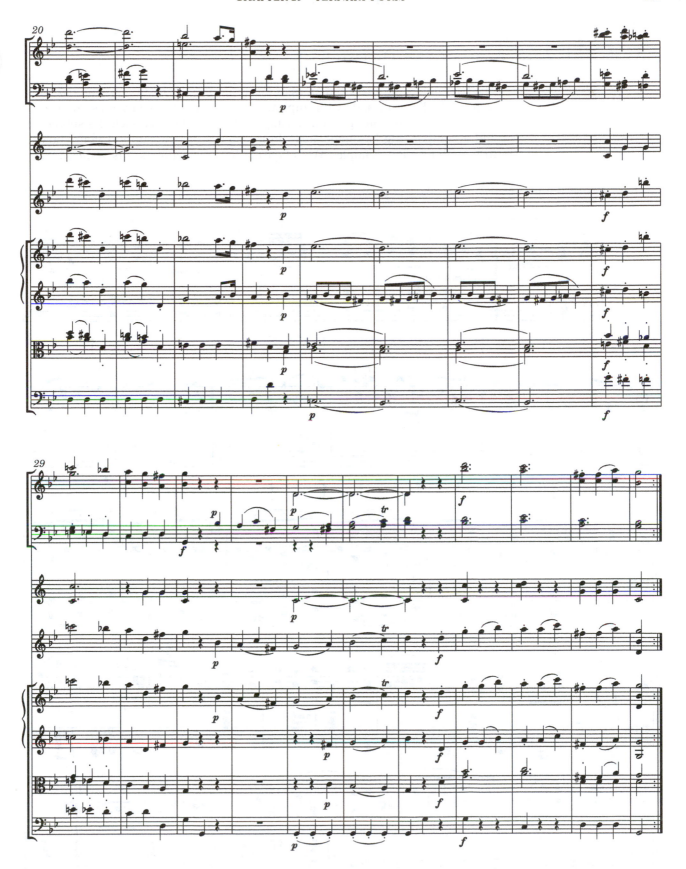

EXERCISE 25.5 Analysis and Dictation

The bass line is omitted from areas of this example. Notate the missing bass notes (arrows) by listening and by the implications of the given upper voices. Analyze the piece in its entirety and provide a complete formal label that includes subsections and accompanying harmonic areas. In a sentence or two, support your choice of form with relevant examples. What type of phrase structure occurs in mm. 1–8?

Brahms, Waltz in E minor, *Waltzes for Piano*, op. 39, no. 4

EXERCISE 25.6 Aural Identification and Analysis of Ternary and Binary Forms

We now listen to and answer some more questions about ternary and binary forms without the aid of a score. Provide a formal diagram and formal label. Include subsections in your diagram. Support your answers carefully in a short paragraph. An incomplete score follows for mm. 1–5. Notate the missing bass line.

Schumann, "Winterzeit I," *Album für die Jugend*, op. 68, no. 38

PLAYING

EXERCISE 25.7 Figured Bass

Add the inner voices to the given soprano, bass, and figures. Analyze using two levels. Be able to sing the bass while you play the other voices.

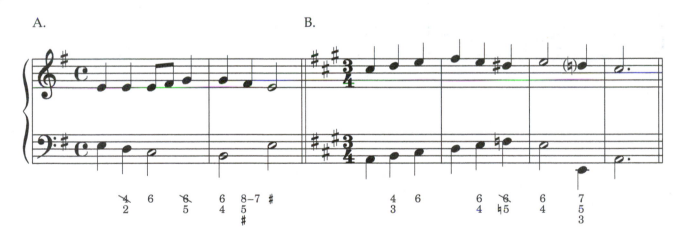

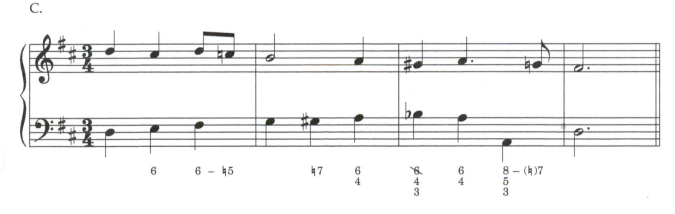

EXERCISE 25.8 Road Map

A musical outline follows that includes instructions for your keyboard composition and the length of each section. Analyze.

establish
tonic
contrapuntally

move to ♭VI
through passing
$V_3^4/♭VI$

establish ♭VI harmonically
for 2–3 mm. End up on
$V^7/♭VI$. Treat it as a Ger $_5^6$
and resolve to V–I in new key.

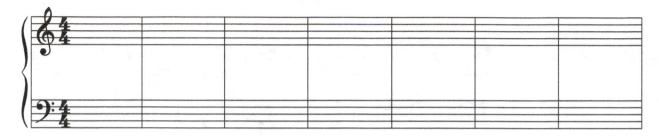

begin A2 (–3/+4) +applied $_5^6$;
treat arrival as minor tonic

use D2 (–5/+4) to mod.
to III of this key.

expand +6 with V in this new key;
end w/PAC. What key is this?

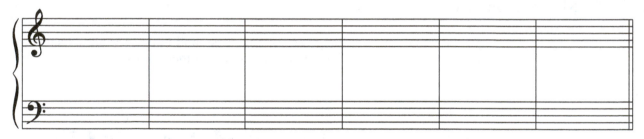

Rondo

LISTENING

EXERCISE 26.1 Aural Analysis

You will hear a rondo, for which no score is included. Answer the following questions and complete the tasks:

Beethoven, Piano Sonata no. 8 in C minor, "Pathétique," op. 13, *Allegro*

1. Notate mm. 1–8 of the soprano melody of the refrain.

2. Discuss the tonal and phrase/formal structure of the refrain. Consider modulations, sequences, and unusual phrase characteristics.
3. The B section is in a major key. Based on your knowledge of rondo form, suggest Beethoven's most likely tonal possibility or possibilities.
4. What harmonic procedure occurs in the B section?
5. Shown are the upper voices for a passage within the B section. Notate the missing bass voice and provide roman numerals (mm. 43–53).

6. Are there significant changes in repetitions of the refrain? Describe.
7. In what key is the C section? What contrapuntal technique characterizes this section?
8. Is this a five- or seven-part rondo? If seven, what changes occur in the repetition of the B section?
9. The closing measures of the movement are reproduced next. What formal label might you apply to this section? Provide roman numerals for these measures. Why might Beethoven have briefly tonicized the key that he does in mm. 200–206?

EXERCISE 26.2 Potpourri of Binary, Rondo, and Ternary Forms

You will hear three movements; no scores are included except for excerpts that accompany specific questions. Answer the following questions.

A. Haydn, Piano Sonata in D major, Hob XVI.19, Finale

    1. Make a formal diagram that includes important key areas.
    2. Do recurrences of material remain the same or change?

B. Haydn, String Quartet in G minor, op. 20, no. 3, Hob III.33, Menuetto, *Allegretto*

    1. Make a formal diagram that includes important keys.
    2. Below is the incomplete score of mm. 1–10. Notate the bass, give roman numerals, and then make a phrase–period diagram.

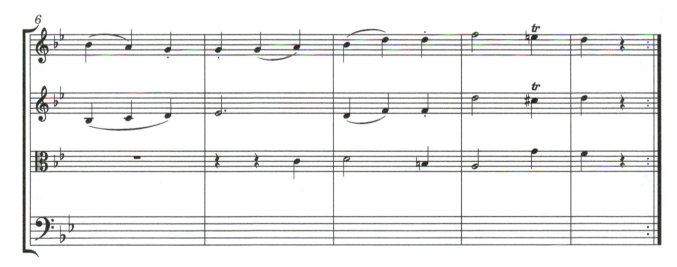

3. What contrapuntal device does Haydn employ later in this large section?
4. Next is the music that occurs near the close of the first large section. Notate the bass and provide roman numerals.

5. The music that occurs near the end of another formal section follows. Notate the bass. What is the harmonic techique in this excerpt?

EXERCISE 26.3 Aural Analysis

You will hear a rondo, for which no score is included. Answer the following questions and complete the tasks:

Beethoven, Piano Sonata no. 9 in E major, op. 14, no. 1, *Allegro commodo*

1. There is a transition between the refrain and the first episode; from what material is it derived?
2. There is a transition that moves to the C section. What crucial harmonic change occurs at the beginning of the transition, and how does it help prepare the key of G major?
3. The key of the C section is G major. Is this unusual, and if so, why?
4. What rhythmic effect occurs in the final statement of the refrain?
5. Make a formal diagram that includes the prevailing key of each section. Make sure that you have answered the preceding questions, since they will guide your listening.

EXERCISE 26.4 Potpourri of Aural Analysis of Binary, Rondo, and Ternary Forms

You will hear two movements; no scores are included. Answer the following questions.

A. Schumann, *Kreisleriana*, op. 16, no. 3

1. Make a detailed formal diagram that includes the form and keys of any subsections.
2. What harmonic technique occurs in the opening section of the piece?

B. Mozart, Sonata no. 3 in A major for Flute and Piano, K. 12, *Allegro*

1. Make a formal diagram.

2. Make a phrase–period diagram of the opening period (the meter is $\frac{3}{8}$, felt as one beat per measure).

3. The material that follows the opening period is closely related to the opening material, yet is deployed differently; discuss.

EXERCISE 26.5 Analysis and Listening

You will next hear a movement from a Schubert string quartet; no score is included. Answer the following questions.

Schubert, String Quartet no. 11 in E major, op. 125, no. 2, D. 353, *Allegro vivace*

1. Make a formal diagram.
2. Make a phrase–period diagram for mm. 1–12. Discuss unusual features.
3. What chromatic harmony is tonicized in the following section? *Hint*: Compare the opening sonority of that section with the end of the preceding section; focus on the motion in the cello part.

PLAYING

EXERCISE 26.6 Reduction

The following example contains various chromatic harmonies, in particular, Neapolitan and augmented sixth chords. Reduce the texture by verticalizing it into four voices, then play the homophonic progression.

Mozart, String Quartet no. 15 in D minor, K. 421

CHAPTER 27

Sonata Form

LISTENING

EXERCISE 27.1 Analysis and Dictation

Analyze the form of this movement and answer the following questions. In addition, there are a few "bare spots" in the music, areas where the bass line is missing. Notate the bass line for these areas, marked with brackets.

Mozart, Piano Sonata in F major, K. 332, *Allegro*

1. What key is implied (in addition to F major) in mm. 1–4?
2. What contrapuntal and metric techniques occur in mm. 5–9?
3. What key is implied at the beginning of the transition? What about at the end of the transition? What key actually occurs at the STA?
4. What harmonic technique occurs in mm. 60–65? (Identification of this technique will aid in notating the missing bass line.)
5. What is the motivic relationship between the FTA theme and the theme in mm. 86–88?
6. Explore thematic/motivic relationships between mm. 89–93 and the opening two measures of the development.
7. What key is strongly implied in mm. 118–126? Is this key ever realized?
8. Does anything unusual occur in the FTA and the STA of the recapitulation? If so, describe.

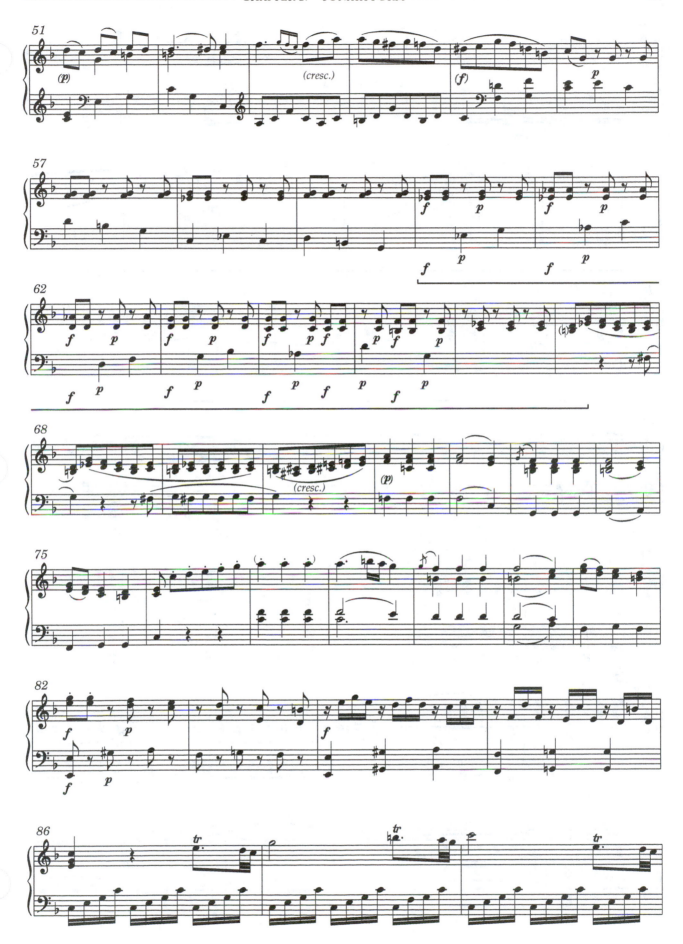

EXERCISE 27.2 Aural Analysis

You will hear a sonata movement with no score provided. Answer the series of questions. Begin by making a detailed form chart.

Mozart, Piano Sonata in A minor, K. 310, *Allegro maestoso*

Exposition

1. What type of sequence is implied in the FTA?
2. Name the type of transition. Near the end of the transition, what unusual key is implied? (Be specific.)
3. In what key is the STA? Is this a monothematic sonata?
4. Is there a closing section? If so, how many subsections occur within the closing section?

Development

5. What key opens the development? What thematic material is used in this section?
6. The development comprises two large sequences. What types are they. (Be careful, the first sequence is quite spread out.)
7. What harmony immediately precedes the V of the retransition and continues to expand V within the retransition?

Recapitulation

8. Compare the opening of the transition in the recapitulation to the opening of the transition in the exposition. Describe the difference in texture between these two places.
9. In what key is the STA of the recapitulation?
10. If there is a closing section in the recapitulation, compare it to the exposition: Are there any significant changes in the recapitulation's closing section (other than the obvious transposition to the tonic)?

EXERCISE 27.3 Aural Analysis

You will hear a sonata movement with no score provided. There are two types of tasks in this exercise. First you must answer a series of questions similar to those in Exercise 27.2 that will accompany each movement. The second task involves identifying formal sections and their keys. As you listen to the movement your instructor will call out numbers that represent points in the formal structure. You should answer the questions that correspond to these numbers.

A. Haydn, Symphony no. 45 in F♯ minor, "Farewell Symphony," Hob I.45, *Allegro assai*

In mm. 1–16 (essentially one large phrase), the harmony changes every two measures except for a couple of spots: identify each harmony in the blanks provided.

mm.	1–2	3–4	5–6	7–8	9	10	11–12	13	14	15–16
	___	___	___	___	___	___	___	___	___	___

1. Name the formal segment. What key is it in?
2. Name the formal segment. What key does it begin in?
3. Name the formal segment. What key is it in? What is the origin of this material?
4. Name the formal segment. Has this been heard before and, if so, how does it differ from its earlier appearance?
5. Name the formal segment. What is unusual about it and why?
6. What type of transition occurs in the exposition? To what tonal area does it lead? A sequence appears in it; what type?
7. In what tonal area does the exposition close?
8. How long is the retransition?

B. Beethoven, Piano Sonata no. 3 in C major, op. 2, no. 3, *Allegro assai*

1. Make a formal diagram that includes important keys.
2. Do mm. 1–8 form a period? Support your answer.
3. Shown is the incomplete score from the opening of which formal section? Notate the bass line and provide roman numerals.

CHAPTER 28

New Harmonic Tendencies

LISTENING

EXERCISE 28.1 Dictation

Notate bass and soprano voices, and provide a roman numeral analysis. Finally, in a few sentences describe the type of ambiguity involved.

EXERCISE 28.2 Dictation and Analysis

Notate the bass voice, and provide a roman numeral analysis. Finally, in a few sentences describe the type of ambiguity involved.

A. Brahms, "An die Nachtigall" ("To the Nightingale"), op. 46, no. 4

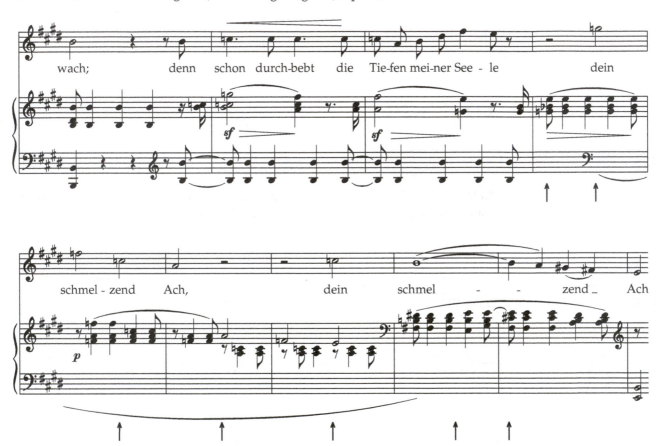

B. Beethoven, Symphony no. 2 in D major, op. 36, *Allegro molto*
Provide missing bass notes.

EXERCISE 28.5 Dictation

Determine the goals of harmonic motion for the following modulating passages, where note values below the staff indicate harmonic rhythm. Then notate the bass and soprano and provide roman numerals. Expect both diatonic and mixture pivots as well as enharmonic diminished sevenths. Use figured bass notation to label embellishing tones. Finally, add logical inner voices, focusing on enharmonic diminished sevenths.

A.

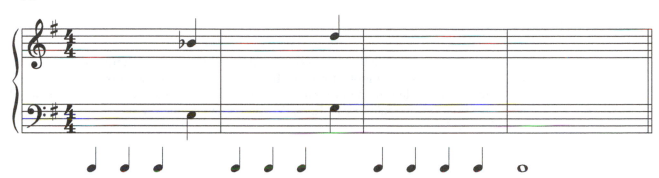

B.

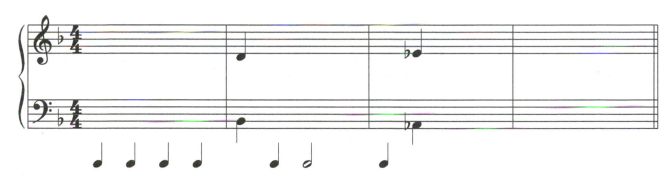

EXERCISE 28.6 Dictation

Notate both the bass and soprano in these progressions, which modulate by enharmonic diminished sevenths. Analyze, marking the pivot carefully. Begin by determining the new key; then work backward from the cadence until you encounter the diminished seventh chord. *Hint*: A diminished seventh chord will often appear twice, first in its usual diatonic context, and then later in its enharmonic "chameleon-like" guise, to prepare the new key.

A.

B.

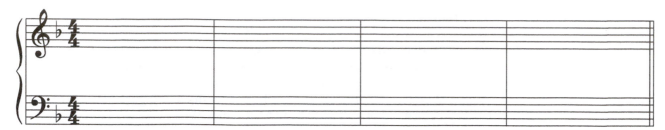

EXERCISE 28.7 Dictation

Listen to and notate the outer voices of these examples, which modulate by using the three types of pivot chords we have discussed: diatonic, mixture, and enharmonic. Provide roman numerals and interpret the pivot chord. The possible tonal destinations in major are ii, ♭II, iii, IV, V, ♭VI, vi; in minor, the possibilities are III, iv, v, and VI.

A.

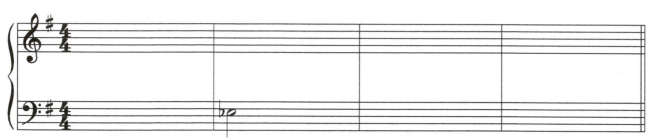

B.

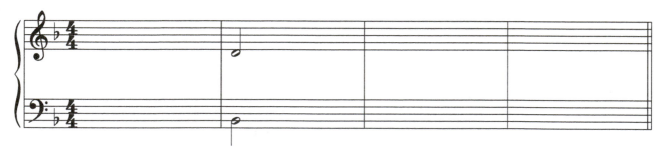

C.

EXERCISE 28.8 Dictation

Notate both the bass and soprano in the following progression, which modulates by means of enharmonic diminished sevenths. Analyze, marking the pivot carefully. Begin by determining the new key; then work backward from the cadence until you encounter the diminished seventh chord. *Hint*: A diminished seventh chord will often appear twice, first in its usual diatonic context, and then later in its enharmonic "chameleon-like" guise, to prepare the new key.

upbeat

EXERCISE 28.9 Dictation

Listen to and notate the outer voices of these examples, which modulate by using the three types of pivot chords we have discussed: diatonic, mixture, and enharmonic. Provide roman numerals and interpret the pivot chord. The possible tonal destinations in major are ii, ♭II, iii, IV, V, ♭VI, vi, and VI; in minor, the possibilities are III, iv, v, and VI.

A.

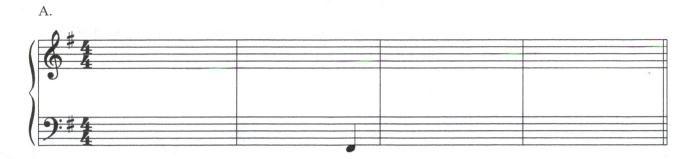

B.

C.   begins on beat 3

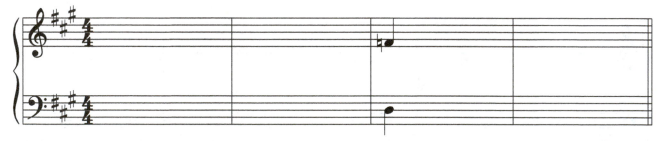

PLAYING

EXERCISE 28.10 Warm-up and Review

Complete the following tasks.

A. Modulate from E major to ♭III by using modal mixture in the home key to prepare the new key. You may write out a basic sketch of what you will be playing. Analyze your work. Also include in your example:

1. A D2 (–5/+4) or A2 (–3/+4) sequence in either key. You may use either a diatonic or an applied chord sequence.
2. A tonicization of the Neapolitan.
3. An expansion of the pre-dominant area in ♭III that includes both the Ger$_5^6$ and Ger^7 chord.

B. Add inner voices to the following unfigured bass and soprano melody. Analyze and transpose to one other key of your choice.

EXERCISE 28.11 New Harmonic Procedures and Chromatic Chords

Complete the following tasks in four voices; analyze.

A. In D major and B♭ major play the progression I–iv–iv⁶–V–♭VI–ii°⁶₅–I (begin with $\hat{5}$ in the soprano).

B. In G major, play a progression in which tonal ambiguity arises because of the confusion between the tonic and IV.

C. Modulate from E♭ major to D major using an enharmonic augmented sixth chord.

EXERCISE 28.12 Figured Bass and Illustration

A. Figured Bass

Using four voices, realize the given figured bass, which begins off-tonic. Be aware of other types of ambiguity, including plagal relations, the reciprocal process, and semitonal voice leading, as well as enharmonic modulation.

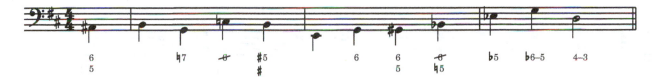

B. Play a progression in F major that begins off-tonic. You may wish to stabilize a chord such as vi for at least two measures before moving to the tonic.

EXERCISE 28.13 Warm-up and Review

Continue the following progressions based on the pivot-chord instructions. Transpose to two other keys of your choice.

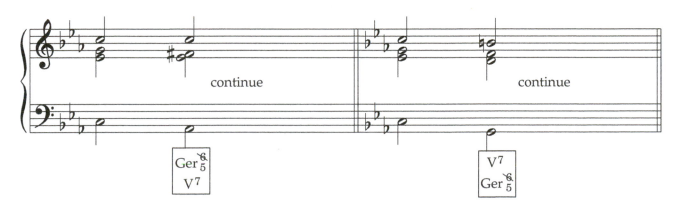

EXERCISE 28.14 Enharmonic Modulation by Means of Diminished Seventh Chords

A. Use the diminished seventh chord D–F–A♭–C♭ to modulate from E♭ major to C major.

B. Interpret each member of the diminished seventh chord C♯–E–G–B♭ as a root that leads to its own tonic. Be able to spell the chord correctly in each of the four keys. Then, play a progression that begins in one of the keys and includes the diminished seventh as a pivot that leads to one of the other distantly related keys.

EXERCISE 28.15 Diminished Seventh Enharmonic Modulation

Study the following examples that enharmonically reinterpret a diminished seventh chord to modulate to distant keys. Then, play the short progressions and specify the key to which the diminished seventh leads. Finally, play longer progressions (approximately 6–8 chords) that establish the initial key, C major. Modulate by means of the diminished seventh chord and close with a strong cadence in the new key.

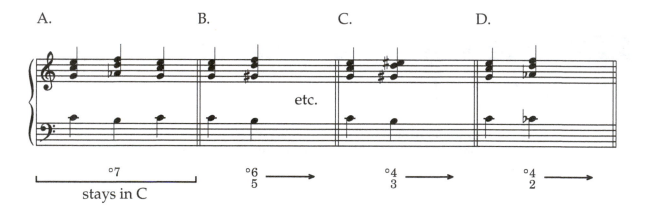

The Rise of Symmetrical Harmony in Tonal Music

LISTENING

EXERCISE 29.1 Analysis and Dictation

Listen to the following examples and study the given upper voices. Then notate the bass and provide a roman numeral analysis.

A.

B.

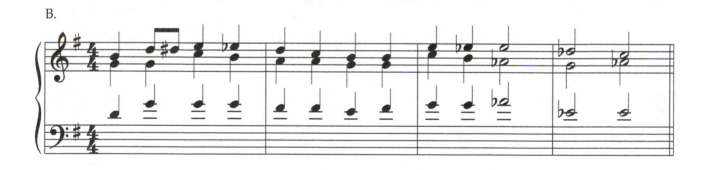

C.

EXERCISE 29.2 Analysis and Dictation

Provided are the upper parts of examples. Listen to and study what is given, then notate the bass and provide a roman numeral analysis.

A. Beethoven, Bagatelle in G minor, op. 119, no. 1

B. Haydn, String Quartet in G minor, op. 74, no. 2, Hob III.74, *Andante grazioso*

C. Schumann, *Klavierstücke*, op. 32, Scherzo
   Be aware that there is an enharmonic modulation.

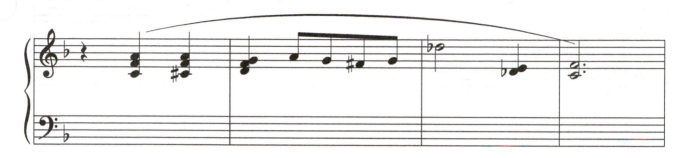

EXERCISE 29.3 Variations and Expansion of a Harmonic Model

You will hear a model, which is followed by a series of variations, or expansions, on the model. Notate the outer voices and provide a roman numeral analysis.

Model:

Expansion 1

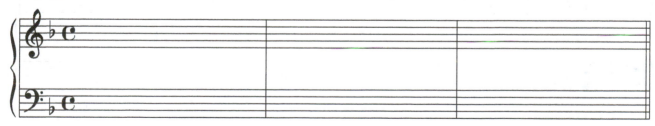

Expansion 2

Expansion 3

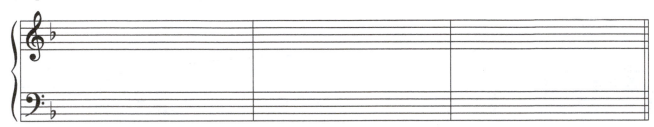

Expansion 4

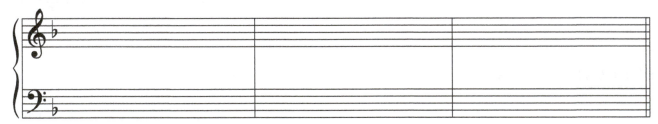

EXERCISE 29.4 Analysis and Dictation

Notate the missing soprano and bass voice for the following excerpts, which illustrate common-tone harmonies. Add logical inner voices.

A.   B.

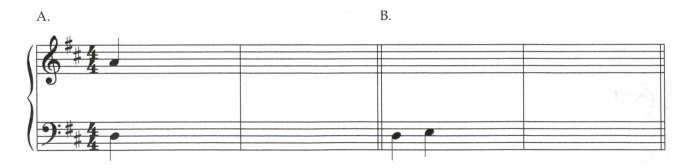

C. Beethoven, Variation XII, *32 Variations in C minor*, WoO 80

EXERCISE 29.5 Analysis and Dictation

Notate the missing soprano and bass voice for the following excerpts that illustrate augmented triads, altered dominant seventh chords, and common-tone chords (diminished sevenths and augmented sixths). Add logical inner voices.

A.

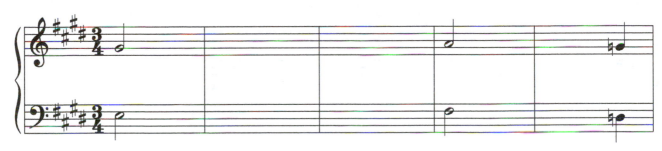

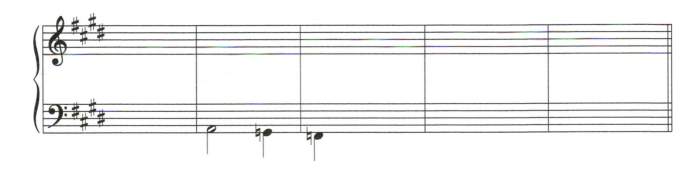

B.

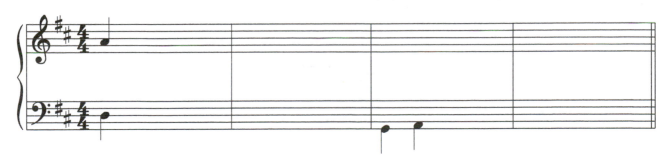

EXERCISE 29.6 Variations and Expansion of a Harmonic Model

The following model is followed by seven variations, or expansions. Notate the outer voices and provide a roman numeral analysis.

Model:

Expansion 1   Expansion 2

Expansion 3   Expansion 4

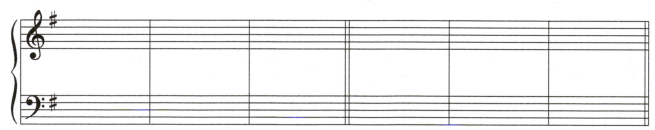

Expansion 5

Expansion 6

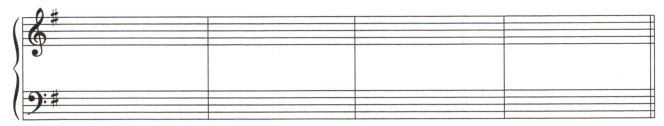

Expansion 7

EXERCISE 29.7 Semitonal Voice Leading

Given are the outer voices of four implied dominant seventh chords whose roots are minor thirds apart. Determine the roots for each chord, then add the missing chordal members in the inner voices. Notice how each chord connects to the next by common-tone or half-step motion. Transpose the four-chord pattern down a whole step and up a whole step. *Extra credit*: Sing one of the outer voices while playing the other three.

EXERCISE 29.8 Augmented Triads

Indicate the function of the augmented triads in the following progression. Then play the progression as written and transpose to any two other keys.

EXERCISE 29.9 Altered Dominant Seventh Chords

Play the following cadential patterns containing altered dominant sevenths. Transpose to major keys with signatures up to and including two sharps and two flats.

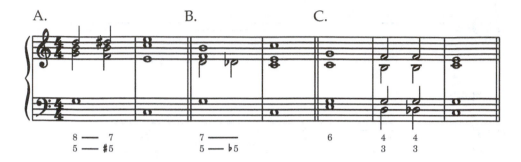

EXERCISE 29.10 Common-Tone Chords

Play the given progression as written and in another major key of your choice. Determine whether common-tone (embellishing) diminished seventh chords are used in neighboring or passing functions and whether they expand the tonic or the dominant.

EXERCISE 29.11 Figured Bass and Metrical Realization

Analyze the following two progressions. Then, based on the harmonic rhythm, contrapuntal expansions, and required metrical placement of certain harmonies, add a meter and rhythms. Expect to encounter enharmonic modulations, altered dominant sevenths, and various types and expansions of the augmented sixth chord.

EXERCISE 29.12 Figured Bass

A. Realize the given figured bass in four voices. Be able to sing either bass or soprano parts while playing the remaining three parts.

B. Warren, "We're in the Money"
   Sing only the tune while realizing the other voices at the keyboard. Analyze.

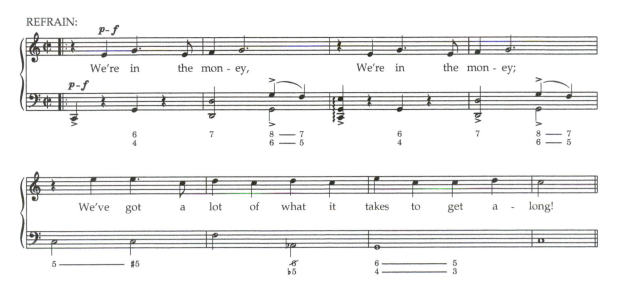

CHAPTER 30

Melodic and Harmonic and Symmetry Combine: Chromatic Sequences

LISTENING

EXERCISE 30.1 Sequence Identification from the Literature

You will hear a variety of diatonic and chromatic sequences. All but the first two are taken from the literature. Label each sequence. (*Note:* There may be more than one sequence in an excerpt.)

A. _____

B. _____

C. Chopin, Piano Concerto in F minor, op. 21, BI 43, *Allegro*

_____

D. Chopin, Piano Concerto in E minor, op. 11, BI 53, *Allegro*

_____

E. Beethoven, String Quartet no. 7 in F major, op. 59, no. 1, *Allegro*

_____

F. Schubert, Trio in B♭ major, D. 898, *Allegro moderato*

_____

EXERCISE 30.2 Analysis and Dictation of Diatonic and Chromatic Sequences

Label the sequence type, bracket begin and ending points of the sequence on the incomplete score, then notate the bass line.

A.

B.

EXERCISE 30.3 Analysis and Dictation of Diatonic and Chromatic Sequences

Label the sequence type; bracket beginning and ending points of the sequence on the incomplete score; then notate the bass line.

A.

B.

EXERCISE 30.4   Analysis and Dictation of Diatonic and Chromatic Sequences from the Literature

Label the sequence type; bracket begin and ending points of the sequence on the incomplete score; then notate the bass line.

A. Beethoven, Piano Sonata no. 12 in A♭ major, op. 26, Scherzo

B. Beethoven, Symphony no. 3 in E♭ major, "Eroica," op. 55, *Allegro con brio*

C. Schumann, Symphony no. 2 in C major, op. 61, *Allegro* (in two)

EXERCISE 30.5 Dictation of Sequences

Identify the sequence type and notate the bass voice.

A.

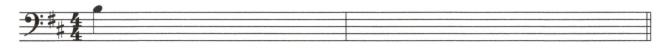

B.

C.

D.

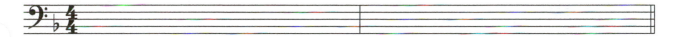

EXERCISE 30.6 Dictation of Sequences

Identify the sequence type and notate the bass voice.

A.

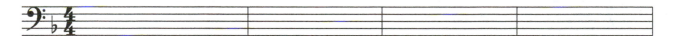

B. Mendelssohn, Symphony no. 3 in A minor, "Scottish," op. 56, *Allegro, un poco agitato*

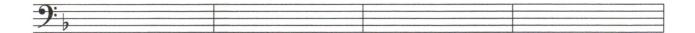

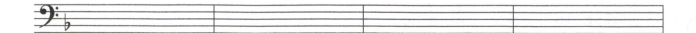

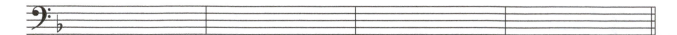

EXERCISE 30.7 Dictation

The contrary-motion chromatic progressions prolong either the tonic, dominant or the pre-dominant function. Notate outer voices, provide roman numerals, and bracket and label the expanded harmonic function.

A.

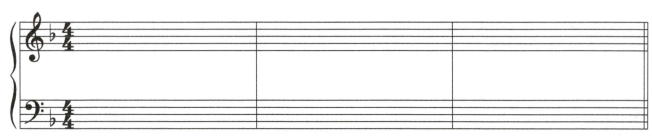

B.

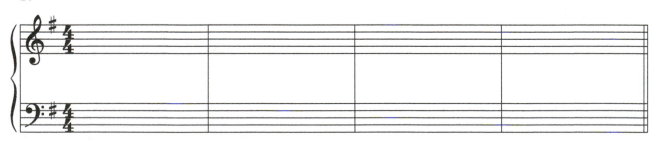

C.

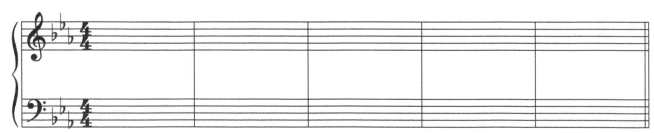

EXERCISE 30.8 Expansion and Variation of Model Progressions

Study the following harmonic models. Each is followed by a series of expansions and/or variations. On a separate sheet of manuscript paper, notate outer voices and provide roman numerals. Expect chromatic sequences and modulations.

Model A:

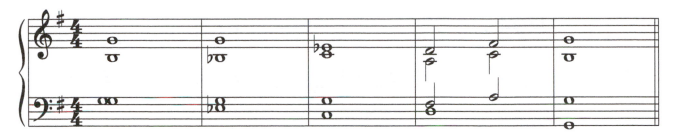

Model B:

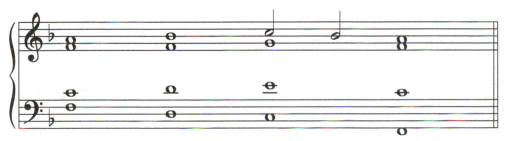

Model C:

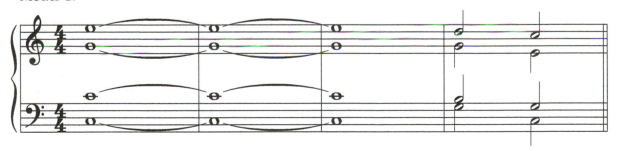

PLAYING

EXERCISE 30.9 Sequences

Identify each sequence type. Realize Exercises A and C in three voices and Exercise B in four voices.

A.

B.

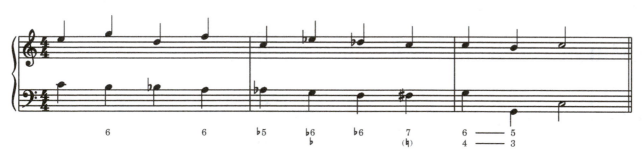

C.

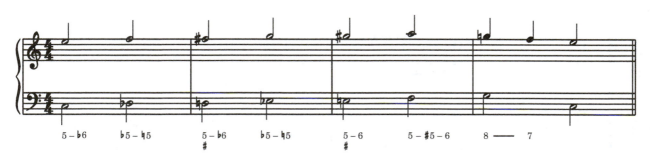

EXERCISE 30.10 Chromatic Voice Exchange and Enharmonic Modulation in Sequence

Continue the following sequence using chromatic voice exchange (to the key of A♭).

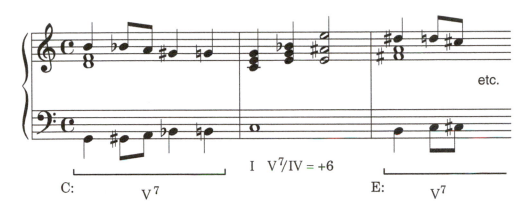

EXERCISE 30.11 Figured Bass

Realize the following soprano and figured bass in keyboard style. Analyze. Be able to sing either outer voice while playing the remaining three.

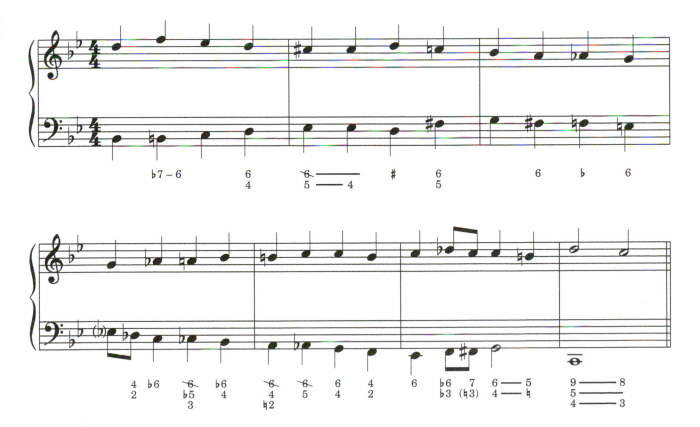

CHAPTER 31

At Tonality's Edge

SINGING

EXERCISE 31.1 Singing Sequential Motions That Evenly Divide the Octave

Using scale degree numbers or solfège, sing (or play on your instrument) the sequential progressions, and continue until you return to the starting tonic. You will need to alter scale degree numbers and solfège syllables when you enter a new tonal area. If you play the progressions on your instrument, transpose each to two additional keys of your choice. You will need to consider octave shifts in order to maintain a single register as much as possible.

EXERCISE 31.2 Analysis and Dictation: Potpourri of Various Types of Tonicization

The following examples tonicize or modulate to diatonic or chromatic keys. Add missing bass pitches. Analyze. Modulatory techniques include the following:

1. pivot chord (diatonic, mixture chord, or enharmonic (diminished seventh or German sixth)
2. sequence (diatonic or chromatic)
3. sequential progression

A.

B.

EXERCISE 31.3 Analysis and Dictation: Potpourri of Various Types of Tonicization

The following examples tonicize or modulate to diatonic or chromatic keys. Add missing bass pitches. Analyze. Modulatory techniques include the following:

1. pivot chord (diatonic, mixture chord, or enharmonic (diminished seventh or German sixth)
2. sequence (diatonic or chromatic)
3. sequential progression

A.

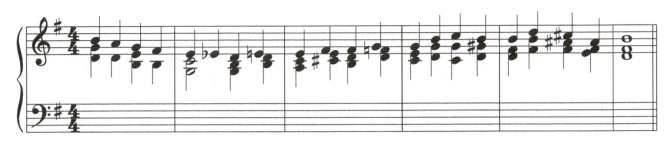

B.

EXERCISE 31.4 Analysis and Dictation

You will hear two excerpts from Alexander Scriabin's piano preludes. Notate the bass and provide a roman numeral and second-level analysis.

A. Scriabin, Prelude in A♭ major, op. 11, no. 17

B. Scriabin, Prelude in C major, op. 35, no. 3

EXERCISE 31.5 Outer-Voice Dictation

Notate the outer voices for the following chromatic modulations. Analyze.

A.

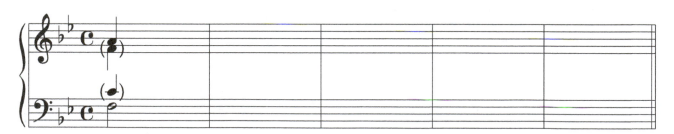

B.

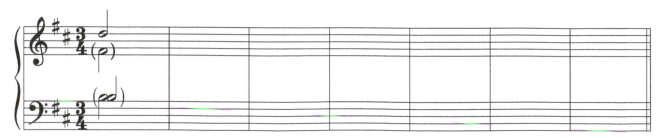

C.

D.

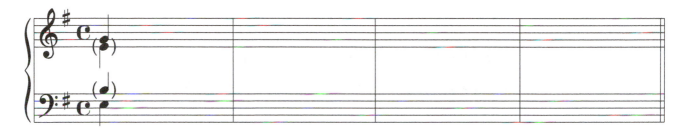

E.

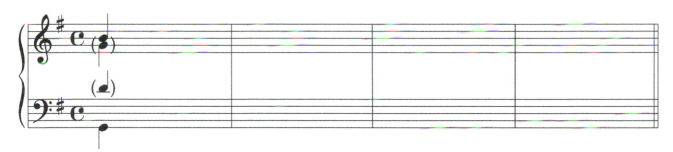

PLAYING

EXERCISE 31.6 Sequential Progressions

Continue the following short chromatic progressions for at least two repetitions. The result will be longer sequential progressions that divide the octave equally. Discuss the chords within each progression as well as the overall octave division.

A.

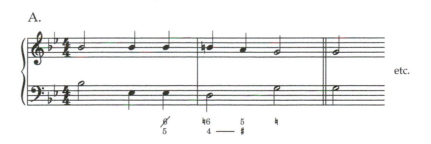

etc.

EXERCISE 31.7 Brain Twister

Employ an F-major triad in the various contexts and keys detailed here. Play each example in four voices. Each progression should establish the tonic and close with a cadence and contain approximately eight to ten chords. Use the F-major triad:

    A. as a mixture chord in A major

    B. as a pre-dominant in E minor

    C. as part of a descending chromatic 5–6 sequence in G major

    D. tonicized in D minor

    E. expanded through voice exchange in B♭ major

    F. as an applied chord in A minor

EXERCISE 31.8 Driving the Omnibus

Play the progression in Example A in keyboard style as written, and then transpose to the key of F major (you'll be starting on C^7 since this omnibus expands the dominant). Then try leaving the sequence at various points, treating the first chord of any measure as a V^7 (see Example B) or as a Ger^6 (see Example C).

A.

B.

C.

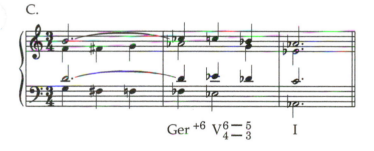

EXERCISE 31.9 Brain Twister

Use the following sonorities (or their enharmonic equivalents) in at least two different ways. (*Hint*: Recall that enharmonic changes permit different harmonic destinations.)

    A. C♯–E–G–B♭

    B. E♭–G–B♭–D♭

    C. C–D–F♯–A♭

The Pitch Realm

SINGING

EXERCISE 1A.1 Matching Pitch Classes

Listen to the pitch, then sing the pitch class you hear on "la" in a comfortable register.

EXERCISE 1A.2 Echoing Pitch Patterns

Listen to the short patterns, then sing them back on "la."

EXERCISE 1A.3 Pitch-Class Identification

Say the pitch-class name of each of the following pitches. In order to maintain a steady pulse, set a metronome at 60 with one pitch per click. Increase the speed as follows for one note per click: 88, 108, 126. Try two notes per click as follows: 60, 66, 76.

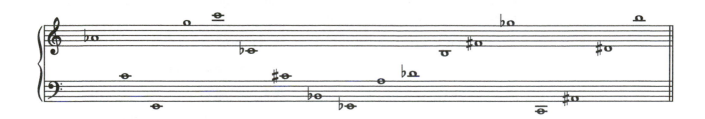

EXERCISE 1A.4 Pitch-Pattern Identification

Say the pitch-class names of each of the pitches in the two- to four-note groups. Try some variations, such as reading the pitches within a pattern backwards, or mix up the order of the given patterns. The goal is immediate reading comprehension.

EXERCISE 1A.5 Singing Scales

In a comfortable register, be able to sing a one-octave major scale beginning on any given pitch in both ascending and descending forms. Use scale degrees or solfège.

EXERCISE 1A.6 Singing Scales

In a comfortable register, be able to sing any of the three forms of the minor scale beginning on any given pitch in both ascending and descending forms. Use scale degrees or solfège.

EXERCISE 1A.7 Singing Scale Fragments

Be able to sing any three- to five-note stepwise fragment from any major or minor scale using pitch names. You will be given $\hat{1}$ each time. For example, given the instruction to sing $\hat{3}$–$\hat{2}$–$\hat{1}$ in the key of B♭ major, you would be given the pitch B♭, and then you would sing "D–C–B♭," each note being a whole step from the other. Below are sample patterns to sing:

A. In G minor, sing $\hat{5}$–$\hat{4}$–$\hat{3}$–$\hat{2}$–$\hat{1}$.   B. In A major, sing $\hat{7}$–$\hat{1}$–$\hat{2}$–$\hat{3}$.

C. In F major, sing $\hat{6}$–$\hat{5}$–$\hat{4}$–$\hat{3}$.   D. In C (melodic) minor, sing $\hat{6}$–$\hat{5}$–$\hat{4}$–$\hat{3}$.

E. In D major, sing $\hat{5}$–$\hat{6}$–$\hat{7}$–$\hat{1}$.   F. In E (melodic) minor, sing $\hat{8}$–$\hat{7}$–$\hat{6}$–$\hat{5}$.

G. In C major, sing $\hat{1}$–$\hat{4}$–$\hat{3}$ H. In D (harmonic) minor, sing $\hat{1}$–$\hat{7}$–$\hat{1}$–$\hat{3}$

I. In A major, sing $\hat{1}$–$\hat{3}$–$\hat{5}$–$\hat{6}$–$\hat{5}$ J. In B (melodic) minor, sing $\hat{1}$–$\hat{3}$–↓$\hat{1}$–$\hat{7}$–$\hat{6}$–$\hat{5}$

K. In E major, sing $\hat{1}$–↓$\hat{5}$–↑$\hat{1}$–$\hat{2}$–$\hat{3}$ L. In B♭ major, sing $\hat{3}$–$\hat{5}$–$\hat{1}$–$\hat{4}$–$\hat{3}$

EXERCISE 1A.8 Sight-Singing Paradigms

Sing the following short models in D major.

EXERCISE 1A.9 Sight-Singing

Using scale degree numbers and then solfège, sing the following short major mode melodic fragments in a comfortable register. Follow this procedure before you sing:

1. Determine the key.
2. "Scan" the melody, looking for the following:

   a. literal repetitions of patterns (e.g., scale degrees $\hat{1}$–$\hat{7}$–$\hat{1}$–$\hat{3}$–$\hat{5}$; $\hat{1}$–$\hat{7}$–$\hat{1}$–$\hat{3}$–$\hat{5}$)
   b. modified repetitions of patterns (e.g., scale degrees $\hat{1}$–$\hat{2}$–$\hat{3}$; $\hat{2}$–$\hat{3}$–$\hat{4}$; $\hat{3}$–$\hat{4}$–$\hat{5}$)

3. Give yourself scale degree $\hat{1}$, then sing $\hat{1}$–$\hat{3}$–$\hat{5}$ before you sing the fragment.

Major mode:

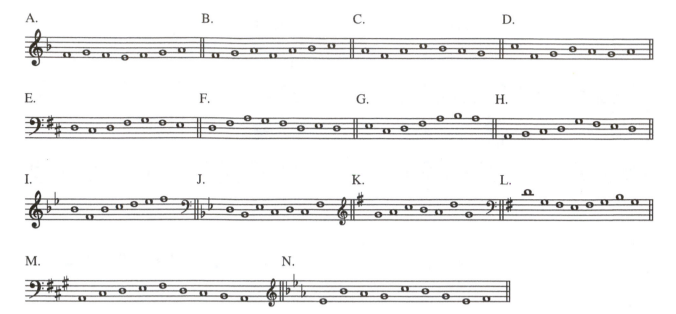

Minor mode:

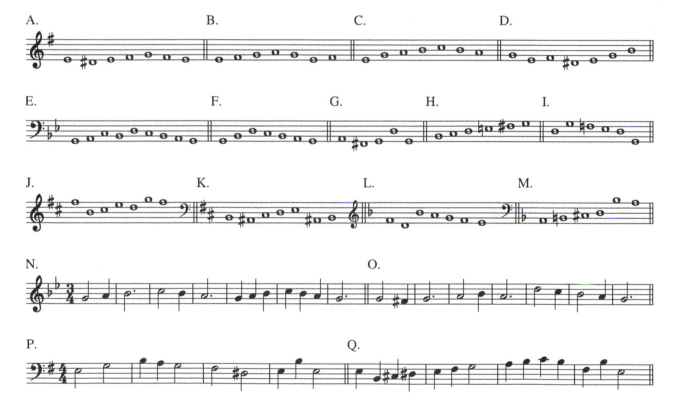

Longer examples in major:

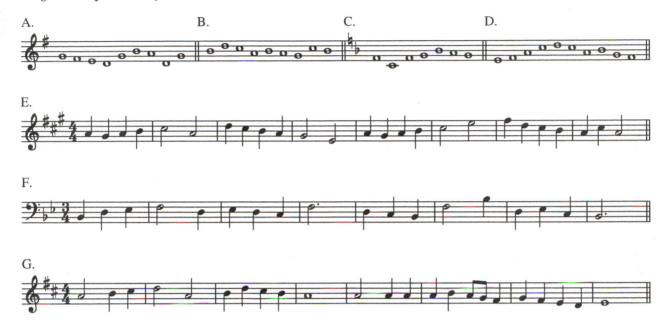

LISTENING

EXERCISE 1A.10 Half Versus Whole Steps (I)

Sing the two pitches that you hear in a comfortable register. Determine whether the pitches lie the intervallic distance of a half step or a whole step from one another. You may wish to listen in terms of function: a half-step relationship will sound like leading tone to tonic ($\hat{7}$–$\hat{8}$), or vice versa. A whole-step relationship will sound like the beginning ascent of a scale ($\hat{1}$–$\hat{2}$) or the ending descent ($\hat{2}$–$\hat{1}$). Identify using "H" or "W."

A. ____ B. ____ C. ____ D. ____ E. ____ F. ____ G. ____ H. ____ I. ____ J. ____

EXERCISE 1A.11 Half Versus Whole Steps (II)

This exercise is identical to Exercise 1A.10, but this time you will notate the second pitch of the pair of pitches.

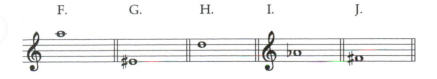

EXERCISE 1A.12 Aural and Visual Comparison

You will hear melodic fragments. Circle the score that corresponds with what was played.

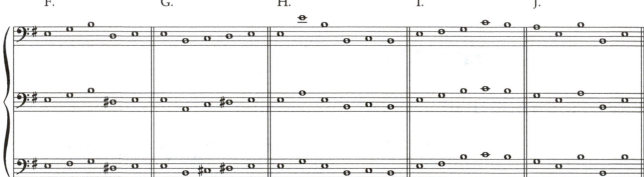

EXERCISE 1A.13 Aural and Visual Comparison

Determine for each exercise which of the three given patterns best represents what is played.

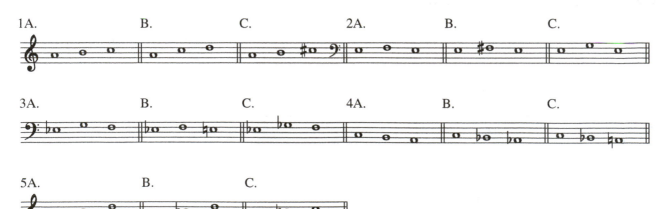

EXERCISE 1A.14 Correction

The notated melodies contain one or more errors. Listen to the recording, then rewrite the melody correctly.

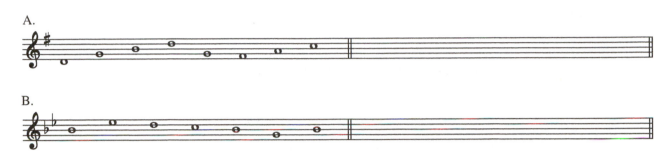

MELODIC DICTATION

Now let's begin to hear, memorize, and notate (called dictation) longer melodies. Here are some things to keep in mind as you take dictation.

1. Don't write down each note as soon as you hear it. This is not a good way to develop your ear because, by focusing on a single pitch, you lose all sense of the musical context.

2. In addition, there are practical reasons why you wouldn't want to notate as the music is being played. If you make a mistake in notating one of the pitches, each following pitch might also be incorrect. Or, if the example is played at a faster tempo, you will find that you are remembering and writing only a few notes at a time.

3. An important goal is to develop a long-range memory. You will find it particularly satisfying to hear a musical passage; store its formal, melodic, and harmonic contents in your memory; and then leisurely reconstruct it on paper or on your instrument.

Let's go through the process of listening. For now, you'll be given $\hat{1}$ before the melody is played.

- *Acclimating:* Begin by quietly singing $\hat{1}$, and then $\hat{1}$–$\hat{3}$–$\hat{5}$ to situate yourself in the key.
- *Memorizing:* Listen to the example. Immediately sing it back on a neutral syllable, such as "la." The goal is to memorize the entire tune in one or, at most, two playings.
- *Analyzing:* Step back and begin to operate on, or *analyze*, what you have memorized:
  - What is the first pitch? If it is not $\hat{1}$, sing down to $\hat{1}$ by step (scalewise singing).
  - What is the contour? Are there many leaps?
  - Is the melody made up of a single unified thread of pitches, or is it a combination of two or more separate units?
  - Determine scale degree numbers for important points in the melody, like the opening and closing.
  - Sing back the entire tune using scale degree numbers.

• *Notating*

- Write down the scale degree numbers.
- Notate the pitches of the melody by converting the scale degree numbers into pitches of the given key.

EXERCISE 1A.15 Melodic Dictation

Notate scale degree numbers for the major-mode melodic fragments. You will hear scale degrees 1̂–3̂–5̂ before each example.

A. ____ ____ ____ ____   B. ____ ____ ____ ____

C. ____ ____ ____ ____ ____ ____ ____   D. ____ ____ ____ ____ ____ ____

E. ____ ____ ____ ____ ____ ____ ____   F. ____ ____ ____ ____ ____

EXERCISE 1A.16 Melodic Dictation

Notate scale degree numbers for the minor-mode fragments. You will hear scale degrees 1̂–3̂–5̂ before each example.

A. ____ ____ ____ ____ ____ ____   B. ____ ____ ____ ____ ____ ____

C. ____ ____ ____ ____ ____ ____ ____   D. ____ ____ ____ ____ ____

E. ____ ____ ____ ____ ____ ____ ____   F. ____ ____ ____ ____ ____ ____

EXERCISE 1A.17 Melodic Dictation

Notate scale degrees of the minor-mode melodies.

A. ____ ____ ____ ____ ____ ____   B. ____ ____ ____ ____ ____ ____

C. ____ ____ ____ ____ ____   D. ____ ____ ____ ____ ____

E. ____ ____ ____ ____   F. ____ ____ ____ ____ ____ ____

PLAYING

EXERCISE 1A.18 Half and Whole Steps

Play half and whole steps above and below the following pitches: D, G, F, B, A♭, E♭, B, C♯.

Give yourself the starting pitch and sing half and whole steps above and below the given pitches. In order to become fluent with this task and to sing in tune, view the given pitch as a scale degree within a key. For example, in order to sing a half step above D, consider D to be 7̂ in the key of E♭, and resolve this leading tone to 8̂, which is E♭. Similarly, in order to sing a whole step below D, consider D to be 2̂ in C major and then fall to 1̂, which is C.

EXERCISE 1A.19 Scales

We will use the "tetrachordal" fingering for scales: The four fingers of your left hand (beginning with the smallest finger (finger numbers 5–4–3–2) will play the first four notes of a scale (referred to as the first tetrachord), and the four fingers of your right hand will play the next four notes of the scale beginning with the index finger (finger numbers 2–3–4–5). Shown is an illustration in D major:

D	E	F♯	G	A	B	C♯	D
LH: 5	4	3	2	RH: 2	3	4	5

Mix up the activities as follows:

- Play each scale in ascending and descending forms.
- Sing as you play.
- Play the major scale in keys through 2 sharps and 2 flats.
- Play two notes; then sing the next two, playing the following two, and so on.
- Jump immediately to any scale degree in a scale.

EXERCISE 1A.20 Identification of Notes

Using alternating hands, find and play the Gs on the keyboard. Begin by locating middle C and identifying all the Gs, first by descending in octaves and then by ascending. Continue this exercise in the same manner with the following pitch classes: D, C♯, A, F♯, B, E, C, B♭, E♭, F, and A.

EXERCISE 1A.21 Matching Pitches

Play the following pitches on the keyboard and then sing each pitch. Begin by playing the pitches in the middle of the piano, then branch out and play pitches in other registers (i.e., in different octaves above and below the original octave). When you sing these pitches, you will need to find a comfortable register.

A   F   B   E♭   G   C♯   A♭   D   F♯   B♭   E

EXERCISE 1A.22 Bass and Treble Reading

Play the following pitches on the keyboard and then sing each pitch in a comfortable register. Begin by playing the pitches in the middle of the piano, then branch out and play pitches in other registers (i.e., in different octaves above and below the original octave). When you sing these pitches, you will need to find a comfortable register. Ledger lines appear in this exercise.

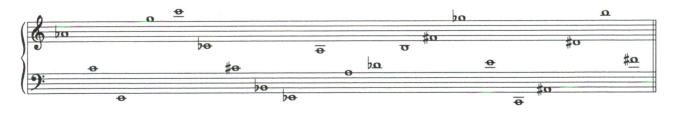

EXERCISE 1A.23 Half and Whole Steps

Be able to play half and whole steps above and below the following pitches: B♭, D♭, E, F♯, B, G♯, G♭. Then, give yourself the starting pitch and sing half and whole steps above and below those pitches.

To become fluent with this task and to sing in tune, view the given pitch as a scale degree within a key. For example, to sing a half step above D, consider D to be $\hat{7}$, and resolve this leading tone to $\hat{8}$, which is E♭. Similarly, to sing a whole step below D, consider D to be $\hat{2}$ in C major and then fall to $\hat{1}$, which is C.

EXERCISE 1A.24 Playing Major Scales Derived from Nontonic Pitches

Construct the major scale derived from the scale degree function of the given pitch. For example, given the pitch G and $\hat{5}$, count down five scale degrees to C and then play a C major scale.

Given pitch:	C	F♯	A	B♭	E	B	D	C♯	B
Given scale degree:	$\hat{4}$	$\hat{3}$	$\hat{7}$	$\hat{4}$	$\hat{3}$	$\hat{3}$	$\hat{3}$	$\hat{7}$	$\hat{3}$

EXERCISE 1A.25 Playing Melodic Minor Scales from Nontonic Pitches

Construct the minor scale derived from the scale degree function of the given pitch. For example, given the pitch G and $\hat{5}$, you count down five scale degrees to C and then play a C minor scale.

Given pitch:	A	D	F	B♭	B♭	F♯	B	G	D
Given scale degree:	$\hat{4}$	$\hat{3}$	$\hat{3}$	$\hat{3}$	$\hat{6}$	$\hat{5}$	$\hat{2}$	$\hat{3}$	$\hat{5}$
				(descending form)					

EXERCISE 1A.26 Keyboard Scale Fragments

A. Given the following two- or three-note scale fragments, play the major scale(s) of which they are members. *Hint:* Remember that half steps occur both between $\hat{3}$ and $\hat{4}$ and between $\hat{7}$ and $\hat{8}$.

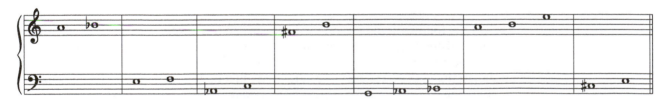

B. In the following example, you are given two-note scale fragments. Play the minor scale(s) of which they are the members.

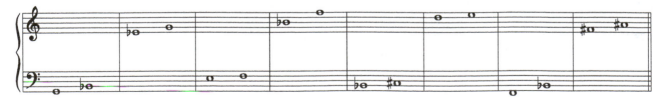

Pulse, Rhythm, and Meter

SINGING

EXERCISE 1B.1 Rhythmic Warm-up

Perform the following rhythmic patterns as follows:

1. Clap the given beat value (for example, if the quarter note receives the beat [i.e., gets one beat], the half note would receive two beats; if the half note receives the beat, then the quarter note would receive half a beat.)
2. While clapping the beat, say the rhythm pattern on a neutral syllable (for example, "ta").

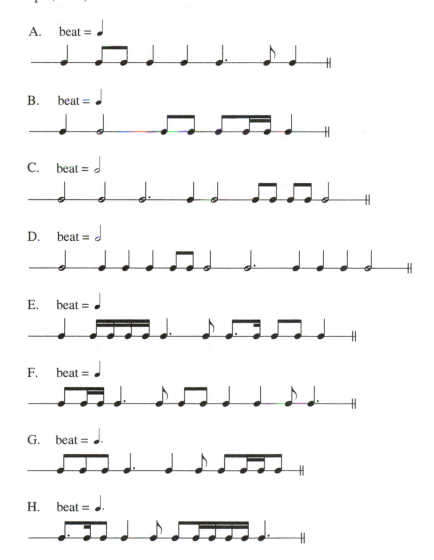

EXERCISE 1B.2 Singing Melodic Fragments

Clap the assigned beat value while singing the following melodic fragments.

EXERCISE 1B.3 Singing Rhythmic Fragments in the Major and Minor Modes

Begin by singing major and minor ascending and descending scales in a comfortable octave. Then clap and sing the rhythmic pattern that appears in each exercise. Repeat the pattern on the next-higher scale degree, making sure to sing only the diatonic pitches from the scale in which you began. Continue the pattern until you reach the tonic one octave above the initial tonic. Then return to the tonic by descending the scale, and continue to sing and clap each pattern.

EXERCISE 1B.4 Toward Meter

Perform the following rhythmic passages. Then determine how many of each of the given rhythmic durations would be required to represent the total length of each passage.

CONDUCTING PATTERNS

The vast majority of college-level music programs require that students learn basic conducting patterns. You'll use conducting when singing, directing other students in musicianship classes, and especially when playing with ensembles. We'll learn only three patterns here: duple, triple, and quadruple. You can then use these patterns for many meters, including compound meters such as $\frac{6}{8}$, $\frac{9}{8}$, and $\frac{12}{8}$, which are also often conducted in two, three, and four, respectively. Here are a few requirements:

1. Conduct with your right hand (even if you are left-handed).
2. Use efficient motions:
   - conduct within an imaginary box of about 12 x 12 inches,
   - move mostly your forearm (not your entire arm).
3. Consider that the imaginary conducting box has a firm bottom and that each beat will touch the bottom of the box and rebound just a bit. This point, which marks the precise beginning of the beat, is called the ictus.

A downward motion of your forearm always indicates a *downbeat* (i.e., beat 1 of a measure). An upward motion of your forearm always indicates an upbeat (i.e., the last beat of a measure). Beats between the downbeat and upbeat are indicated by moving your forearm to the right or left.

The following diagrams summarize these conducting patterns.

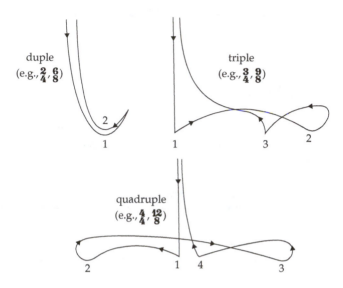

EXERCISE 1B.5 Conducting and Singing Fragments in Rhythm and Meter

This exercise presents melodic fragments in a meter, with a rhythmic pattern given below. First, practice the conducting patterns for $\frac{2}{4}$, $\frac{3}{4}$, $\frac{4}{4}$, and $\frac{6}{8}$. Then, using "ta" or another rhythmic syllable, conduct the meter and say the rhythm. Finally, conduct the meter and sing the scale degrees in rhythm. Continue each pattern until you return to the tonic.

A. $\frac{2}{4}$ etc.

B. $\frac{6}{8}$ etc.

C. $\frac{4}{4}$ etc.

D. $\frac{3}{4}$ etc.

EXERCISE 1B.6

Perform each exercise and determine the meter, then supply an appropriate meter signature and bar lines. All but the first example begin on downbeats, but some of the characteristic metrical groupings (e.g., beams) are missing. Discuss this in a sentence or two. Once you have determined the meter for each example, rewrite it using proper notation. There may be more than one possible meter for some examples.

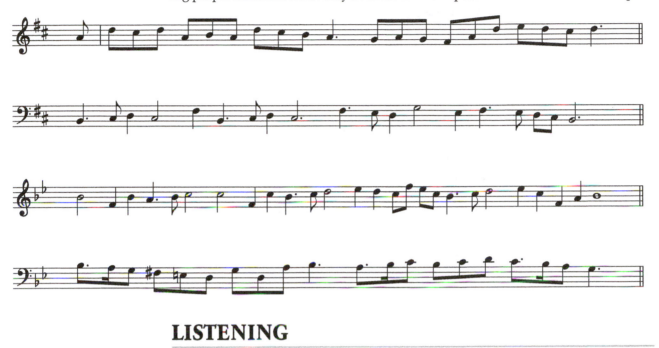

LISTENING

EXERCISE 1B.7 Rhythmic Completion

Incomplete rhythmic patterns are given. Listen to each example, notating the missing rhythms.

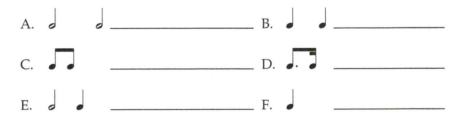

EXERCISE 1B.8

Notate both pitch and rhythm for the following short melodic fragments.

EXERCISE 1B.9 Rhythmic Dictation

Notate the short rhythmic patterns using the given note value as the beat. You will hear the tempo of the beat before each exercise is played.

A. beat = ♩

B. beat = ♩

C. beat = 𝅗𝅥

D. beat = ♪

EXERCISE 1B.10 Melodic Dictation

Notate both the pitch and rhythm of the short melodic fragments. The note value that receives the beat is given, and you will hear the tempo of the beat before the exercise is played.

A. beat = ♩ B. C.

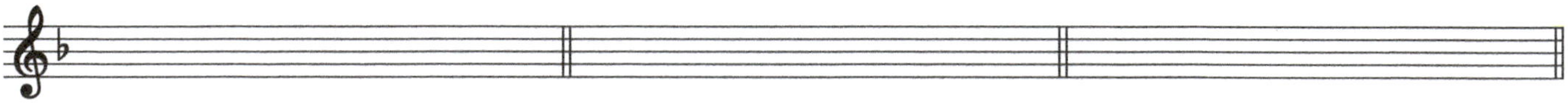

D. beat = 𝅗𝅥 E.

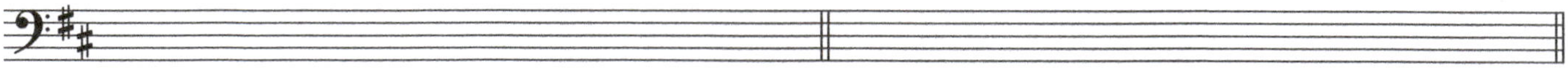

EXERCISE 1B.11 Rhythmic Dictation

Determine the meter, then notate the measures whose rhythms are missing.

EXERCISE 1B.12 Rhythmic Dictation

Determine an appropriate meter for the following rhythmic patterns. Provide the meter signature, bar lines, and notate the rhythms.

A. Schubert, "Schwanengesang," D. 744

B. Couperin, "Les Nations," Premier Ordre, Chaconne

C. Hummel, Bagatelle in C major

EXERCISE 1B.13 Rhythmic Dictation

Notate the rhythmic patterns based on the given meter.

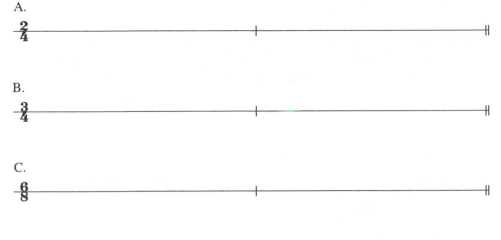

EXERCISE 1B.14 Identification and Conducting

Determine the meter for each example by conducting. Begin by finding the down-beat then counting pulses until the next downbeat. Conduct during the performance of the exercise.

A. Schubert, Impromptu in A♭ major, D. 935_____

B. Mozart, Clarinet Quintet in A major, K. 581, I_____

C. Mozart, Piano Sonata in D major, K. 576, *Allegro*_____

D. Schubert, "Der Müller und der Bach," *Die schöne Müllerin*, D. 795_____

E. Schubert, String Quartet no. 3 in B♭ major, D. 36, Minet_____

F. Haydn, String Quartet in B♭ major, op. 64, no. 3, Minuet_____

EXERCISE 1B.15 Meter and Mode Identification: Simple Meters

Identify the meter and mode (major or minor) of each of the following excerpts. First, identify the basic pulse, then locate the regularly recurring accented beat that is followed by one or more weak beats. Next, determine the generic meter, which will be duple or triple. Finally, refine your decision by assigning $\frac{2}{4}$ or $\frac{3}{4}$.

Example:

Schumann, "Einsame Blumen," *Waldscenen*, op. 82	Meter: $\frac{2}{4}$	Mode: Major
A. Traditional, "Amazing Grace"	Meter: _____	Mode: _____
B. Beethoven, Piano Sonata, op. 28, *Andante*	Meter: _____	Mode: _____
C. Haydn, String Quartet, op. 64, no. 5	Meter: _____	Mode: _____
D. Beethoven, Piano Sonata, op. 14, no. 1, *Andante*	Meter: _____	Mode: _____

EXERCISE 1B.16 Meter and Mode Identification: Simple and Compound Meters

This exercise requires you to identify both simple and compound meters. Your choices are $\frac{2}{4}$, $\frac{3}{4}$, $\frac{4}{4}$, $\frac{6}{8}$, and $\frac{9}{8}$. Each exercise contains a recurring rhythmic pattern. Based on the meter you choose, notate the rhythmic pattern.

A. Haydn, String Quartet in G minor, op. 74, no. 3, Hob III.74, *Allegro*

B. Wagner, "Liebestod," from *Tristan und Isolde*

C. Brahms, Intermezzo in E minor, op. 119, no. 2

D. Bach, Minuet II, from Suite no. 1 in G major for Cello, BWV 1007

E. Schubert, Moment Musical no. 6, D. 780

F. Beethoven, Symphony no. 7 in A major, op. 92, *Allegretto*

EXERCISE 1B.17 Rhythmic Dictation

Determine the meter, then notate the rhythmic patterns.

A.

♩ = beat ——— ‖

B.

♩ = beat ——— ‖

C.

♩ = beat ——— ‖

D.

♪ = beat ——— ‖

EXERCISE 1B.18 Rhythmic Dictation

Notate the rhythms perfomed.

A. $\frac{4}{4}$

B. $\frac{3}{4}$

EXERCISE 1B.19 Melodic Dictation

Determine the mode (major or minor) and meter, then notate both pitch and rhythm of the following exercises.

A.

B.

PLAYING

EXERCISE 1B.20 Keyboard: Scale Fragments in Both Hands

Using both hands, which are placed one octave apart, play the following scale degree patterns. Then, play the pattern in one hand while singing it. Finally, try playing and/or singing the exercises by beginning one hand before the second hand.
Start the second hand as the first plays the third note of each pattern. Try singing
and playing this way as well. Such canons are common in tonal music.

Scale degrees in A minor: $\hat{1}$ $\hat{2}$ $\hat{3}$ $\hat{2}$ $\hat{1}$ in B♭ major

Scale degrees in D minor: $\hat{3}$ $\hat{2}$ $\hat{1}$ $\hat{2}$ $\hat{3}$ in E♭ major

Scale degrees in G minor: $\hat{5}$ $\hat{4}$ $\hat{3}$ $\hat{2}$ $\hat{1}$ $\hat{2}$ $\hat{3}$ in D major

EXERCISE 1B.21 Two Notes in Each Hand

Simultaneously play the following pairs of scale degrees in the hand requested. As
you play, sing first the lower and then the higher pitch. Choose a comfortable
singing range.

A. Play $\hat{1}$ and $\hat{5}$ (using fingers 1 and 5) in the following keys:

Using the right hand: G major, B♭ major, E major
Using the left hand: D minor, B minor, F minor

B. Play $\hat{1}$ and $\hat{3}$ (using fingers 1 and 3) for the following keys:

Using the right hand: C major, B♭ major, D major
Using the left hand: A minor, E minor, G minor

C. Play $\hat{2}$ and $\hat{5}$ (using fingers 2 and 5) for the following keys:

Using the right hand: A major, B major, G major
Using the left hand: C minor, D minor, B minor

D. Play $\hat{1}$ and $\hat{4}$ (using fingers 1 and 4) for the following keys:

Using the right hand: A major, B major, G major
Using the left hand: C minor, D minor, B minor

E. Play $\hat{2}$ and $\hat{4}$ (using fingers 2 and 4) for the following keys:

Using the right hand: B♭ major, F major, A major
Using the left hand: B minor, C♯ minor, A minor

EXERCISE 1B.22 Filling in Gaps

Return to Exercise 1B.21, and fill in each of the given scale degree distances with
the remaining scale steps.

EXERCISE 1B.23 Scales in Rhythm

Play the major and three forms of minor scales (natural, harmonic, and melodic) in keys with three sharps and three flats. Determine a probable meter for each exercise. Use the tetrachordal fingering.

EXERCISE 1B.24 Scale Fragments in Rhythm

Sing each fragment in rhythm. As you sing, tap the beat (for simple meters, it will be the quarter note; for compound, the dotted quarter note). Then play the melodic fragments in rhythm on the piano with either hand) while you sing. Next, play the melodic fragments in rhythm on the piano with either hand while tapping the beat with the free hand. Finally, determine a possible meter for each example and conduct that meter while playing the melodic fragments.

Intervals

SINGING AND PLAYING

EXERCISE 1C.1 Intervals Within a Key from $\hat{1}$

Play a pitch at the piano and consider it to be $\hat{1}$ in both a major and its parallel minor. Sing the interval required, and call out the scale degree names. Work through the list in the order presented, then give yourself a different pitch, and work through the list again.

Intervals ABOVE the given pitch:
M2
P5
m3
M6
m7
P4
P8
M6
M7

Intervals BELOW the given pitch:
m3
P5
M3
M2
P4
m6
m7
P8

EXERCISE 1C.2 Intervals Within a Key from Any Scale Degree

Play a pitch at the piano and consider it to be the scale degree given, then sing intervals based on the required scale degree.

A. Treat the given pitch as $\hat{2}$, sing UP to the requested scale degrees, and call out the specific interval's name that is created. The mode of the scale (major or minor) is specified when $\hat{3}$, $\hat{6}$, and $\hat{7}$ are involved.

$\hat{2}$ up to $\hat{3}$ (in major)
$\hat{2}$ up to $\hat{5}$
$\hat{2}$ up to $\hat{6}$ (in minor)
$\hat{2}$ up to $\hat{3}$ (in minor)
$\hat{2}$ up to $\hat{7}$ (in major)

B. This time, treat the given pitch as $\hat{4}$.
$\hat{4}$ up to $\hat{5}$
$\hat{4}$ up to $\hat{7}$ (in major)
$\hat{4}$ up to $\hat{1}$

C. This time, treat the given pitch as $\hat{5}$.
$\hat{5}$ up to $\hat{7}$ (lowerd form, in minor)
$\hat{5}$ up to $\hat{6}$ (in major)
$\hat{5}$ up to $\hat{1}$
$\hat{5}$ up to $\hat{7}$ (raised form)
$\hat{5}$ up to $\hat{6}$ (raised form)

D. This time, treat the given pitch as $\hat{3}$.
$\hat{3}$ (in minor) down to $\hat{1}$
$\hat{3}$ (in minor) down to $\hat{2}$
$\hat{3}$ (in major) up to $\hat{4}$
$\hat{3}$ (in major) up to $\hat{6}$
$\hat{3}$ (in minor) up to $\hat{1}$
$\hat{3}$ (in major) down to $\hat{7}$

EXERCISE 1C.3 Position Finding

Sing the following scale degree patterns in major keys. Boxed pairs of scale degrees require you to "shift tracks," reinterpreting the final pitch of the original pattern with a new scale degree number. You must then begin to sing in the new key, using the pattern of whole and half steps required.

For example, given the following pattern and the beginning key of C major:

$$\hat{1}-\hat{2}-\hat{3}-\boxed{\hat{2}}\ \boxed{\hat{1}}-\hat{2}-\hat{3}-\boxed{\hat{2}}\ \boxed{\hat{1}}-\hat{2}\text{-etc.}$$

you would sing:

$$\text{C-D-E-}\boxed{\text{D}}\ \boxed{\text{D}}\text{-E-F}\sharp\text{-}\boxed{\text{E}}\ \boxed{\text{E}}\text{-F}\sharp\text{-G}\sharp\text{-F}\sharp\text{-etc.}$$

A. $\hat{1}-\hat{2}-\hat{3}-\boxed{\hat{4}}\ \boxed{\hat{1}}-\hat{2}\text{-etc.}$

B. $\hat{1}-\hat{5}-\hat{4}-\hat{3}-\boxed{\hat{2}}\ \boxed{\hat{1}}-\hat{5}\text{-etc.}$

C. $\hat{1}-\hat{2}-\hat{3}-\hat{1}-\boxed{\hat{7}}\ \boxed{\hat{1}}-\hat{2}-\hat{3}-\hat{1}-\hat{7}\text{-etc.}$

D. $\hat{1}-\hat{5}-\hat{4}-\boxed{\hat{3}}\ \boxed{\hat{1}}-\hat{5}\text{-etc.}$

EXERCISE 1C.4 Singing Melodies

Sing the following melodies. Remember to scan each melody before singing.

A.

B.

C.

EXERCISE 1C.5 Determining Meter in Longer Melodies

Sing the following melodies. Determine the meter and add the meter signature and bar lines.

A.

B.

LISTENING

EXERCISE 1C.6 Aural Identification and Notation of Seconds, Perfect Fifths, and Octaves

In each example you will hear intervals in either melodic (successive) or harmonic (simultaneous) settings. You will hear the given pitch alone, followed by the interval. For harmonic intervals, the given pitch will always be the lower pitch of the interval. Notate the missing pitch, and identify the resulting interval. Your choices are m2, M2, P5, and P8. You might wish to employ the following listening procedure:

1. Determine the approximate size of the interval; major and minor seconds are small intervals, the fifth is a medium-size interval, and the octave is a large interval.
2. Differentiate between major and minor seconds in both harmonic and melodic contexts. Think about:

   - For intervals played harmonically, determine the level of dissonance. Minor seconds are very dissonant and major seconds are less dissonant.
   - For intervals played melodically, imagine that they are two pitches in a *major* scale; a *major* second will sound like $\hat{1}$ moving to $\hat{2}$ (or vice versa) and a minor second will sound like $\hat{7}$ to $\hat{1}$ (or vice versa).

EXERCISE 1C.7 Notating Seconds, Fifths, and Octaves

The first note of a melodic interval is given. Label the interval you hear and notate the second note that forms that interval. Your choices are m2, M2, P5, and P8.

EXERCISE 1C.8 More Seconds, Fifths, and Octaves

The second note of a melodic interval is given. Label the interval you hear and notate the first note that forms that interval. Your choices are m2, M2, P5, P8, and compounds.

A.   B.   C.   D.   E.   F.   G.   H.   I.   J.

EXERCISE 1C.9 More Melodic Seconds, Fifths, and Octaves

You will now hear descending seconds, fifths, and octaves. Label all intervals; compound intervals are included in this exercise.

1st note given   2nd note given

A.   B.   C.   D.   E.   F.   G.   H.   I.   J.

EXERCISE 1C.10 Harmonic Seconds and Fifths

You will hear intervals played harmonically. Notate and label intervals. For Exercises A–E, the lower note is given and for F–J, the upper.

A.   B.   C.   D.   E.   F.   G.   H.   I.   J.

EXERCISE 1C.11 Identifying and Notating Seconds and All Perfect Intervals

A mix of ascending and descending seconds, fifths, and octaves occur. To these intervals we add the perfect fourth. Notate and label intervals. For exercises A–E, the first note is given and for F–J, the second.

EXERCISE 1C.12 Identifying and Notating Major and Minor Thirds and the Tritone

The lower note for melodic ascending intervals is given. Notate the second pitch and label the interval. Since the diminished fifth and augmented fourth are impossible to distinguish aurally, notate them both. Refer to compound thirds as major or minor tenths.

EXERCISE 1C.13 More Thirds and Tritones

This exercise is identical to Exercise 1C.12, except that the second note, rather than the first note, is given.

EXERCISE 1C.14 Yet More Thirds and Tritones

This exercise is similar to Exercise 1C.13, but now descending thirds and tritones occur. For exercises A–E, the first note is given and for F–J, the second.

EXERCISE 1C.15 Melodic Thirds and Tritones

Notate the ascending and descending thirds and tritones that occur. For Exercises A–E, the first note is given and for F–J, the second.

EXERCISE 1C.16 Harmonic Thirds and Tritones

Notate the thirds and tritones that are played harmonically. For exercises A–E, the lower note is given and for F–J, the upper.

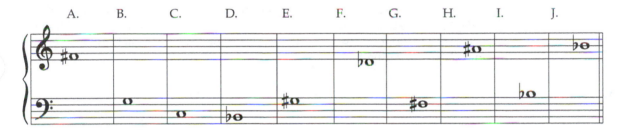

EXERCISE 1C.17 Intervals: Seconds, Thirds, Fourths, Fifths, Octaves, and Tritones

Notate and label the harmonic intervals that you hear. The lower note is given in A–E, the upper in F–J. On a separate sheet of manuscript paper, renotate each interval enharmonically by changing the *upper pitch*.

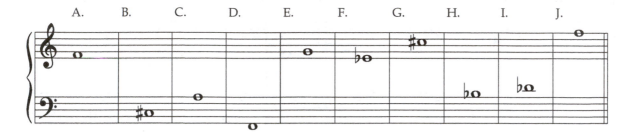

EXERCISE 1C.18 Intervals: Major and Minor Sixths and Sevenths; Review of Seconds, Thirds, Fourths, Fifths, and Tritones

You will hear ascending melodic forms of the m2, M2, m3, M3, m6, M6, and m7, M7, P4, P5, and tritone. The first note is given; notate the second note and label the interval. On a separate sheet of manuscript paper, renotate each interval enharmonically by changing the *lower pitch*.

EXERCISE 1C.19 Notation of Diatonic Melodies

You will hear short melodic fragments (approximately eight notes). Once you are given the tonality, quietly sing $\hat{1}$–$\hat{3}$–$\hat{5}$–$\hat{3}$–$\hat{1}$ to give yourself a tonal footing. Then memorize each fragment. Finally, use scale degree numbers to notate the fragment.

A. _____   B. _____

C. _____   D. _____

E. _____   F. _____

EXERCISE 1C.20 Notation of Melodic Fragments

This time you are to notate the pitches on staff paper (noteheads without stems are adequate, since rhythm is not involved at this point) in the following keys.

A. E minor   B. F major   C. F♯ minor

D. C major   E. G minor   F. D major

Include an analysis of scale degrees and the intervals between each pair of pitches.

EXERCISE 1C.21 Identifying All Intervals

You will hear a mix of melodic, harmonic, and ascending and descending intervals. Identify each on a separate sheet of manuscript paper.

EXERCISE 1C.22 Major and Minor Sixths and Sevenths; Review of Seconds, Thirds, Fourths, Fifths, and Tritones

This exercise is identical to Exercise 1C.18, except that the second pitch descends.

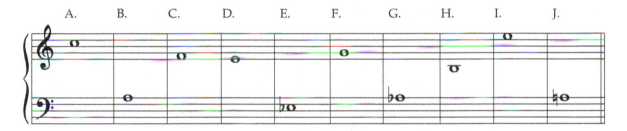

EXERCISE 1C.23 Major and Minor Sixths and Sevenths, and Review of Seconds, Thirds, Fourths, Fifths, and Tritones

This exercise is similar to Exercise 1C.22, but now intervals are presented harmonically. Identify each interval you hear on a separate sheet of manuscript paper.

PLAYING

EXERCISE 1C.24 Scales and Intervals

Using one finger on each hand, play the following scale degree pairs in these keys: Ab, A, Eb, and E major and F, F#, C, and C# minor. Be able to identify the melodic interval. Scale degrees:

$\hat{1} + \hat{4}$

$\hat{1} + \hat{6}$ (use harmonic/natural minor)

$\hat{2} + \hat{4}$

$\hat{2} + \hat{6}$ (major only)

$\hat{1} + \hat{7}$ (above; use all forms of minor)

$\hat{5} + \hat{3}$

EXERCISE 1C.25 Playing Major, Minor, and Perfect Intervals

Be able to sing or play on your instrument any major, minor, or perfect interval above a given pitch.

EXERCISE 1C.26 Two-Voice Step Motions in Parallel Motion on the Keyboard

Play in a steady tempo the two-voice exercises that focus on scalar seconds in major and minor keys up to and including four sharps and four flats. The lowest note in each exercise, $\hat{1}$, should be played using the thumb in the right hand and the fifth finger in the left hand. Play adjacent notes with adjacent fingers. Be able to sing one part while playing the other.

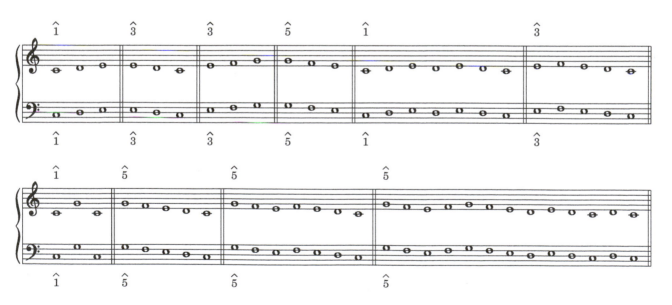

EXERCISE 1C.27 More Major, Minor, and Perfect Intervals

- Using the given pitches, play the intervals requested *above* each given note.
- Identify the inversion.
- Next, increase and decrease the size of each interval by a half step and identify the resulting interval. (Remember, you can increase the size of an interval by raising the upper note or lowering the lower note, and you can decrease the size of an interval by lowering the upper note or raising the lower note.)

Construct above the pitch D: P5, m3, M6
Construct above the pitch B♭: M2, M7, P4
Construct above the pitch G: M6, P4
Construct above the pitch F♯: M3, M7, P5

EXERCISE 1C.28 Intervals from Scales

Sing and/or play all possible perfect, major, and minor intervals within major and minor keys. That is, perform all intervals between all possible scale degree combinations. For example, build intervals above and below each scale degree, such as from 1̂, as follows: ascending: 1̂–2̂, 1̂–3̂, 1̂–4̂, . . .; and 7̂–1̂, 6̂–1̂, 5̂–1̂; as well as descending: 1̂–7̂, 1̂–6̂, 1̂–5̂, . . .; and 2̂–1̂, 3̂–1̂, 4̂–1̂, ... Continue this exercise by beginning on each of the seven scale degrees in both major and minor modes.

EXERCISE 1C.29 Playing and Singing

Given the following series of pitches, find a comfortable register in which you can sing the required intervals above and below the given pitch. Then complete the following tasks:

A. given E: Play and sing major and minor thirds and perfect fifths.
B. given A♭: Play and sing major and minor thirds, tritones, and perfect fifths.
C. given B: Play and sing all major and minor seconds and thirds and perfect intervals.
D. given E♭: Play and sing all perfect intervals and major and minor seconds and thirds.

EXERCISE 1C.30 Two-Voice Exercises in Parallel Motion: Seconds and Thirds

Play the following short melodies; duplicate the pitches at the octave in the left hand. Play each exercise in a steady tempo as written and in G and E major and minor.

The lowest note in each exercise, 1̂ should be played by using the thumb in the right hand and the fifth finger in the left hand. Play adjacent notes with adjacent fingers. Be able to sing one part while playing the other. Finally, play the left hand a sixth or tenth below what is written in the right hand, using the diatonic pitches from the key you are in. The result will be parallel sixth and parallel tenth motion. Reverse this process so that the right hand plays tenths and sixths above the left hand's given pitches.

A.   B.   C.

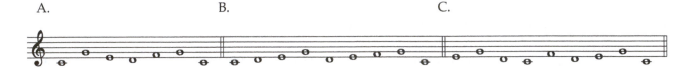

EXERCISE 1C.31 Interval Combinations

Play the various interval combinations that follow, transposing each by the required interval until you return to the starting pitch pattern (unless specified differently). You will need to employ enharmonic notation to return to the tonic (e.g., if you were to transpose the pitch D by major thirds, you could write either D–F♯–A♯–D or D–F♯–B♭–D; notice that a diminished fourth (shown in bold) occurs in both versions). Be able to identify each interval in the given pattern. *Extra credit:* Play the first pitch, and sing each subsequent pitch.

   A. Transpose by ascending major seconds.
   B. Transpose by ascending major thirds.
   C. Transpose by descending major seconds.
   D. Transpose by ascending perfect fourths (only four repetitions).
   E. Transpose by ascending major seconds.
   F. Transpose by descending major thirds.
   G. Transpose by descending perfect fifths (only four repetitions).

A.   B.   C.

D.   E.   F.   G.

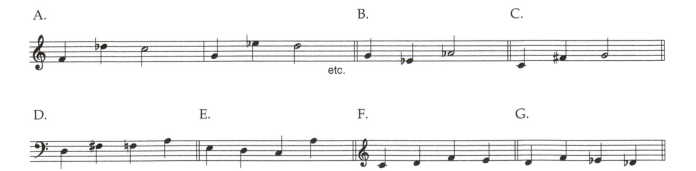

Triads, Inversions, Figured Bass, and Harmonic Analysis

SINGING

EXERCISE 1D.1   Singing Root-Position Triads

Sing (arpeggiate on "la") root-position major, minor, and diminished triads from any pitch.

EXERCISE 1D.2   Arpeggiation of Inverted Triads

Given any pitch, sing or play root-position major, minor, or diminished triads. Next, arpeggiating from the root-position triad, sing or play first-inversion triads then second-inversion triads, ending with root position. For example, to arpeggiate a minor triad from the pitch D, you would sing or play D–F–A, F–A–D, A–D–F, and end by ascending to root position (D–F–A).

EXERCISE 1D.3   Reinterpreting Pitches to Create Triads

Given a pitch, treat it as the root, the third, or the fifth of a major, minor, or diminished triad. For example, given the pitch G, consider it to be the root of major, minor, and diminished triads. Then treat it as the third of an E♭-major triad and the third of E-minor and E-diminished triads. Finally, treat G as the fifth of C-major and C-minor triads and as the fifth of a C♯-diminished triad.

EXERCISE 1D.4   Singing Triads from Given Scale Degrees

Complete the following tasks in the order given:

1. Arpeggiate a tonic triad (I) upward from the root to the fifth.
2. Sing a dominant triad (V), also beginning with the root. (This should be easy, for the root of the dominant triad is the fifth of the tonic triad.)
3. Return to the tonic triad, arpeggiating it downward from the fifth.
4. Sing the subdominant triad (IV), arpeggiating downward from scale degree 1 (its fifth, and the root of the preceding tonic) to scale degree 4 (its root) and then up again.
5. Reestablish the tonic triad by arpeggiating it up and down, beginning with its root.

Thus, you'll sing:

$\hat{1}$–$\hat{3}$–$\hat{5}$ $\hat{5}$–$\hat{7}$–$\hat{2}$–$\hat{7}$–$\hat{5}$ $\hat{5}$–$\hat{3}$–$\hat{1}$ $\hat{1}$–$\hat{6}$–$\hat{4}$–$\hat{6}$–$\hat{1}$ $\hat{1}$–$\hat{3}$–$\hat{5}$–$\hat{3}$–$\hat{1}$

I   V   I   IV   I

EXERCISE 1D.5 Singing Melodies

Sing the following tunes that outline the tonic (I) and dominant (V) triads.

EXERCISE 1D.6 Completing Triads

Given are two of the three members of a triad. Based on the instructions, add the missing member to create a complete root-position triad.

A. Add a single pitch *above* the given pitches to create the required root-position triad.

B. Add a single pitch *below* the given pitches to create the required root-position triad.

C. Add a single pitch *inside* the given pitches to create the required root-position triad.

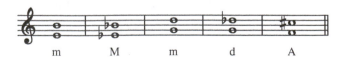

EXERCISE 1D.7 Completing Inverted Triads

Given are two of the three members of a triad. Based on the instructions, add the missing member to create a complete *inverted* triad.

A. Add a single pitch *above* the given pitches to create the required inverted triad.

m   M   m   M   m   d   m   A

B. Add a single pitch *below* the given pitches to create the required inverted triad.

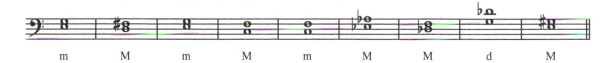

m   M   m   M   m   M   M   d   M

C. Add a single pitch *above* the given pitches to create the required inverted triad.

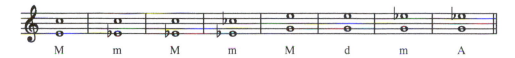

M   m   M   m   M   d   m   A

LISTENING

EXERCISE 1D.8 Identifying Chord Quality

Identify the type of root-position triad that you hear (major, minor, diminished). Sing, by arpeggiating, each triad after you have labeled it.

A. _____   B. _____   C. _____   D. _____   E. _____   F. _____

EXERCISE 1D.9 Aural Discrimination of Triad Members and Constructing Triads

Each of the given pitches is either the root, the third, or the fifth of a major, minor, or diminished triad. Listen to the pitch and then to the triad. Identify the type of triad and whether the given pitch is the triad's root, third, or fifth. Notate the triad, labeling the type of triad and the function of the given pitch.

A. B. C. D. E. F. G. H.

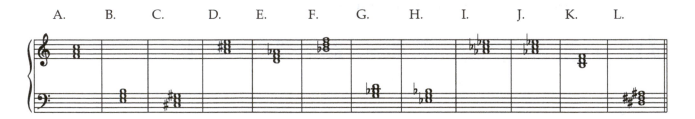

EXERCISE 1D.10 Aural and Visual Analysis of Root-Position Triads (I)

Listen to and identify each of the following close-position triads. Your choices are major (M), minor (m), diminished (d), and augmented (A). Then renotate each given triad on the opposite staff as follows:

- Major becomes diminished, and vice versa.
- Minor becomes augmented, and vice versa.

A. B. C. D. E. F. G. H. I. J. K. L.

EXERCISE 1D.11 Aural and Visual Analysis of Root-Position Triads (II)

Listen to and identify each of the following open-position triads. Again, your choices are major (M), minor (m), diminished (d), and augmented (A). Then renotate on a separate sheet of manuscript paper each given triad as follows:

- Major becomes diminished, and vice versa.
- Minor becomes augmented, and vice versa.

A. B. C. D. E. F. G. H. I. J. K. L. M.

EXERCISE 1D.12 Hearing and Writing Root-Position Triads

Each of the following pitches is the root of a triad. Listen to the recording and notate in close position the type of triad you hear. Next to each triad, write a four-voice version in open position.

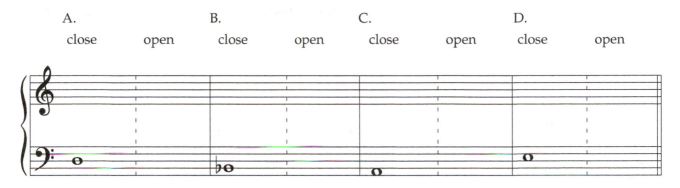

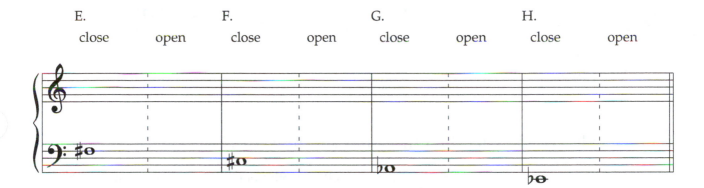

EXERCISE 1D.13 Hearing Root-Position and First-Inversion Triads

The bass is given for first-inversion triads (i.e., the third of major, minor, diminished triads is given as the bass) and root-position triads. Add the two missing upper voices you hear to create complete triads. All chords are performed as follows: The bass is played first, with the upper voices played together one beat later. Notate the missing chordal members in close position above the bass.

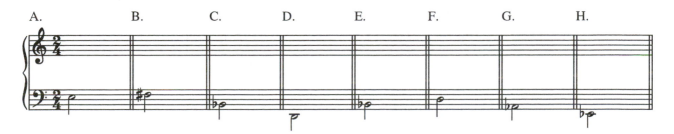

EXERCISE 1D.14 Constructing Triads

A series of pitches is given, each of which is either the root, third, or fifth of a major, minor, or diminished triad.

1. Listen to the given pitch, and then the triad that includes the pitch. Determine the type of triad and whether the given pitch is the triad's root, third, or fifth.
2. Notate the triad in close position.

Sample solution:

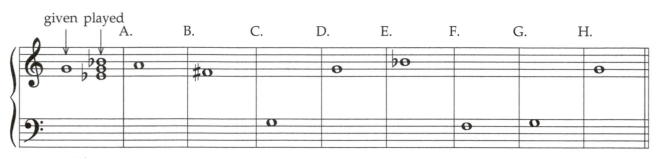

E♭ major
third is given

EXERCISE 1D.15 Triad Identification and Bass Voice

Label the bass member (B) as R, 3rd, 5th (root, third, and fifth, respectively), and chord quality (Q) as M, m, or d.

A. ____|____   F. ____|____
    B   Q   B   Q

B. ____|____   G. ____|____
    B   Q   B   Q

C. ____|____   H. ____|____
    B   Q   B   Q

D. ____|____   I. ____|____
    B   Q   B   Q

E. ____|____   J. ____|____
    B   Q   B   Q

EXERCISE 1D.16 Triad Identification: Aural Recognition

This exercise is identical to Exercise 1D.15, but now you must also identify the member of the chord that is in the soprano (S) in addition to bass (B) and quality (Q).

A. ___|___|___
     B   S   Q

F. ___|___|___
     B   S   Q

B. ___|___|___
     B   S   Q

G. ___|___|___
     B   S   Q

C. ___|___|___
     B   S   Q

H. ___|___|___
     B   S   Q

D. ___|___|___
     B   S   Q

I. ___|___|___
     B   S   Q

E. ___|___|___
     B   S   Q

J. ___|___|___
     B   S   Q

PLAYING

EXERCISE 1D.17 Building Triads at the Keyboard

First with the right hand and then with the left hand, play the following arpeggiation exercises as written (in broken chords) and as vertical chords. Be able to retrace your steps by descending as well. Transpose the patterns to major and minor keys up to five flats and sharps. Use the fingerings provided.

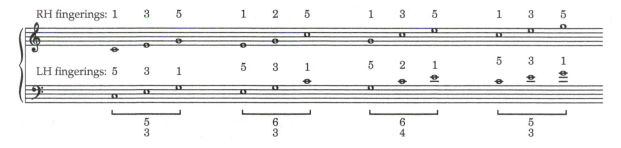

EXERCISE 1D.18 Keyboard: Triads in Various Spacings: Three Voices

Seven sets of two notes of a root-position triad are shown. Determine the missing chordal member and play it below the soprano voice to create a three-part texture. If a fifth is given, the triad could be major or minor since the third of the chord is not specified; be able to play both triad types. Finally, be able to sing the missing note before playing it.

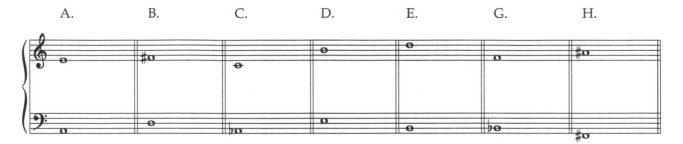

EXERCISE 1D.19 Building Triads at the Keyboard Using Figured Bass

In three voices, construct triads from the figured bass. Play the bass voice with the left hand and the upper two voices with the right hand. Remember that figured bass indicates intervals above the bass but does not indicate spacing. Be aware of accidentals. Identify root and triad type for each example.

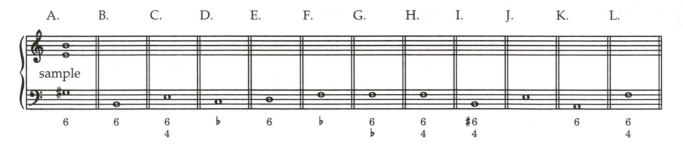

EXERCISE 1D.20 Playing in Keyboard Style

Given are both incomplete and complete three-voice root-position triads. Create complete four-voice sonorities with doubled roots. After playing the chords in keyboard style, revoice the right-hand notes to create three different voicings.

EXERCISE 1D.21 Building Triads

The following intervals require a third pitch to make a triad. The lowest note is the bass, from which you will construct major, minor, and diminished triads. For example, given a perfect fifth, only a root-position triad is possible since the interval of a fifth is not formed with the bass in inverted triads. Similarly, the fourth would belong only to a second inversion triad ($^6_4$).

However, if a third or sixth is given, there is more than one type of triad to which they may belong. For example, the third occurs in both a root-position triad ($^5_3$) and a first-inversion triad ($^6_3$). Further, depending on the specific type of third, fifth, or sixth given, several triads are possible. For example, given C and E♭, you could construct C minor, C diminished, A♭ major (in $^6_3$ position), and A diminished (in $^6_3$, position) triads.

Determine the missing pitch, say the triad and its position, and then play it. Where there are two or more possibilities, play them all (see examples). Finally, spread out each triad, playing the bass in the left hand and the upper voices with the right.

examples:

exercises:

EXERCISE 1D.22 Triads in Various Spacings: Three Voices

Two voices are given; add one pitch to create triads. Depending on the given interval, create $^5_3$, $^6_3$, and $^6_4$ major, minor, and diminished triads. Each example presents the opportunity to make triads of at least two different qualities. Add the third pitch either above or below the given right-hand pitch.

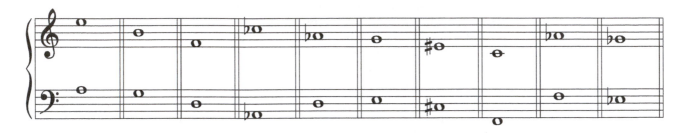

EXERCISE 1D.23 Figured Bass in Three Voices

Realize the figured bass by adding the two missing notes in the right hand. Play each harmony in two different voicings.

EXERCISE 1D.24 Outer Voices and Keyboard Style

You are given a right-hand note and its chordal function, the root of the triad appears in the bass. Complete each triad by adding the missing note. Then, add a doubled root in your right hand as close to the other two notes as possible to create a four-voice texture, as shown is the sample solution. Finally, arpeggiate the right hand through the three various voicings while sustaining the left-hand note.

Sample solution:

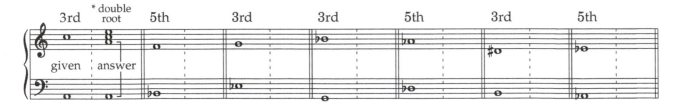

Seventh Chords and Harmonic Analysis

SINGING AND PLAYING

EXERCISE 1E.1 Performing Seventh Chords

Sing and play root-position Mm, MM, mm, dm, and dd seventh chords from any pitch.

EXERCISE 1E.2 Building Seventh Chords

Add a single pitch *above* or *below* the given pitches as specified to create the required *root-position* seventh chords.

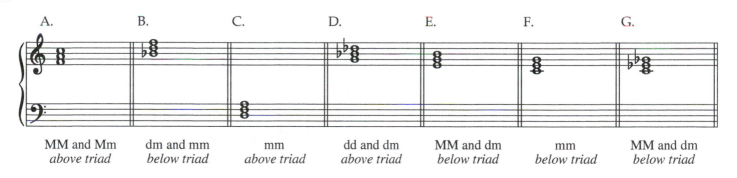

A.	B.	C.	D.	E.	F.	G.
MM and Mm	dm and mm	mm	dd and dm	MM and dm	mm	MM and dm
above triad	*below triad*	*above triad*	*above triad*	*below triad*	*below triad*	*below triad*

EXERCISE 1E.3 Constructing Seventh Chords

Given are two pitches, both of which will be members of one *or more* seventh chords. Add *two* more pitches in order to create the required seventh chord. Do not enharmonically alter the given pitches. For example, given C and F♯, do not change F♯ to G♭.

Sample solution:

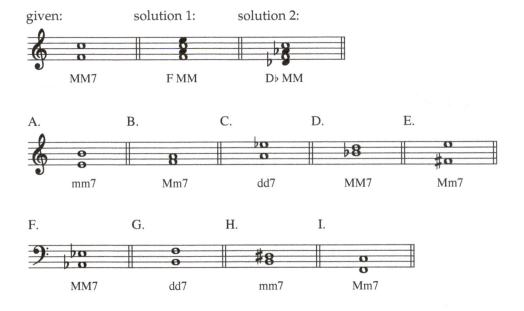

EXERCISE 1E.4 Sing and Play

Play either the upper or lower voice while singing the other voice; reverse. Try playing both voices together.

EXERCISE 1E.5 Singing Major-Minor Sevenths in Inversion

Given that Mm seventh chords occur more often than other seventh chords do, you must be familiar not only with their root-position sound but also with the sound of their inverted forms. Be able to arpeggiate from root position through each inversion until you return to root position. For example, given a B♭ Mm chord, you would sing B♭–D–F–A♭, D–F–A♭–B♭, F–A♭–B♭–D, A♭–B♭–D–F, B♭–D–F–A♭.

EXERCISE 1E.6 Singing and Playing Major-Minor and Minor-Minor Seventh Chords from Given Pitches

Given any pitch, treat it as the root, third, fifth, or seventh of a Mm or mm seventh chord. For example, given the pitch C, consider it to be the root of each of the specific seventh chords. Then, consider C to be the third of a Mm 7 chord (which would be built on A♭) then as the third of a mm 7 chord (which would be built on A), and so on. You may either sing or play the resulting chords.

EXERCISE 1E.7 Singing Seventh Chords from Given Scale Degrees

Choose a major key, play its tonic pitch, and arpeggiate an ascending and descending MM seventh chord constructed above $\hat{1}$. Continue singing seventh chords built on the other diatonic scale degrees in the following manner: $\hat{1}$–$\hat{3}$–$\hat{5}$–$\hat{7}$–$\hat{5}$–$\hat{3}$–$\hat{1}$, $\hat{2}$–$\hat{4}$–$\hat{6}$–$\hat{1}$–$\hat{6}$–$\hat{4}$–$\hat{2}$, $\hat{3}$–$\hat{5}$–$\hat{7}$–$\hat{2}$–$\hat{7}$–$\hat{5}$–$\hat{3}$, and so on. Do the same for a minor-mode key.

LISTENING

EXERCISE 1E.8 Identifying Chord Quality

Identify the type of root-position seventh chord (Mm, MM, mm, dm/ø7, dd/°7). Then, when you listen to each exercise, consider the musical characteristics of each chord presented earlier. Sing the chord's root once you hear it played, then arpeggiate the chord in order to determine its type.

A. _____   B. _____   C. _____   D. _____   E. _____   F. _____   G. _____   H. _____

EXERCISE 1E.9 Seventh-Chord Identification

One pitch is added above or below the given triad. Complete the following tasks:

1. Identify the given triad.
2. Listen to the recording and identify the seventh-chord type.
3. Notate the missing pitch.

above:

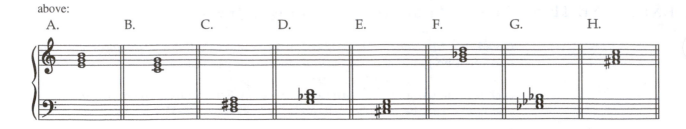

below:

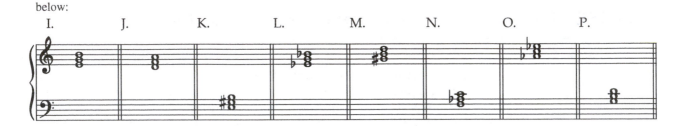

EXERCISE 1E.10 Seventh-Chord Completion

You will hear seventh chords of the following qualities: Mm, mm, MM, dm, and dd. Based on what you hear, construct root-position seventh chords above the notated roots, first in close position, then in an open position.

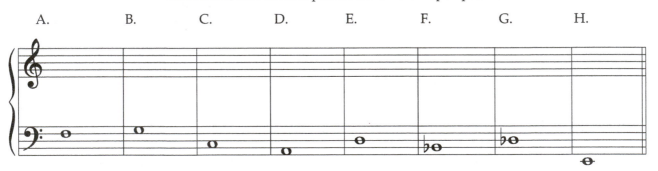

EXERCISE 1E.11 Seventh-Chord Completion

Listen to the following examples and add the two missing pitches to complete the root-position seventh chord you hear. The lowest pitch is the root. Identify each seventh chord (see the two sample solutions). Your choices are MM, Mm, mm, dm, and dd. Finally, provide a plausible roman numeral and key in which each seventh chord would function (there will be multiple possibilities for some of the chords).

Sample solutions:

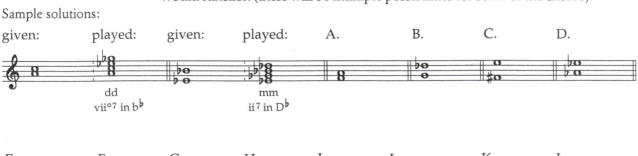

EXERCISE 1E.12 Triads and Seventh Chords in Various Textures: Aural Identification

We will now continue developing aural and analytical skills using various textures. Let's begin by varying the texture, that is, by altering spacing, instrumentation, density, register, and rhythmic pattern. All chord members will be present, but one or more members will be doubled or even tripled.

1. For A–D, identify the type of sonority (triads and seventh chords). All chords are in root position.
2. For E–H, identify the type of sonority and the member of the chord in the bass. (*Hint:* The only inverted sonorities you will hear are triads and the Mm seventh chord.)
3. For I–L, complete the tasks in (2), but now two sonorities will be played. Identify which member of the triad or the Mm seventh is in the bass, and sing the bass.

Use figured bass notation to denote inversions ($^6_3$, $^6_4$ for triads; $^6_5$, $^4_3$, $^4_2$ for seventh chords).

A. chord quality _____

B. chord quality _____

C. chord quality _____

D. chord quality _____

E. chord quality _____   chord member in bass _____

F. chord quality _____   chord member in bass _____

G. chord quality _____   chord member in bass _____

H. chord quality _____   chord member in bass _____

I. chord qualities _____ _____   chord members in bass _____ _____

J. chord qualities _____ _____   chord members in bass _____ _____

K. chord qualities _____ _____   chord members in bass _____ _____

L. chord qualities _____ _____   chord members in bass _____ _____

EXERCISE 1E.13 Seventh-Chord Completion

Each of the given pitches is either the root, third, fifth, or seventh of Mm, MM, mm, dm7, or dd7 seventh chords. Listen to the given pitch, then to the root-position seventh chord in close position. Identify both the type of seventh chord and the pitch's placement as the root, third, fifth, or seventh of the chord.

EXERCISE 1E.14 Constructing Seventh Chords

You will hear the given pitch followed by an open-position seventh chord played in root position or one of the inversions.

1. Determine the type of seventh chord and whether the given pitch is the chord's root, third, fifth, or seventh.
2. Notate the missing pitches in close position and label the chord.
3. Renotate each chord a minor sixth higher than its original position.

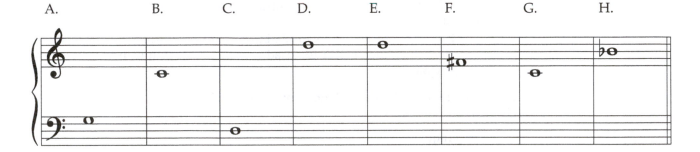

PLAYING

EXERCISE 1E.15 Major-Minor Seventh Chords

Three notes of dominant seventh chords are given. The root is in the bass. Play the missing member in the right hand with the other two given notes. Return to the beginning of the exercise, play the given voices, then sing the missing voice.

EXERCISE 1E.16 More Major-Minor Seventh Chords

Given are three notes of major-minor seventh chords, but the bass may or may not be the chord's root. From the three given notes, determine the missing member of a dominant seventh chord and play it in the right hand. Play the right-hand notes in two different spacings as shown in the example. Return to the beginning of the exercise, play the given voices, then sing the missing voice.

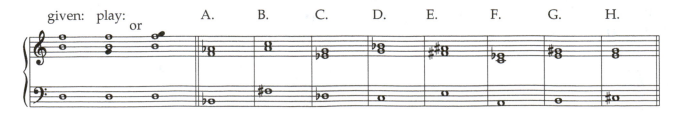

EXERCISE 1E.17 Adding Missing Voices

In the following exercise, the bass is the root of a specified type of seventh chord. At the keyboard, add the two missing voices below the soprano to create the required chords in close spacing.

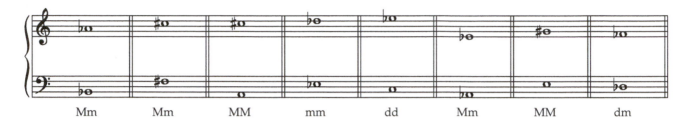

Mm   Mm   MM   mm   dd   Mm   MM   dm

EXERCISE 1E.18 Sing and Play

Play the following example using two hands. Then play one part while singing the other; reverse.

Invertible Counterpoint, Compound Melody, and Implied Harmonies

PERFORMING

EXERCISE 2.1 Singing and Playing Invertible Counterpoint

Sing one voice while playing the other in the following short exercises. Then swap the pitches in each voice to create invertible counterpoint. Now repeat the exercise, this time singing and playing the opposite voices. Analyze the implied harmonies in each exercise. *Note*: All these exercises expand the tonic. Play each exercise in major and in the parallel minor and transpose to two other keys of your choice. Exercise A is completed for you.

The Motive

LISTENING

EXERCISE 3.1 Hearing Motivic Elaborations

Each example given is an elaboration of a basic 1:1 contrapuntal structure. Listen to each example then notate only the outer-voice 1:1 skeleton, omitting all elaborating pitches and motives.

Analyze. Then, in a sentence or two, describe the *single* main motivic component used in each exercise (e.g., "the motive is a passing, dotted rhythmic figure").

A.   upbeat

B.

C.